Cornbread Nation  4

The Best of Southern Food Writing

Cornbread Nation 4

The Best of Southern Food Writing

Edited by Dale Volberg Reed and John Shelton Reed
General Editor, John T. Edge

Published in association with
The Southern Foodways Alliance

The University of Georgia Press ■ Athens and London

Published by The University of Georgia Press
Athens, Georgia 30602
© 2008 by the Southern Foodways Alliance,
Center for the Study of Southern Culture, University of Mississippi
All rights reserved
Designed by Anne Richmond Boston
Set in 10.5 Adobe Minion
Printed and bound by Maple-Vail
The paper in this book meets the guidelines for permanence and durability of the
Committee on Production Guidelines for Book Longevity of the Council on
Library Resources.
Printed in the United States of America
12   11   10   09   08   P   5   4   3   2   1

Library of Congress Cataloging-in-Publication Data
    Cornbread nation 4 : the best of Southern food writing / edited by Dale Volberg Reed
and John Shelton Reed.
        p.   cm.
    ISBN-13: 978-0-8203-3089-1 (pbk. : alk. paper)
    ISBN-10: 0-8203-3089-2 (pbk. : alk. paper)
    1. Food writing. 2. Food habits—Southern States. I. Reed, Dale Volberg. II. Reed,
John Shelton. III. Southern Foodways Alliance. IV. Title: Cornbread nation four.
TX644.C68 2008
394.1'20975—dc22   2007039041

British Library Cataloging-in-Publication Data available

The recipes in this book have not been kitchen tested for this publication.
Copyrights and acknowledgments appear on pages 303–306, which constitute
a continuation of the copyright page.

Contents

Cornbread Nation 4

The Best of Southern Food Writing

Introduction

In his classic *American Cooking: Southern Style* (1971), the late Eugene Walter offers a charming little poem that asks where the South is, and answers that it can be found in everything Southerners cook and eat. We wanted to begin with this poem, but some lawyer at Time-Life Books wouldn't let us.

So we'll begin instead with an apothegm from our friend Lisa Howorth, who once observed that we Southerners can be identified by what goes into our mouths and what comes out of them. What we eat and how we prepare it, what we say and how we say it—for as long as there have been Southerners to be identified, these have usually sufficed to do the job.

Which makes it apt that, since its founding in 1999, the Southern Foodways Alliance (SFA) has brought Southerners together to eat Southern food and to talk about it.

The SFA has also collected a good many written words on the subject in three volumes of an occasional publication called *Cornbread Nation*. The first, edited by John Egerton and published in 2002, was boldly subtitled "The Best of Southern Food Writing." Lolis Eric Elie edited the second (2004), on barbecue, and Ronni Lundy the third (2005), on Appalachian food.

In preparing *Cornbread Nation 4* we reverted to the organizing principle and the subtitle of the first volume in the series—actually, to that volume's lack of an organizing principle. That is, we didn't start with a particular theme; rather, we sought articles about Southern food, cooks, and eaters that were unusually well written or unusually interesting or, as it turned out, gratifyingly often, both. We began with a wealth of papers that had been presented at SFA symposia and field trips, added a few dozen articles that we recalled having read somewhere or other, and threw in a score or two from the clipping files of the SFA's redoubtable director, John T. Edge. Finally, a call for suggestions from people on the SFA's email list yielded nearly a hundred more possibilities. From this pile we chose the selections you see here.

A few of our decisions were dictated by space limitations. David Leite's article on Ricky Parker, for instance, has been included in place of a much longer—and hilarious—account of Leite's barbecue apprenticeship (available online at leitesculinaria.com), and "The Natural" by Brett Anderson, "Crab Man" by Robb Walsh, and "Molly Mooching on Bradley Mountain" by Mary Hufford had to be substantially abridged. (Interested readers should consult the original publications.) On the other hand, although there were no recipes in earlier editions of *Cornbread Nation*, some of the articles we selected were greatly enhanced by accompanying recipes, and it seemed perverse to leave them out on some obscure point of principle.

In the end, of course, the selections were our own, and they reflect our own interests and tastes, as readers and eaters. We're a little hesitant about that subtitle, but "Some of the Best of Southern Food Writing" seemed awkward. Mourning the sometimes almost arbitrary omissions, we consoled ourselves by reflecting that there will be future volumes in this series, and that any reader who disagrees with our choices can edit the next one.

Although we did not start with a theme for this collection, in fact (as our table of contents reveals), *several* themes emerged from the choices we made. This is not surprising, given that the SFA's symposia and field trips served as starting points in our search for material. For example, after a memorial tribute to Edna Lewis, one of the great Southern cooks, we begin with some essays on the Gulf Coast, from Apalachicola to Beaumont, with the focal point in New Orleans and Acadiana. Given the glories of its food, this region would almost certainly have been well represented in any case, but it is not immaterial that the SFA's field trips in 2005 and 2006 were to New Orleans and the Florida Panhandle.

Shortly after the New Orleans field trip, hurricanes Katrina and Rita tore through much of this territory, and the devastation they wrought evoked some eloquent tributes to what was lost, as well as some fine journalism about how people were dealing with the catastrophe. Coupled with the material we already had on Louisiana and the Gulf Coast, we had so much in hand that we thought about doing an entire collection on the subject—before and after—although, in the event, as you see, we settled for two sections in a broader volume.

The first of the two Gulf Coast sections includes a splendid photo-essay on the oystering industry of the Apalachicola Bay by the SFA's resident documentarian, Amy Evans. If a picture is indeed worth a thousand words, Evans is by far the major contributor to this volume, another reason why "The Best of Southern Food *Writing*" isn't strictly accurate.

In the "interlude" that makes up the third section, we move on to the South Carolina Lowcountry. That we found ourselves with two pieces on Charleston and environs was purely accidental: the SFA had not had a field trip there. But these essays remind us, if a reminder is needed, why such a visit was overdue, and in fact one was held shortly after this volume went to the publisher. (Look for more on the food of coastal Carolina in the next edition of *Cornbread Nation*.)

On the other hand, the section we've called "Sweet Things" does reflect the SFA's recent activities. The organization's 2005 symposium and field trip focused on sugar and the South, and the three essays in this section began as presentations at the symposium.

So did Bill Ferris's appreciation of the Moon Pie and Tom Hanchett's disquisition on soft drinks, both of which wound up in the next section, "Corndog Nation." If we apply Dwight Macdonald's well-known discussion of high, folk, and popular culture to the subject at hand, it is plain that several essays in this volume treat the South's high cuisine, the chefs who prepare it, and the restaurants that serve it. Others are clearly examining the foodways of the Southern folk. But the Moon Pie, RC Cola, Vienna sausage on saltines, hotdogs, Waffle House, and a cookbook with recipes calling for Velveeta cheese and canned mushroom soup? All this is "popular" cuisine, in Macdonald's sense of that word, and as a rule it gets no more respect from foodies than tail fins got from Macdonald. But it's fun to write about, and to read about. If it shouldn't be treated solemnly, it can be taken seriously, as two or three of these essays do—and ironic respect may be better than none at all.

We've come to think of the next two sections as the heart of the book. "Downhome Food" brings together a number of essays and three fine poems by Michael McFee to examine and mostly to celebrate some of those "food-ways of the Southern folk"—ingredients and dishes that range from greens to chitlins, catfish to barbecue, moonshine to morels. "Downhome Places" looks at some of the places, often funky ones, that preserve them.

It probably doesn't get more downhome than the Mississippi jails discussed, from the inside, by Bernard Lafayette, whose talk, like several pieces in this volume, came from a presentation to the 2004 SFA symposium, which took as its theme "Southern Food in Black and White." A recurring question at that symposium, treated explicitly by Shaun Chavis and at least by implication in a couple of other essays, is whether there is any difference between "black food" and "white food" in the South. You can judge for yourself, but it seems to us that the answer must be, essentially, no; that the table is one place—maybe *the* one place—where the cliché "it's not about race, it's about class" actually holds true. At any rate, that's our rationale for not having a Jim Crow section in this book.

Finally, the section we've entitled "Compare and Contrast" is something of a grab bag, a residual category for pieces that didn't really fit anywhere else, but many of them do seem to involve food, cooks, or eaters somehow at the margins of the South, or engaged in interesting ways with other cultures—German, Jewish, Italian, French, Yankee, what have you.

We've closed the book with a benediction. By a preacher. Very Southern, to be sure. Maybe it should have come at the beginning, and we could have called it grace. Anyway, those of us tempted to make a religion out of food could probably use a taste of the real thing.

Amen, and bon appétit.

Dale Volberg Reed
John Shelton Reed
Chapel Hill, North Carolina

Famed cook and food writer Edna Lewis, who died on February 13, 2006, at her home in Decatur, Georgia, was a founding member of the Southern Foodways Alliance, and received the SFA's Jack Daniel's Lifetime Achievement Award in 1999. This excerpt from The Taste of Country Cooking, *first published in 1976, is followed by her menu for an early spring dinner.*

Spring

Edna Lewis

Each season had a particular interesting feature, but spring held something special. After the long spell of winter we welcomed the first warm day of February, heralding the coming of spring.

Often a mother hen would surprise us with a healthy brood of baby chickens that she had hatched in the hay loft and somehow gotten down to the ground. They would be chirping and pecking in the snowy slush of the barnyard. We would pick them up and carry them and the mother in to the kitchen and place them in a wooden box behind the cookstove which served as a nursery for early hatched chickens, baby calves, pigs, and lambs that were too weak and unaggressive to compete for food. All such animals would be kept in the kitchen until the severe cold weather was over and they were strong enough to feed themselves. The quiet routine of the kitchen would give way to the sounds of chirping, pip pip, and baa baa. We were so excited about our kitchen guests that we would set about adopting the most unusual ones for ourselves and we would keep watch over our pick sometimes for a year, or until it was sold, which would be a sad day for us. But there was always a good reason given why it had to be sold. All the realities of life were explained to us as we grew up.

Further evidence of spring would be the arrival of the noisy killdeer, running over the ground as if it were on roller skates, signaling that it was time to begin ploughing. It continued to call out "kill dee, kill dee" during the ploughing season.

I will never forget spring mornings in Virginia. A warm morning and a red sun rising behind a thick fog gave the image of a pale pink veil supported by a gentle breeze that blew our thin marquisette curtains out into the room, leaving them to fall lazily back. Being awakened by this irresistible atmosphere we would hop out of bed, clothes in hand, rush downstairs, dress in a sunny spot, and rush out to the barn to find a sweet-faced calf, baby pigs, or perhaps a colt. We always stopped by the hen house to look at the setting hens sitting in their row of nests along the wall. They had to be checked often to see if the eggs were moist enough to hatch properly. I can still remember the moist smell of chickens hatching and making quiet, cuddly noises. The mother hen would fuss and ruffle her feathers, very annoyed at my mother for lifting her from the nest to sprinkle the eggs. There would be guineas setting under the woodpile where no one could reach and they would appear one day with a brood that was so swift of movement that one could only get a glimpse of them scampering through the weeds.

This was truly a time of birth and rebirth in barnyard, field, and forest. Early-morning visits to the barnyard extended into the woods as well, which was just across the stream from the barn. The quiet beauty in rebirth there was so enchanting it caused us to stand still in silence and absorb all we heard and saw. The palest liverwort, the elegant pink lady's-slipper displayed against the velvety green path of moss leading endlessly through the woods. Birds flitting back and forth knowing it was spring and looking for food, a spider winding in his catch while his beautiful dew-laden web shimmered and glistened in the early-morning sunshine, the early-morning sound of the mournful dove, the caw caw of a crow looking for food.

A stream, filled from the melted snows of winter, would flow quietly by us, gurgling softly and gently pulling the leaf of a fern that hung lazily from the side of its bank. After moments of complete exhilaration we would return joyfully to the house for breakfast. Floating out to greet us was the aroma of coffee cooking and meat frying, mingled with the smell of oak wood burning in the cookstove. We would wash our hands and take our places on the bench behind the table made for the children.

Breakfast was about the best part of the day. There was an almost mysterious feeling about passing through the night and awakening to a new day. Everyone greeted each other in the morning with gladness and a real sense of gratefulness to see the new day. If it was a particularly beautiful morning it was expressed in the grace. Spring would bring our first and just about only fish—shad. It would always be served for breakfast, soaked in salt water for an hour or so, rolled in seasoned cornmeal, and fried carefully in home-rendered lard with a slice of smoked shoulder for added flavor. There were crispy fried white potatoes, fried onions, batter bread, any food left over from supper, blackberry jelly, delicious hot coffee, and cocoa for the children. And perhaps if a neighbor dropped in, dandelion wine was added. With the morning feeding of the animals out of the way, breakfast was enjoyable and leisurely.

Another pleasure was following the plough. I loved walking barefoot behind my father in the newly ploughed furrow, carefully putting one foot down before the other and pressing it into the warm, ploughed earth, so comforting to the soles of my feet. As I listened to my father sing one of his favorite songs, the chickens from the hen house would flock behind me, picking up all kinds of worms and bugs that were turned up by the plough. The noisy killdeer was still around, guarding her tiny speckled eggs in a nest she had made of small stones. Now and then the plough would turn up roots of a sassafras bush, which we would carry into the house and make into a tea for breakfast the next morning. We also enjoyed tea made from a bush that grew along the streams; used only while in the bud stage, it was known as sweet bud.

Planting season was always accompanied by the twilight arrival of the whippoorwill repeating breathlessly and rapidly "whippoorwill! whippoor-will!" Because of the longer hours of daylight, field work could extend into the evening, and dinner was served at midday. First spring meals would always be made of many uncultivated plants. We would relish a dish of mixed greens—poke leaves before they unfurled, lamb's-quarters, and wild mustard. We also had salad for a short period made of either Black-Seeded Simpson or Grand Rapids, loose-leaf lettuce that bolted as soon as the weather became warm. It was served with thin slices of onion before they begin to shape into a bulb—the tops used as well—in a dressing of vinegar, sugar, and black pepper. It was really more of a soup salad. We would fill our plates after finishing our meal and we adored the sweet and pungent flavor against the crispy fresh flavor of the lettuce and onions.

One usually thinks of lamb as a spring dish, but no one had the heart to kill a lamb. The lambs were sold at the proper time and the sheep would be culled—some sold and a few butchered. My mother would usually buy the head and the forequarter of the mutton, which she cooked by braising or boiling and served with the first asparagus that appeared along the fence row, grown from seed the birds dropped. There were the unforgettable English peas, first-of-the-season garden crop cooked and served in heavy cream along with sautéed first-of-the-season chicken. As the new calves came, we would have an abundance of milk and butter, as well as buttermilk, rich with flecks of butter. Rich milk was used in the making of gravies, blanc mange, custards, creamed minced ham, buttermilk biscuits, and batter breads, as well as sour-milk pancakes. And we would gather wild honey from the hollow of oak trees to go with the hot biscuits and pick wild strawberries to go with the heavy cream.

Freetown was a beehive of activity, with everyone caring for crops of new animals, poultry, and garden, gathering dandelions and setting them to wine. People also helped each other by trading seed, setting hens, and exchanging ideas as well. Although this was a hectic time and visiting was put off for a calmer time of year, the neighbors still found time for unforgettable pleas-antries. I remember when I was very little, our neighbor Mrs. Towles came over one bright afternoon and invited me for tea as she often did. As I walked along the path behind her, we came upon a nest of colored candy Easter eggs. I had never seen anything so beautiful in all my five years of life. I asked her how did she think they had gotten there, and she replied casually, "I guess the Easter Rabbit must have left them there for you."

As the weather warmed up and we moved toward summer, the main crops were planted—corn, beans, melons, and peanuts. Sweet potato plants were ready for pulling from the hotbed—a structure made of four-by-four-by-three boards stationed in a corner of the garden. The bed was made by filling in a six-inch layer of fresh stable horse manure that was then covered over with a four-inch layer of dry oak leaves and a few twigs of green pine needles. A four-inch layer of old hay was added, and that was topped with a five-inch layer of clean, dry sand. The bed was then covered with a piece of old blanket or canvas and left to heat up for a few days. When the temperature in the hotbed reached seventy degrees, specially selected sweet potatoes were inserted into the sand and the cover replaced. The bed was aired daily, every afternoon when the temperature was at its highest, and sprinkled lightly with warm water during incubation. When the plants reached a height of five inches, the bed was left uncovered so that the plants could toughen before setting them in the open ground. Very often other vegetable seed was sown in the bed alongside the potatoes—those were the days before hybrid seed. We would always save our own seed and plant it from year to year. A few of the vegetables we planted are seldom seen today, such as cymlings, almost flat, rounded, white squash with scalloped edges that matured early and was usually served fried; butter beans; a leafy green known as rape; black-eyed peas served puréed; parsnips, salsify, and root celery. The common herbs were sage, purple basil, chervil, horseradish root, and wild thyme. No homestead was complete without an orchard and a grape arbor bearing fragrant sweet dessert grapes. Some of the fruits we loved best and thought most flavorsome for preserving and keeping were Stayman Winesap apples; Kieffer pears, which were sweet and juicy; a variety of deliciously sweet cherries—blackheart, sour red, and a bluish pink one called Royal Ann; fragrant round, red plums, as well as damsons; and that famous old fruit, the quince. Almost all these fruits we served stewed or used as a filling for cake, as well as preserving. The garden also included a gooseberry bush. Flowers, too, were an integral part of every homestead, especially perennials such as cowslips, Virginia bluebells, sweet myrrh, rambling roses, and our favorite geranium (which, incidentally, had its origin in Africa, as did the guinea hen, wheat, and many other good things that are part of our table today).

Planting season in Freetown was particularly hectic because everyone planted their crops, set their chickens, and everything else according to the sign of the zodiac. These signs appeared only once in each month and lasted for two or three days. So the ground had to be ready to plant then; if you missed the proper sign, the crop would be thrown back for a month. It was said that seed that blossomed should be planted when the moon was light, whereas vegetables grown underground should be planted in the dark of the moon. Some of these practices still go on today. There used to be a big sigh of relief when planting was over, but then we would plunge right into the work of cultivation and raising the new crop of hatched chickens, turkeys, and barnyard animals, at the same time as we watched the hay ripen and looked toward hay-cutting time.

I remember in spring how the bobwhite used to walk around as a decoy, calling "bobwhite, bobwhite" to his mate as she sat nearby on her first hatch. We felt happy to hear him calling out, thinking that somehow this made everything complete, and we would answer him back, saying, "Bobwhite, bobwhite! Are your peaches ripe?"

An Early Spring Dinner

Braised Forequarter of Mutton

Thin-Sliced Skillet-Fried White Potatoes

Skillet Wild Asparagus

*Salad of Tender Beet Tops, Lamb's-Quarters, and Purslane
Garnished with Chopped Chervil*

Yeast Rolls

Butter

Blanc Mange Garnished with Raspberries

Special Butter Cookies

Coffee

Louisiana and the Gulf Coast Before

Tabasco
Edmund McIlhenny and the Birth of a Louisiana Pepper Sauce

Shane K. Bernard

Tabasco. Almost every English-language dictionary includes the word as a proprietary term along with other select trademarks, such as Xerox, Kleenex, and Band-Aid. The condiment itself has appeared on dinner tables at the White House, gone to war with U.S. soldiers in their MREs (Meals, Ready-to-Eat), and flown into orbit aboard Skylab, the Space Shuttle, and the International Space Station. It has appeared in numerous TV programs and movies, from Charlie Chaplin's 1917 classic *The Immigrant,* to a 1997 episode of *The X-Files,* to the notorious 2003 flop *Gigli.* When noted Dixieologists John Shelton Reed and Dale Volberg Reed compiled *1001 Things Everyone Should Know about the South,* they included Tabasco sauce as one of the South's major culinary contributions, calling it the "gold standard" of pepper sauces.

None of this would be the case if not for a single Louisiana entrepreneur: Edmund McIlhenny, inventor of Tabasco brand pepper sauce. Although his story has been told countless times in brief by journalists and advertising agents, much of what has been written about Edmund and the early years of Tabasco sauce derived solely from hearsay and legend. Now, however, an examination of Edmund's business and personal papers in the McIlhenny Company archives has for the first time yielded a more accurate early history of this global culinary icon from rural Louisiana.

Edmund McIlhenny was born in Hagerstown, Maryland, on October 15, 1815, to a middle-class family. His father, John McIlhenny, a local politician, merchant, and tavern keeper who served on the board of the local bank, died from Asiatic cholera on Edmund's seventeenth birthday. As Edmund recalled over a half-century later in an autobiographical sketch (written in third person), "Soon after the death, . . . his second son Edmund, though only seventeen, decided to go to work to assist his mother in the care and education of his younger brothers."

What happened to Edmund over the next nine years is unknown, although some evidence suggests he may have worked in Baltimore's financial industry. In 1841 at age twenty-six, however, he surfaced in New Orleans, where, armed with letters from his father's friends, he secured a job at the Bank of Louisiana. There he worked his way up from bookkeeper to "general agent," a position of enormous trust whose duties consisted of monitoring the bank's five branches at Baton Rouge, St. Francisville, Donaldsonville, Opelousas, and Alexandria.

Through his own thrift and industry Edmund accrued a small fortune by the late 1850s, when he purchased these branches and became an independent banker. During the same period he acquired a reputation as a bon vivant, joining the elite Louisiana and Orleans clubs—racing his boat *The Secret* as a member of the Southern Yacht Club and riding his prize mare "Fashion" through the streets of New Orleans. In confidential documents he recorded his worth in 1860 at $112,000 (about $2.5 million at present-day value).

New Orleans society regarded Edmund, now in his early forties, as one of its most eligible bachelors: his name appeared in the locally published booklet *Bliss of Marriage; or, How to Get a Rich Wife*, which (despite its title) listed both the region's unmarried ladies and gentlemen with their estimated individual wealth.

Family tradition explains why Edmund christened his yacht *The Secret*: the "secret" was that Edmund had fallen in love with young Mary Eliza Avery, daughter of his closest friend, prominent Louisiana attorney and planter Daniel Dudley Avery. Judge Avery, as he was later known, resided in Baton Rouge and through his wife's family owned a sugar plantation deep in the Teche country at a place called Petite Anse Island, today called Avery Island.

Edmund's love for Mary Eliza grew, and after she turned twenty in 1858 he wrote to Judge Avery, "My long and intimate intercourse with your family has resulted in an honest and devoted love for your daughter, Mary. Save by inference from my attention, she is unaware of my feelings. I respectfully ask your permission to make them known to her." Judge Avery refused to answer the entreaty, disapproving of a prospective son-in-law only five years his junior. He finally consented, however, when Mary Eliza—who knew of Edmund's feelings and his letter to her father—threatened to elope. The couple were wed on June 30, 1859, at St. James Episcopal Church in Baton Rouge.

Edmund and Mary Eliza honeymooned at Pass Christian for several months and then took up residence on Rampart Street. Around December 1859, Mary Eliza became pregnant, and she and Edmund traveled to Avery Island in May 1860 to await the birth. It came in September at Marsh House, the Avery homestead on the island. They named the child Sara, nicknamed "Sadie," the first of eight children, two of whom would die as infants.

Two months later Lincoln became president and the nation quickly plunged into civil war. The now intertwined Avery and McIlhenny families sought refuge from the conflict on their isolated plantation. Around this time an event occurred on the island that forever altered its history: the discovery of solid rock salt only sixteen feet beneath the island's surface.

With its salt supply cut off by a Union blockade, the South regarded this find as a "gift from Heaven," as Ella Lonn wrote in *Salt as a Factor in the Confederacy*. Unable to operate his banks because of the war, Edmund put his financial skills to work helping his in-laws run the salt works. "My duty is at the mine," he wrote to Mary Eliza, "and I must necessarily be absent from you."

As many as five hundred teams of horses from throughout the lower South descended on the island daily to be loaded with salt. Ironically, this activity transformed the Averys' obscure plantation retreat into a military target. In November 1862, two Union gunboats and a transport ship loaded with foot soldiers moved up Bayou Petite Anse with orders to destroy the island's salt works. The attack failed miserably, and the island remained beyond Union control until April 1863, when General Nathaniel P. Banks invaded south Louisiana. With Southern troops withdrawing rapidly to the north, the McIlhennys and Averys abandoned the island and sought self-imposed exile in Texas. They left on April 15, 1863, barely two days before Union troops captured the salt works.

In Texas, Edmund worked as a civilian employee of the Confederate military. He initially served in the commissary office at Galveston, overseeing supplies for the stronghold—an office of consequence, given that before his arrival there had been a mutiny over substandard provisions. He later transferred to the paymaster's office, traveling by rail and stage across Texas to distribute funds to Southern troops. Edmund rarely saw his wife and daughter during his wartime service, even though they lodged with his Avery in-laws in Houston, Brenham, Austin, and elsewhere in southeast and central Texas.

At war's end Edmund returned with his family to Avery Island. His in-laws emerged from the conflict with their sugarcane fields and salt mines intact, but Edmund's banks were in financial and physical ruin. Having lost his antebellum wealth, Edmund spent months alone in New Orleans looking for work, but no one wanted to hire a middle-aged former independent banker, especially when young carpetbaggers could be had so inexpensively. Edmund dejectedly returned to the island, moved into the Avery residence, and occupied his time tending the family's fruit and vegetable garden.

It was during this period that Edmund first experimented with making a red pepper sauce. What spurred him to do so remains unclear because he left behind no personal account of the matter. Furthermore, his wife and children later could not agree about such basic details of the story as when and from whom he obtained his peppers. But their accounts exhibit several common elements. For example, they agree that Edmund got the peppers in New Orleans from a soldier, possibly named Gleason, who had recently returned to the United States from Mexico. Edmund planted seeds from these peppers on Avery Island and used their fruit to invent a pepper sauce for the family table. He bottled this homemade sauce in used cologne bottles and eventually shared it with friends in New Orleans, who urged him to market it commercially in local groceries.

Whatever the peppers' origin, in 1868 Edmund grew his first commercial crop. Although he made no sauce that year, he used the crop of 1868 and that of the next year to produce 658 bottles of pepper sauce in 1869. In 1870 he produced 1,012 bottles; in 1871, 2,896 bottles; and in the banner year of 1872, 15,084 bottles. Production peaked in 1889, when Edmund manufactured 41,472 bottles.

Edmund made his sauce in a factory located on a gentle slope across the lawn from Marsh House. Known as "the Laboratory," the building consisted of a three-story stucco tower and a rectangular two-story brick and clapboard structure. According to family tradition, the Laboratory originated in the antebellum period as a *pigeonnière* (pigeon house); during the Civil War, however, Confederate soldiers added the tower's third story as an observation deck and built the brick and clapboard section as a barracks or supply depot.

Claiming the Laboratory as his workplace, Edmund used the tower's base as his business office and its adjoining rooms for concocting Tabasco sauce. The manufacturing process was complicated and time-consuming. Edmund crushed ripe red peppers with an ordinary potato masher and blended the resulting "mash" with granulated salt from the island's mine. He packed this mixture into jars or "tight molasses barrels" and aged it for at least thirty days. Edmund then removed a crusty layer of mold, transferred the mash into larger jars, and added French white wine vinegar. He aged this mixture for at least another thirty days, removed a new layer of mold, and forcibly worked the red pulp through a series of increasingly finer sieves in order to extract a liquid free of skins or seeds. The outcome was a refined red pepper sauce ready for bottling and consumption. (The product's renowned three-year aging process in white oak barrels would develop only after Edmund's lifetime.)

Edmund originally called his condiment "Petite Anse Sauce," but he changed the trademark after Judge Avery objected to this use of his plantation's name. As a result, Edmund rechristened his product "Tabasco"—a word of Mexican-Indian origin supposedly meaning "land where the soil is humid" or "place of coral or oyster shell." According to one of his children, Edmund chose this name because he found it "euphonious," but the choice may have been influenced by historically strong commercial ties between the port of New Orleans and the Tabasco region of Mexico.

Prior to the coming of the railroad in the 1880s, Edmund shipped his finished sauce by horse and wagon to nearby New Iberia. From there steamboats carried it down Bayou Teche, across several coastal bays, against the current up Bayou Plaquemines, and down the Mississippi to New Orleans. In the city grocers introduced his sauce to local Reconstruction-era consumers.

The meandering trip to New Orleans resulted in many broken bottles and much spoiled sauce. Edmund solved these problems by using sturdier bottles, sanitizing corks in alcohol, and sealing bottle tops in green wax. (Modern screw-top Tabasco bottles sport a green neckband in homage to the days when Edmund topped off his bottles with green wax.)

In 1870 Edmund entered into a business relationship with an unsung hero of early Tabasco history: John C. Henshaw, a former Union officer and distant Avery relative, who resided in New York City. Edmund wanted to sell Tabasco sauce outside south Louisiana and, noting Henshaw's splendid reputation among the Averys as an entrepreneur, he asked Henshaw to serve as his first Tabasco salesman. Edmund chose wisely, because Henshaw, in modern parlance, was "a real go-getter" who energetically set about introducing Tabasco sauce in the major cities of the Northeast. Edmund so admired Henshaw's dynamism that he shortly appointed him the sole Tabasco agent for Maryland, Pennsylvania, New Jersey, New York, Massachusetts, and the District of Columbia.

Henshaw soon negotiated an amazingly successful agreement with E. C. Hazard and Company of New York City, one of the largest food manufacturers and distributors in nineteenth-century America. Hazard quickly became Edmund's largest customer, ordering in 1872, for example, over 10,500 bottles of Tabasco sauce, which it supplied at wholesale to grocers in the Northeast and beyond. As a result, Tabasco sauce advanced dramatically toward becoming a nationally recognized product.

In addition, Henshaw proposed that Edmund obtain his bottles, stoppers, labels, crates, and other supplies from highly competitive manufacturers in the industrial Northeast. He correctly asserted that these manufacturers could provide such items more cheaply than less efficient firms in New Orleans, even when factoring in shipping costs. Furthermore, it was Henshaw who suggested that Tabasco bottles carry a warning label for the uninitiated. "Caution—This sauce should always be mixed with your gravy, vinegar, or other condiment, before using," read the new rectangular label on the back of each bottle. "One or two drops are enough for a plate of soup, meat, oysters, &c., &c."

In 1876 Edmund and Henshaw abruptly ended their association following a business dispute, and Henshaw died shortly thereafter. Edmund never appointed another regional salesman. Instead, he went it alone, processing orders from grocers, restaurateurs, and individual consumers nationwide while continuing to rely on E. C. Hazard and Company as a wholesale distributor.

Although Edmund first exported a small quantity of Tabasco sauce in late 1873 and early 1874 (to England and France), he did not export the product in notable quantities until later in that decade. Overseas grocers initially gave the sauce a mixed reception. The renowned London firm of Crosse and Blackwell declined to carry the product, advising Edmund that a glut of sauces on the British market would render Tabasco sauce "unprofitable." Meanwhile, Henry L. Sherlock & Sons of Liverpool eagerly advised Edmund of its wish "to be appointed sole agent in the United Kingdom . . . and for the Continent."

Although Crosse and Blackwell grossly miscalculated Tabasco sauce's potential, the British firm correctly observed that the product faced vigorous competition. Its chief early rival, Maunsel White's Concentrated Essence of Tobasco Pepper, hailed from New Orleans and appeared on the market as early as 1864.

Rumor has maintained that Edmund obtained both his peppers and his sauce recipe from White, a prominent New Orleans businessman who owned nearby Deer Range plantation. Yet no contemporary evidence points to White as the source of Edmund's peppers, and White's and Edmund's recipes are known to be different. The *New Orleans Daily True Delta* newspaper and the planters' journal *De Bow's Review* noted that White's recipe (of which White made no secret) called for his concoction to be boiled. Edmund, on the other hand, boiled none of his ingredients, but allowed them to ferment naturally.

The dissimilar appearance of the two rival sauces underscored their different methods of preparation. As Edmund wrote to his wife from New Orleans in 1870 after visiting a grocery, "Mr. Henning has the M. W. [Maunsel White's] for sale. . . . [It is] indifferently put up, and I was surprised to find that the colored pulp settles down more than half, leaving a muddy looking fluid above. There is a row of it on Henning's shelves just beneath mine, and the contrast in style and appearance is decidedly in my favor, and Henning says he sells 25 of mine where he sells one of the M.W."

Edmund's pepper sauce business grew steadily during the two decades after its inception, yet it remained a largely one-man operation. Edmund occasionally received help from one or two Avery Island freedmen, however, or from his wife and children. As Edmund's youngest daughter, Marigold, recalled in

1952, "My father would take me out of school when he would have a good order so I could help, and I would label the bottles. . . . The labels came in big sheets . . . and my father put the mucilage, gum arabic, on the back of it, and then I would cut them, cut them in sections and make the diamond, the Tabasco label, and then the caution label for the other side. . . . [My cousin] said, 'I can label just as good as Marigold. I don't see why you don't take me out of school.' But she wasn't a little pepper sauce girl."

Suffering from gout and other ailments, Edmund McIlhenny died at Avery Island on November 25, 1890, at age seventy-five. In the autobiographical sketch that he dictated late in life to his daughter Sadie, Edmund made no reference to Tabasco sauce, but reminisced instead only about his heyday as a banker. His widow and children valued the entire Tabasco operation, including its factory and trademark, at a mere $14,250, only a fraction of Edmund's antebellum worth.

Edmund's heirs recognized the potential of the business, however, and soon expanded the island's pepper fields from about five to sixty-five acres. By 1911 pepper fields covered about 450 acres. Edmund's eldest sons, John Avery McIlhenny and Edward Avery McIlhenny, presided successively over the operation and adopted modern business methods, such as legally incorporating the company, issuing shares of stock to family members, building a larger factory, increasing worldwide exports, and creating brand awareness through advertising. In 1894, for example, John McIlhenny commissioned a Vaudeville-type musical called *The Burlesque Opera of Tabasco* that toured the country to promote the condiment. By the turn of the twentieth century, consumers both in America and abroad widely regarded Tabasco sauce as *the* preeminent red pepper seasoning.

McIlhenny Company remains a private corporation owned solely by Edmund's descendants, and it continues to manufacture Tabasco sauce exclusively on Avery Island. The company employs hundreds of workers, markets Tabasco sauce in twenty-one languages and dialects, and exports the product to over 160 countries and territories. It can produce over 700,000 bottles of sauce daily (twice the number Edmund made during his entire twenty-two-year career as a pepper sauce manufacturer). This global culinary icon began over 135 years ago with one Louisianian, Edmund McIlhenny, and his homespun recipe for a fiery condiment called "Tabasco."

Boudin and Beyond

Mary Tutwiler

The blackened door of the small, old smokehouse behind Johnson's Grocery was propped with a stick. Talya Frugé sidled through the narrow opening, a clanking washtub filled with sausage on her hip. Coils of fresh garlic sausage hung from wooden dowels racked across the ceiling. She set the tub down.

Her laced work boots braced on the packed dirt floor, Talya, twenty-one, swung a wooden rod into place at shoulder height, and began the slow, deliberate process of looping yards of sausage evenly over the length of the dowel.

Once the smokehouse was filled, she struck a match to light a small oak fire in a dented metal cradle, clamped the door shut, and left the sausages to smoke slowly until the next morning, when they were taken down and heaped in a red-brown pile on the meat counter.

Johnson's Grocery in Eunice, Louisiana, started in 1937 by Arneastor Johnson, makes smoked sausage "the old way," said current owner, Wallace Johnson, seventy-four. Wallace, along with his brothers Steven and Matthew and, up until his death, Joe, have adhered to the tradition of the old smokehouses of the Cajun prairie.

Once the great grasslands of Louisiana, the Cajun prairies lie to the north and west of Lafayette, extending as far north as Evangeline parish and west to Calcasieu. Beginning in the 1770s a sparse population of settlers began founding communities called *anses*, or coves.

The heavy clay a few feet below the topsoil broke the wooden plows of early cotton farmers, so these descendants of Acadian refugees and Napoleonic soldiers garrisoned in the Louisiana territories turned to cattle ranching. The Crowley-Eunice highway (Louisiana 13) bisects the once-open grasslands where Cajun cowboys ran herds of cattle, ranges now squared off into quadrants of rice fields. The yields are still measured, as the locals tell it, by how much gravy it will take to cover an acre of rice.

Punctuating the skyline are rice silos built in the style of German Catholic churches, a nod to German settlers of the 1850s, and smokehouses, practicing a method of food preservation dating back to the Native Americans who once inhabited these prairies. For hungry travelers looking for superlative sausage, and an oddity, a stuffed pig's stomach that's sometimes called chaudin, the highway leads right up to Eunice, 45 minutes to an hour northwest of Lafayette, and nearly to Wallace Johnson's door.

"When I was a boy, before we opened up the store we had a little bitty farm. Three acres. We had a few cows, cotton, a few hogs," Wallace Johnson said, describing life on the Cajun prairie in the 1930s. "A few families would get together. Daddy would get a hog, we'd have a hog kill. You'd kill it, scald it, clean it, pass round the meat, make salt meat, marinated meat, smoked bacon, boudin."

Smoking and salting were the only ways to keep meat from spoiling. While farmers could get together and share a cow, beef is too lean and doesn't respond well to smoking. The meat turns out dry, like jerky. Corn-fed pork, on the other hand, bathed in pure white lard, rises to its glory when preserved with a little hickory smoke.

"We moved to this location in 1948," Wallace said. "Before that we were four blocks up the street, on the old Crowley-Eunice highway. We had very little refrigeration in the store, just an old stand-up ice box where we kept milk, some bologna. We didn't sell fresh meat.

"Then in 1946—we were still at the old store—Daddy bought some meat equipment. We bought our meat from Boo Ledoux. We'd go and get three or four pounds of ground meat, three or four T-bones, and some round steaks. Boo was a rodeo rider. I call him the last of the Cajun cowboys around here."

Today, Johnson's Grocery has a modern facade (Wallace said he missed the sound of the old screen door as it swung shut with a bang), but its boot-polished wooden floors attest to the age of the midcentury grocery.

The butcher counter, all the way in the back, is where the action is. Butcher Keith Jacobs is always busy, slipping chunks of pork shoulder into a marinade or sawing up delectable smoked ribs for a customer's dinner.

From the 1940s smokehouse out back come a variety of types of smoked sausage: pork, pork with garlic, "mixed" (pork and beef), mixed with garlic, beef, turkey, and andouille (a smoked sausage of chunky ground pork), ponce (smoked, sausage-stuffed pig stomach), bacon, ribs, and beef jerky. Johnson's Grocery carries rabbit and turtle meat, a variety of other fresh meats, home-made hog's head cheese (a gelatinous pork pâté,) boudin (sausage made of pork, rice, and gravy), and cracklins (fried pork fat with a little meat), as well as fresh baked sweet potatoes, which sit, still warm and fragrant, on the counter.

"We knew some farmers who would butcher, they'd make boudin, they'd bring it to the store," Wallace said while he leaned on the corner of the old meat cooler. "Nobody was selling boudin back then. Daddy would sell it. This was on Saturdays. We'd sell it all by that afternoon.

"As it got better, it was good business for us. It got so we were making fifteen to eighteen hundred pounds of boudin. One Saturday before Christmas we had people lined up in the store past the checkout counters in the aisles all the way out the door.

"As things went on other stores started selling boudin. We don't sell as much on Saturdays as we used to, but we make it every day now, and on Saturday we make eight hundred pounds of boudin."

Back in a little kitchen just off the meat-cutting floor, a big covered kettle simmered on a stove. An old-fashioned white porcelain drip coffee pot sat on the next burner. Wallace led me into the kitchen, a slow smile spreading across his eyes, and fished a link of boudin out of the kettle. Then he handed me a cup of coffee black as Louisiana sweet crude oil.

"You have to have boudin and coffee together," he said. The boudin at Johnson's Grocery is made of very finely ground pork mixed with rice, with a hint of liver in the mix. It is clearly a signature sausage, different from the boudin just down the road at the Eunice Slaughter House, which is different from the boudin in Mowata or Mamou or Pine Prairie.

It was my fourth link of boudin that morning, boudin standing in for coffee cake out here on the prairie, but it wasn't really what I was looking for. I was after a taste of chaudin, a legendary local delicacy made of a stuffed pig's stomach.

The first thing I learned about chaudin—pronounced "show-dahn"—is "that's not what you call it," according to J. R. Gillory at Gillory's Grocery in Pine Prairie. North of Mamou at the northern tip of the Cajun prairie, Pine Prairie is famous for two things, smoked sausage and speeding tickets.

"It's a ponce," J. R. Gillory said.

"Up in Marksville they call it gog," Kenneth Gillory chimed in. "Or gaub."

"That thing you have down south is a green ponce," J. R. added.

Interstate 10 is the great sausage divide. Up north of the east-west highway, all sausage spends some time in a smokehouse. South of Interstate 10, the majority of sausage, sometimes called Cajun sausage, is sold "fresh" (raw) to be grilled, sautéed, or barbecued by the buyer.

"We know in the eighteenth century the Indians living here did have a tradition of smoking meat," said University of Louisiana at Lafayette history professor Carl Brasseaux. "But whether the French and Acadian settlers had a smoking tradition or the Germans and Midwesterners who came along in the nineteenth century brought their own traditions has to be a matter of speculation. I'd say if you're looking for the evolution of smokehouses, it's probably a case of convergent traditions."

At the time the Acadian settlers arrived in the southern part of what is now Cajun country, most of the Native American tribes had disappeared, according to Brasseaux. Thus no smoking tradition. Or perhaps it was the proximity of fresh fish and shellfish, the rich larder of the southern marshes, which obviated the need to preserve meat.

That theory may be proved by the dearth of seafood markets on the prairie. I only found one, in all my wanderings: Ronnie's Seafood Market, in Eunice. Ronnie's specialty, by the way, was home-smoked tasso, smoked pork shoulder, smoked rabbit, and two kinds of cracklins—one with meat, one with the skin still on.

A ponce is a chaudin that has been smoked. An unsmoked chaudin, up on the prairie, is called a green ponce. And to make it all more confusing, many meat markets adhere to the spelling "pounce" for the smoked pig stomach item.

Did they have any ponce at Gillory's? In the meat case, piled up to the top were long red-brown ropes of smoked pork sausage: plain, with garlic, and with jalapeño peppers. I saw smoked turkey wings, smoked pork hocks, smoked andouille, smoked rabbit, boneless stuffed chickens, fresh meat, marinated meat, seasoned and stuffed pork, and beef roast, and, yes, fat brown pockets of stuffed pig stomach.

Could I taste it? "It's not cooked," J. R. Gillory said. "Smoked is smoked, cooked is cooked." Although smoked at a low temperature for twenty-four hours or so, a ponce is still raw and needs to be smothered in brown gravy for a few hours, he said, then served over rice.

I wound up in Basile, home of Nathan Abshire, the great Cajun accordion player. Driving through the piney woods, humming "Pine Grove Blues," Abshire's anthem, I felt sure I would find some ponce on a local menu.

At Redlich's City Cash, butcher James Tibodeaux sent me over to Buck's Fast Stop (at the Exxon station), where they sell plate lunches. "They bought two ponces to cook for their plate lunch a week ago," he said. "By the end of the afternoon we only had one left. Everybody that ate the plate lunch came to buy a ponce to take home." Alas, Buck's, whose ponce is smothered like a roast in a pretty brown gravy, according to Tibodeaux, was finished serving lunches and couldn't say when it would have ponce again.

By this time I was on a mission. Lejune's Sausage Kitchen on Tasso Drive in Eunice is the cleanest sausage-making operation I have ever entered. You could eat the sausage off the floor, which is mopped a couple of times a day, but of course you can't because "smoked is smoked, cooked is cooked."

Kermit and Nita Lejune started the business twenty-four years ago. Today their sons, John and Ryan, and their wives, Tasha and Lechia, make three thousand pounds of sausage a week, which they sell by the box to walk-in customers. They don't ship it or sell it in any other market. You have to go to Tasso Drive to pick it up, but it's worth the trip; it is without peer, even in a region famous for smoked meat. The only two other items on the list are tasso and ponce.

Tasso, down south, comes in paltry little packages to be used as seasoning. Tasso, in smoked-meat country, is cut from the heart of the shoulder. It's a lean cut of pork, the length of a pig's arm, smoked all day long over a fire made of pecan, hickory, or oak.

Their smokehouse was filled with plump ponces, in the middle of a "perfect day for smoking—no humidity. The sausage comes out red, like crawfish," John said, clearly happy with the coming result of the day's smoking. Ponces aplenty, but none ready to eat.

My last shot was one of the most famous boudin stops on the prairie, the Mowata Store. Bubba Frey's store is known by every easy rider from Crowley as the place to pick up superlative boudin for Saturday breakfast on the way to Fred's Lounge in Mamou.

Frey fills his meat case with homemade smoked sausages, bacon, and ponce, but it's the boudin that flies out the door. It's got that perfect balance between meat and rice, heavy on the black pepper, that makes mixing good boudin such a difficult and personal thing.

Frey claimed that the art of fine smoking was perfected by his German ancestors. "I learned from my great uncle Laurence Frey. He made sausage at home." Frey patted some pork sausages he was stuffing. "This recipe here, I'm sure comes from his daddy, who came from Alsace-Lorraine. My great uncle was trilingual. He'd sit on the front porch and talk in German. The brother or the cousin would answer in French. The German influence, that's where the smoking came from. I don't believe the Cajuns knew how to make sausage until the Germans taught them."

Frey was cooking a stew for his lunch place next door. "I grew up on a farm," Frey said. "I grew up eating everything. There were eleven of us—we ate anything you threw at us." He pulled off the lid of a big oval Magnalite pot; curled pieces of meat were bubbling in the brown gravy. "Today's special," he said, forking up a cut of meat, intact. "Tongue."

This story does not have a sad ending. No, I did not find any ponce or chaudin that day, but the tongue at Bubba Frey's was magnificent. Chewy, tender, strange, but delicious. I just hadn't looked in the right place for ponce.

The Pig Stand, in Ville Platte, a mere ten miles east of Highway 13, between Mamou and Pine Prairie, serves ponce every Saturday. Owner Terry Guidry said the ponce is a big seller, drawing in locals for the Saturday plate lunch. The trick, of course, is to resist the famous barbecue, smothered in Pig Stand BBQ Sauce.

On second thought, don't resist, order both. There's no sense not making a pig of yourself when you're in pure pork heaven.

First You Make a Roux

Terri Pischoff Wuerthner

Roux. A simple blend of flour and fat cooked together, roux has been thickening gravies, soups, and sauces for more than five hundred years. It originated with classical French cooking and reached its zenith in the eighteenth century, when Cajuns settling in Louisiana made a discovery: cooking the mixture beyond a light brown color yields an intense, toasted, nutty, smoky flavor. Roux is such an important element of Cajun cooking that a Cajun recipe for almost anything other than a dessert begins with, "First make a roux."

Lard was the original fat used to make roux. In his famous 1651 cookbook François Pierre La Varenne wrote about a *liaison de farine* made with flour and lard, which he called "thickening of flower." "Melt some lard, take out the mammocks; put your flower into your melted lard, seeth it well, but have a care it stick not to the pan, mix some onion with it proportionably. When it is enough, put all with good broth, mushrums and a drop of vinegar. Then after it hath boiled with its seasoning, pass all through the strainer and put in a pot. When you will use it, you shall set it upon warm embers for to thicken or allay your sauces." This mixture eventually became known as *farine frit*, or roux.

One hundred years later the mixture was termed *roux de farine*, and the recipe called for butter instead of lard. After being cooked to a cream color, the mixture was saved for later use, when it would be added to liquid to make a soup or a sauce.

By the mid-nineteenth century roux had become a controversial subject, as some French gastronomes thought it was overused. The great chef Antonin Carême disagreed, saying that those who criticized the use of roux were ignorant men: properly cooked and handled, it was "as indispensable to cooks as ink to writers." Nevertheless, no one paid much attention to roux until the 1970s, when nouvelle cuisine burst onto the scene. Those who watched their begins to brown, the flour has a nutty fragrance that means it's almost done. I could smell it changing and I knew when to get off the bed."

Of course, the length of time a roux takes depends on the depth of color you want to achieve, which in turn depends on what dish you are making. For gumbos, most Cajuns prefer a chocolate roux, though some use blond or peanut butter roux, and others simply cook the roux to a stage somewhere between blond and dark. Light roux is often used with meat, wild game, and birds, while dark roux is paired with light meats such as pork or veal and with fish and shellfish. On the other hand, a holdover from the classic French method of sauce making is to use a blond roux when the accompanying liquid will be milk or cream; a peanut butter roux when the liquid will be chicken, fish, or veal stock; and a chocolate roux when beef stock or stock from game will be used. Personal preferences, however, are the only real rule.

When asked how long it takes to make a roux, a Cajun has one of two answers: as long as it takes either to drink two beers or to brew and drink a pot of coffee. Humorous as these answers are, they are not very helpful. Cooks vary greatly in their estimates of how long it takes to cook a roux, and variables such as how hot the pan is at the start and the heat throughout the cooking process also affect the outcome. In addition, the cooking heat depends not only on the setting of the dial but also on the accuracy of the burner and the thickness of the pan. In short, there are no definitive answers.

The following recipe for roux offers tips on what to look for as the roux progresses through the cooking stages. Refer to these tips when making roux for specific recipes. The best way to ensure that the roux will darken in the suggested amount of time is to heat the pan for two minutes, then heat the oil for another two. (Note: if you are not using a heavy skillet or pot, you may need to cook the roux over medium-low heat.)

Roux
Makes about 1 cup.

¾ cup corn oil or lard
1 cup all-purpose flour

Heat a cast-iron pot or large skillet over medium heat for about 2 minutes. Add the oil and heat for 2 minutes more. Add the flour all at once and whisk or stir constantly to combine. Reduce the heat to low and stir or whisk constantly until the roux takes on the desired color, 20 to 60 minutes.

When the roux reaches the desired color, immediately transfer it to a large plastic or glass bowl to stop the cooking process quickly, stirring

fat and calories believed butter and flour had no place in this new culinary style, and roux was banished from the kitchen. Then, in the 1980s, a revival of interest in Cajun cooking (thanks largely to Chef Paul Prudhomme) brought roux to the front burner once again, and this distinctive combination of flour and oil became widely known.

In classic French cooking, roux is made by blending butter and flour and stirring the mixture constantly for two to five minutes over low heat. Most commonly used in French cooking is light or "blond" roux, the traditional thickener for velouté and béchamel sauces. It is cooked only until the flour begins to take on a pale yellow color. If cooked longer, the flour attains a golden color, which is called "peanut butter roux" in the Cajun tradition. Dark roux, or "chocolate," is obtained when the flour is cooked to a reddish brown stage, the literal meaning of *roux* in French.

The question of roux is complicated by the differences between the Creole and Cajun culinary traditions. Creole cooking is city cooking, while Cajun cooking is country cooking, in which everything is cooked slowly for a long time in one pot. A Creole roux, like a classic French roux, uses flour and butter for its foundation; both usually attain a light color, although a Creole roux is cooked a bit longer than a French roux. Cajun roux, however, uses lard or oil instead of butter. The oil allows it to be cooked longer to achieve a more intense flavor. Sometimes Creole roux is indistinguishable from Cajun roux, since some Creole cooks use oil instead of butter, seeking a richer flavor. By contrast, French roux never uses oil, and it is never cooked for an extended period of time.

The word *roux* today usually refers not to a classic French or Creole roux, but to Cajun roux. This combination of flour and fat is cooked slowly on the stovetop in an iron pot. While a roux can be made in as little as ten or fifteen minutes, it *can* take sixty minutes or more for a Cajun roux to reach the perfect deep color and consistency. Thus it is only a distant cousin to French and Creole roux.

Cajun roux is part of my heritage on my father's side. One of his ancestors, Louis Noel Labauve, emigrated from France to Port Royal, Acadia, in 1678. His descendants were forced from their land by the English in 1755, and in April 1766 they settled in the Saint James area of Louisiana's Acadian Coast, where my father was born. From the time I was a small child I watched my father and grandparents prepare that marvelous mixture of flour and fat, cooked long and slow in an iron pot to an aromatic, nutty brown, the prelude to a fantastic gumbo, fricassee, or étouffée. Later I learned that there are as many ways to make a roux as there are Cajun people. The type of fat used, the type of pot, the length of time it is cooked, and the intensity of heat are all factors that can make a single recipe for roux turn out differently each time.

Lard was traditionally used to make roux, for two reasons. First, nothing in a Cajun kitchen is wasted, and lard was considered a perfectly good food left over from the annual slaughter. Why discard one fat only to use another? Second, lard adds a rich, smooth flavor to both savory and sweet foods. For those who approve of the classic French use of butter but roll their eyes at the mention of lard, I should note that lard is lower than butter in saturated fat (per tablespoon: 5 grams for lard; 7 grams for butter), cholesterol (10 grams, lard; 30 grams, butter), and sodium (0 mg, lard; 90 mg, salted butter). Other time-honored fats used for making roux were the drippings rendered from roast meat and poultry or from bacon, which were strained and saved in a covered can. Drippings, like lard, were considered a food, and they lent a particular character to whichever dishes were made from them. A Cajun woman's cooking was distinguished by the type of fat she used. Today, however, vegetable or peanut oil is often used for the sake of convenience and economy.

Flour is always added to the fat of choice, but the proportions of fat to flour can vary. In his guide to classic French cooking, *Le Guide culinaire*, Auguste Escoffier called for eight parts fat to nine parts flour when making roux, though as a thickener he preferred what he called "pure starch," such as arrowroot, to flour. Cajuns most commonly use equal amounts of fat and flour, although a few use less flour than fat, and others use more. People who want both a thick gravy *and* a dark roux should use four parts flour to three parts oil. Because my own family likes thicker gravies, we tend to use more flour than oil.

Those who use more flour than fat claim that the additional flour compensates for the fact that flour loses its ability to thicken the longer it is cooked. In other words, a dark roux has less thickening power than a light or medium one. A little bit of kitchen chemistry may help explain why a dark roux thickens less successfully. Flour contains an enzyme that interferes with its ability to thicken, but cooking flour in fat inactivates this enzyme, allowing it to thicken the liquid it is in. This happens because cooking the fat coats the starch granules in the flour, causing them to separate and thus to swell and absorb liquid. However, when flour and fat are cooked together for an extended period of time or over high heat, some of the starch in the flour breaks down into dextrins (polysaccharides), which do not have the same thickening power as the full-starch flour before it is broken down by the heat. With less starch in the flour, the roux loses some of its ability to act as a thickener.

Another variable is the heat. Flour and fat cooked over low heat will have less flavor but more thickening power, whereas flour and fat cooked over higher heat or for a long time will have more flavor but less thickening

power. Since lengthy cooking gives more flavor and color to the roux, some people use long-cooked roux for flavor and add a roux cooked for only ten or twenty minutes to thicken the dish at the end. The point to remember is this: a darker roux will result in less thickening power and, thus, a thinner sauce or broth in the dish.

Yet another factor affecting the thickness of roux is the type of pot it is cooked in. Once, while talking to my Cajun cousins, I happened to mention that my roux did not get thick enough. They were puzzled. "Well, you're using a cast-iron pot," they said, "so with the proportions of fat and flour you start with it should be thick." I was too embarrassed to tell them that I was using a heavy pot but not one made of cast iron (sometimes called a "black iron" pot). My cousins simply assumed I was using cast iron because it is so fundamental to both Cajun cooking and making roux. In fact, the roux pot is often contested property when a Cajun couple divorces.

Cast iron also cuts down on the cooking time. A blond roux will take ten minutes in a cast-iron pot and twenty minutes in a non-cast-iron pot; a peanut butter roux will take twenty minutes in a cast-iron pot and thirty minutes in another; and a chocolate roux, thirty minutes in cast iron and forty minutes in a pot made of other materials. I now always use a cast-iron skillet or pot, or at least a very heavy skillet or pot. If the dark color is important, use a cast-iron pot; the iron helps achieve a dark color.

Finally, undivided attention is a primary ingredient of roux, and stirring must be constant. A good roux, particularly a dark one, cannot be rushed. Don't leave the roux to answer the door or telephone. You may get a quick drink of water (or the traditional roux-making drink, a beer), but if you take more than a few seconds, the roux may burn and have to be thrown out. (A roux that develops black, burned specks is fit only for the garbage pail.) A very dark roux must be watched extremely carefully toward the end, because it can burn very quickly at this stage. When it begins to smell like nuts that are being dark roasted, stop the cooking process by removing the roux from the heat or by adding the holy trinity (the Cajun term for the oft-used combination of onion, celery, and bell pepper), which will cool the mixture. Timing is all-important.

This is not to say that every roux takes a long time to cook. In her book *Soul and Spice*, Heidi Cusick-Dickerson recounts an interview with Kevin Belton, a teacher at the New Orleans School of Cooking, who "has fond memories of his mother making roux." He recalls: "My mama made her roux at a high temperature so it didn't take as long. But she couldn't leave it, no matter if the doorbell rang or anything. That meant I had a good fifteen minutes to jump on the bed and she couldn't catch me because she was making the roux. I learned to judge the time by the aroma coming from that roux. Just as it until it cools down a bit. (Do not use stainless steel, which retains the heat for too long.) Adding seasoning vegetables (onion, celery, and bell pepper) at this point can also arrest the cooking process. Be careful, as the roux is very, very hot.

Here is what to look for when cooking the roux: After a few minutes the roux may become foamy and stay that way for several minutes. After about 10 minutes, the roux will start to darken and develop a nutlike fragrance. After about 20 minutes, the roux will begin to cook faster and can easily burn at this point, so watch carefully and lower the heat if necessary. Remember to stir constantly throughout this entire process.

Since roux takes 20 minutes to 1 hour to cook, many people will make up a large batch to keep in the refrigerator or freezer. My grandfather would make several pints of different roux (blond, peanut butter, and chocolate) at one time and keep the jars in the refrigerator to ensure that he always had roux on hand when the desire for gumbo or fricassee hit— which was almost daily. He would remove the roux he intended to use for dinner and let it come to room temperature, then stir the oil on top back into the roux. The amount needed for a given recipe was either used to begin the dish or added to boiling liquid as a thickener toward the end of cooking. Roux made in large batches can be kept in the refrigerator for two months or in the freezer for six.

It is convenient to freeze the roux in ice cube trays in increments of 1 tablespoon; once they are frozen, the cubes can be transferred to freezer bags for storage. When a recipe calls for ¼ cup (4 tablespoons) roux, use 4 cubes of roux. Whenever a soup or stew needs thickening, pop out a cube of frozen roux and add it to the bubbling liquid. For those who wish to make roux in quantity ahead of time, here are some handy quantities: 3 cups oil plus 3 cups flour = 3⅔ cups roux; 1 cup oil plus 1 cup flour = 1 cup plus 3 tablespoons roux. If a recipe calls for a roux made with ½ cup oil and ½ cup flour, use ½ cup of prepared roux. In other words, use a quantity of prepared roux equivalent to the amount of flour called for in a recipe. As a rule of thumb, any roux made with 1 cup flour and 1 cup fat will thicken 5 cups of liquid for a thick gumbo or soup; 6 to 8 cups of liquid for a medium-thick fricassee, étouffée, or stew; and 10 cups of liquid for a thinner gumbo or soup.

Despite all these precautions, making roux is not really difficult once you're armed with the facts. The main thing to remember is to keep the heat low and stir constantly. Above all, enjoy the process of preparing this time-honored blend that makes Cajun food so exciting.

"Johnny" Apple, distinguished political reporter for the New York Times, *bon vivant, and gourmet, was a devoted friend of the Southern Foodways Alliance and a frequent guest at its meetings before his death in 2006. This is one of his many dispatches from Dixie to the* Times.

A Lunchtime Institution Overstuffs Its Last Po' Boy

R. W. Apple Jr.

Sam Uglesich grew up among mariners and fishermen off the coast of Croatia on rocky Dugi Otok, whose name means "long island," surrounded by the azure waters of the Adriatic. Twice he set out for the United States. The first time, he jumped ship in New York, but was caught and sent home. The second time, he made his break in New Orleans, then as now a more permissive city, and got away with it.

Naturally enough, he opened a seafood restaurant in his adopted city, specializing in the local shrimp, soft-shell crabs, lake trout, and oysters. The year was 1924, the place South Rampart Street; Louis Armstrong had played gigs a few doors away.

Three years later, he moved to a modest frame cottage on Baronne Street. There, as the neighborhood around them crumbled, he and his son, Anthony, along with Anthony's wife, Gail, gradually built a reputation of legendary proportions. Grander establishments like Galatoire's, Commander's Palace, and Antoine's loomed larger in the guidebooks, but the exacting standards of little Uglesich's (pronounced "YOU-gull-sitch's")—everything bracingly fresh from lake and gulf and bayou, nothing frozen or imported, and absolutely no shortcuts—generated greater buzz.

Without benefit of advertising, word of Uglesich's big, tan, glistening oysters, its sweet, plump crawfish balls, its searing shrimp Uggie, and its over-stuffed yet feather-light po' boys spread across the city and then across the country. It mattered not to most people that it took no credit cards and served neither dessert nor coffee.

Five days a week, eleven months a year, lines have formed outside the ram-shackle building, which displays a sign from the long-defunct Jax Brewery in one window. On Good Friday this year, customers began arriving at 9 in the morning, even though the restaurant does not open for lunch, the only meal it serves, until 10:30. Soon there were more than two hundred people in line, and the sun was setting as the last of the day's four-hundred-odd clients were being served.

All this with just ten tables inside and six on the sidewalk outside.

Soon Uglesich's will close forever, at least in its present form. Anthony and Gail Uglesich are exhausted, worn out by years of rising at 4:30 and working flat-out all day. Balding, bearlike, Mr. Uglesich, sixty-six, told me he would shut the doors in mid-May, but he has renewed his liquor license, just in case he finds retirement miserable.

"I may go nuts," he said at the end of a particularly brutal day. "I doubt it, but I won't know until I try it. If I do climb the walls, I might try packaging our sauces for retail sale, or maybe do some catering—people are always offering me thousands of dollars to cook for their dinner parties—or reopen here for four days a week, with limited hours and a very limited menu, just appetizers. No more of this, though."

Mrs. Uglesich, sixty-four, a petite woman whose regular customers call her Miss Gail, put the situation bluntly. "Our bodies are telling us we can't take it anymore," she said in the soft, liquid accent that marks her as a New Orleans native. "Anthony has missed only two days' work since we were married, and that was forty-one years ago."

Neither of the Uglesiches' two children—Donna, forty, a businesswoman, and John, thirty-five, author of *Uglesich's Restaurant Cookbook* (Pelican Publishing)—has shown any desire to take over the business. "It's too hard," Mrs. Uglesich said.

With many New Orleans restaurants, including some of the most famous ones, relying these days on frozen crawfish tails and frozen soft-shell crabs and on shrimp and crabmeat imported from Thailand or China, Uglesich's stands out more than ever.

"Look," Mr. Uglesich said, peering through wire-rimmed glasses, "90 percent of the shrimp eaten in this country is imported. Local crawfish costs me $7 a pound, compared with $2.50 imported. People in restaurants here know they can get away with things. But I'd pay $10 for Louisiana crawfish, if that's what it takes. Otherwise, what's going to happen to our local fishermen? When we're gone, I don't know."

Two houses across the street from Uglesich's have been spruced up recently, but otherwise the neighborhood remains pretty insalubrious. A big parking lot for the trucks of Brown's Dairy occupies one corner, weed-filled vacant lots several others; the neighborhood seems miles, not just a few blocks, from both the imposing, pillared mansions of the Garden District and the busy shops and restaurants of the Central Business District.

A few weeks ago Mr. Uglesich was mugged late at night, but he still showed up for work the next day, battered and bruised, to stand in his usual position behind the counter, ready to take orders and to dispense seafood wisdom along with the wines that sat on a shelf behind him. He usually stocks fifteen or twenty labels from France (Trimbach, for example), Australia (Penfolds), and California (Ravenswood). None sells as well as beer or Mrs. Uglesich's horseradish-, lime- and chile-spiked Bloody Marys.

The setup is utilitarian, to put it kindly: concrete floor, sturdy Thonet-style chairs, Formica-topped tables. Mrs. Uglesich makes the sauces and soups at home. Mr. Uglesich brings them to the restaurant in his car. The kitchen gear consists of a single eight-burner range, a fryer, two refrigerators, and several sinks. There are only seven employees in the whole place.

"I was never tempted to get big," Mr. Uglesich said. "I can't find enough good produce as things stand now."

He is a notoriously picky buyer. Many days, he rejects what his suppliers offer him, like soft-shells he considers too small. He claims to be able to tell as soon as a sack hits the ground whether the oysters inside are good enough. He checks every delivery of fish and shellfish with a practiced eye.

Mr. Uglesich buys catfish only from Joey and Jeannie Fonseca in Des Allemands, a tiny place in the swamps southwest of the city; bread only from the 109-year-old Leidenheimer Baking Company; and oysters only from the P&J Oyster Company, which was founded by two fellow Croats, John Popich and Joseph Jurisich.

Uglesich's focuses on relatively few main ingredients. It serves no meat at all, except for the roast beef po' boy, and only two kinds of fish: lake trout and catfish. K-Paul's made redfish famous, Lilette serves delicious drum, and the local pompano has been famous for a century, but Mr. Uglesich sticks to his longtime favorites.

Shrimp rules on Uglesich's tables. In addition to shrimp Uggie, you can order a shrimp po' boy (crisp fried shrimp in a long, toasted bread roll), shrimp and grits (shrimp in a delectably creamy sauce ladled over fried triangles of grits), grilled shrimp and onions, shrimp and country sausage with a Creole mustard sauce, shrimp in bacon with a sweet potato soufflé, firecracker shrimp with barbecue and horseradish sauce, shrimp rémoulade, shrimp Creole, shrimp stuffed with crabmeat, voodoo shrimp, and volcano shrimp, among a long list of other dishes.

Voodoo shrimp, which contains black bean paste and is described on the menu as Asian Creole, and volcano shrimp, which includes ginger, soy sauce, black bean paste, and Chinese red pepper, reflect the influence of recent migrants to south Louisiana, as does the Vietnamese dipping sauce that is now served with the crawfish balls.

Still, it is hard to top the raw oysters on the half-shell served up on a side counter, cold and crisp and bereft of plate in the New Orleans manner, by the estimable Michael Rogers, once voted the fastest oyster opener in town. He makes his own ketchup-based cocktail sauce, but the oysters are so fresh that they almost beg to be eaten plain, with only a squirt or two of lemon juice.

"We heard from the president of the United States, a letter about our plans to close," Mr. Uglesich said, tearing up a bit. "That was very nice. We're nothing special here, just a couple of self-taught cooks. It's only a little hole in the wall."

Paul Varisco thinks otherwise. The owner of a restaurant-supply business, he has eaten lunch at Uglesich's three times a week for years. So often, he said when I caught up with him on Good Friday, "that I must be at least partly Croatian now, instead of Italian, French, and German." One of the restaurant's best-selling specialties, Paul's Fantasy—pan-fried trout with grilled shrimp and cubed, sautéed new potatoes, all fearlessly seasoned—is named for him.

So, I asked, what will he do when Uglesich's closes? "I'll take Anthony out to lunch a lot," he replied, "almost anywhere to keep him out of Gail's hair."

Julia Reed, a writer who lives in New Orleans, is another regular. For her, Mr. Uglesich agreed to open on a Saturday night so she could give a birthday party in honor of her husband, John Pearce. It was a rare event; Mr. Uglesich has played host to private parties only a few times since he first did so in the 1980s, for a bash given by the record executive Ahmet Ertegun for the Fort Worth billionaire Sid Bass and his wife, Mercedes. Oscar de la Renta and Albert Finney were among the guests that time.

Ms. Reed dolled up the place with a giant silver punchbowl to cool the Pol Roger, masses of white lilies, linen tablecloths, and monogrammed napkins. Bottle after bottle of Burgundy (Meursault les Chevalieres 2000 from Joseph Matrot) and Alsatian Riesling (Grand Cru Saering 2001 from Schlumberger) kept thirsts at bay.

The food was vintage Uglesich. One of the restaurant's idiosyncrasies is the liberal use of cheese with shellfish—liked by some and detested by others. Fried oysters with blue cheese opened the Pearce soiree, and I found myself in the first camp while my wife, Betsey, found herself in the second. But there was no dispute about what followed, including shrimp and grits, fried mirliton (a squash) with shrimp rémoulade, and luscious crabmeat au gratin.

Chunky and intensely creamy, the crab dish is "made of all the things you're not supposed to eat," Ms. Reed informed us, including butter, evaporated milk, egg yolks, whipping cream, Swiss cheese, and cheddar cheese. It was divine. I must get the recipe, I thought; it would make a great advertisement for the dairy industry, not to mention a fine starter for my last earthly meal.

Mr. Uglesich saved the best for last. The afternoon before, he had bemoaned the tardiness of soft-shell crabs this year, which he attributed to cold weather. But at 7 o'clock that evening, a supplier showed up with the first of the season, still wiggling in a cardboard box lined with wet newspaper. They were mighty beasts, the size of salad plates, and magnificent when dipped in an egg wash, dredged in plain bread crumbs, and fried until the tops and the legs were crisp and the undersides rich and creamy.

The tartar sauce that came with them was house-made, of course.

Apalachicola

Oysterman A. L. Quick of Eastpoint, Florida, has harvested oysters from the Apalachicola Bay since he was sixteen years old.

All photographs are by Amy Evans and are published by permission of Amy Evans, operating under the auspices of the Southern Foodways Alliance.

Fred's Best Seafood in Eastpoint, Florida.

Gloria Quick shucking oysters at Lynn's Quality Oysters in Eastpoint, Florida. Gloria shucks the oysters that her husband, A. L. Quick, harvests from the Apalachicola Bay.

James Hicks, oyster opener at Papa Joe's Oyster Bar & Grill in Apalachicola, Florida.

Second-generation oyster tong maker Rodney Richards attaches steel-toothed heads to long wooden handles.

A molting crab, harvested by soft-shell crab cultivator Henry Tindell of Eastpoint, Florida.

James Hicks opening an oyster at Papa Joe's Oyster Bar & Grill.

James Hicks holding an opened oyster at Papa Joe's Oyster Bar & Grill.

A man opens oysters as they come in off the Apalachicola Bay.

A docked oyster skiff with tongs resting on the cull board.

Cast net fisherman Pap Bailey with a fresh catch in Apalachicola, Florida.

The shucking stalls at Lynn's Quality Oysters in Eastpoint, Florida.

Fred Millender smokes mullet every day to give to the local fishermen in Eastpoint, Florida.

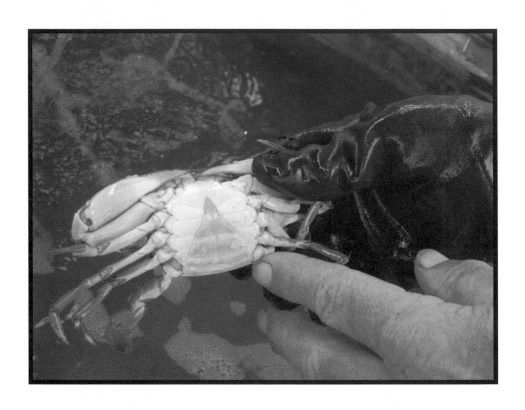

Soft-shell crab cultivator Henry Tindell of Eastpoint, Florida, inspecting one of his crabs.

An oysterman weighs bags of oysters after a day's harvesting on the Apalachicola Bay, Eastpoint, Florida.

Harvesting and culling oysters on the Apalachicola Bay.

The Natural

Brett Anderson

In 1957, a hamburger joint called Big Daddy O's Patio opened in Opelousas. Its owner was a naive, newly married seventeen-year-old, the youngest of thirteen children who grew up on a farm outside of town. He went by Gene Autry Prudhomme, still unaware that Paul was the name on his birth certificate, put there by a baptismal priest who insisted that the boy share a name with a saint.

Save for the fact that Prudhomme ground his own meat to ensure that each hamburger contained the "proper amount of fat for moisture," nothing about Big Daddy O's suggested that its owner would one day become the most famous American restaurant chef in the world. Less than a year after the burger joint's opening, Prudhomme recalled, "I was out of business. . . . It was a quick nine months." His marriage was over as well.

Prudhomme came to New Orleans, not to cook, but to sell magazines. The job took him out west, where he eventually landed back behind the stove. For a decade, he bounced from restaurant kitchen to restaurant kitchen, mostly in Colorado, where the Cajun was never once asked to prepare his native cuisine.

The realization that the food he learned to cook at his mother's hip was foreign to people outside southern Louisiana prompted him in 1970 to move back to New Orleans.

The city, and his profession, would never be the same.

Prudhomme's upward career trajectory hit a steep incline in 1975, when he became the first American-born executive chef at Commander's Palace, and it shot into the stratosphere after he and his second wife, K Hinrichs, opened K-Paul's Louisiana Kitchen, five years later.

At its peak in the 1980s, Prudhomme's profile cast a shadow even over such culinary legends as Julia Child and James Beard, and there was no restaurant-world precedent for the celebrity he enjoyed. The portly chef starred in several cooking shows and home videos, was a regular on local and national TV, appeared on magazine covers, and became a best-selling cookbook author a decade before chefs such as Emeril Lagasse, his heir at Commander's Palace, ushered in the age of the celebrity chef. *Chef Prudhomme's Louisiana Kitchen* (1984—the first of his eight books) is still widely considered a classic.

Today, with his Magic Seasoning Blends spice line, he has ensured that home cooks can closely duplicate the flavors from his kitchen—and he became a pioneering chef-entrepreneur in the bargain. What began with Prudhomme's employees stuffing baggies with homemade spices for sale in the restaurant has mushroomed into a full line of products produced in a thirty-thousand-square-foot plant with fifty-three employees and distribution in all fifty states and twenty-eight foreign countries.

Prudhomme helped ignite a revolution in American gastronomy, inspiring chefs and diners to embrace regional cuisine and fresh, local ingredients. By uncovering opportunities for chefs outside their restaurant kitchens, he transformed his profession. In drawing influences from beyond the parish line, he profoundly altered the dining landscape in New Orleans. And he found a national and international audience for local chefs and restaurateurs, pushing Louisiana, particularly New Orleans, onto the world map of great culinary destinations.

Is K-Paul's a classic New Orleans restaurant? Would New Orleans be a singular dining attraction if Prudhomme had never left Opelousas? Does the cultural saturation of blackening misrepresent Cajun cuisine? It's a measure of the magnitude of his success that enthusiasts continue to debate his impact a quarter-century after his initial splash drenched the town—and more than a decade after he ceded the reins of his restaurant's kitchen.

Today Prudhomme at sixty-five is noticeably trimmer than during his media-star prime—the result of diet and exercise, he says—and you're more likely to find him tending to the business of his spice empire than blackening fish at K-Paul's.

But to truly understand Prudhomme's extraordinary career, you must ask the people who were there. What follows is an oral history—essentially a biographical account of his career, culled from hours of interviews and told entirely in the words of those who either watched his meteoric rise from afar or took part in the restaurateur's wild ride.

It is a long and colorful tale, full of professional twists and personal turns, all leading to one inescapable conclusion: he's come a long way from Big Daddy O's Patio.

Prudhomme: "I went to work at Le Pavillon hotel as a sous chef, working the night shift. A city councilman named Clarence Dupuy used to come in there all the time. He made me a deal to help him open Maison Dupuy hotel in the French Quarter. It was the first time I'd done my version of Louisiana food. When they renovated the French Market area, right below Bella Luna, there was a restaurant and wine and cheese shop run by Jack Duarte. I helped him there. It's where I learned about croissants and that kind of baking. In the meantime, I was [introduced] to Ella Brennan."

Ella Brennan, owner of Commander's Palace: "My family had just moved up to Commander's from Brennan's. We had brought in this chef, and he wasn't going to go where we wanted to go."

Prudhomme: "Ella called me, said, 'Why don't you take the job?' So I was the chef there for five years."

Brennan: "I was very impressed with Paul, his absolute passion for Louisiana food. He was going to sort of work for us as a lunch chef for a while, to see if we liked each other. Well, Paul wasn't in the kitchen a week and he was chef of the whole restaurant."

Prudhomme: "I was the first American they'd hired as an executive [chef]."

Brennan: "The French had intimidated America with their supposed better knowledge of cooking. But we eventually became less intimidated. We started to realize that we had possibly the only indigenous cuisine in the United States."

Gene Bourg, former *Times-Picayune* restaurant critic: "I remember going to Commander's and seeing these bizarre menu descriptions. This is when Paul began using all of these little puns and wordplays in his menu items. He started using words like 'debris,' 'Cajun popcorn.' Nobody knew who he was, because in those days chefs were very anonymous."

Brennan: "It became a totally different menu. There wasn't a thing on the menu that was there before."

Prudhomme: "The gumbo I did at Commander's was a roux gumbo. To my knowledge, it never had been done before. It was chicken and andouille, down-and-dirty Cajun. It was what Mama used to do. I'd go into the country and buy the andouille from the guy I'd known since I was a kid."

Brennan: "Paul was one of the first people I knew to go and get the product that was growing around here and bring it in. We had gone through a period back in the '50s where everything got frozen and packaged. We were trying to get back to what Paul grew up with."

Prudhomme: "I remember [Alice Waters of Chez Panisse in Berkeley] coming to [Commander's]. We sort of fell in love over food. I had never heard anybody be fanatical like I was. 'You raise your own chickens?' I was like, 'Somebody else is doing that?'"

Bourg: "He really opened up the menu at Commander's. That's when Ella and Dick [Brennan] started referring to it as nouvelle Creole."

Brennan: "Paul was trying to make us into Cajuns, and we were trying to make him into a Creole."

Prudhomme: "Sometimes on Sunday we'd serve fifteen hundred, sixteen hundred people."

Emeril Lagasse: "I had tremendous respect for him. He was taking Louisiana cuisine from a place that was considered so country and rustic, making it fashionable and hip."

Brennan: "I remember [food writer] James Villas came to town. He was writing for *Bon Appétit*, and he wanted to do something on gumbo. That's how Paul got his first big publicity, the cover of *Bon Appétit* magazine."

Prudhomme: "Pretty quickly, Ella and I started to help each other. She would teach me about the restaurant business—about, as she says, 'making a buck.' I never cared about that before. [She] changed my mind about making money in the sense that you can have just as much pride in making the proper profit as you can making the best damn dish you've ever tasted. That's why, after I left Ella, I was successful."

A NEW PARTNER

Prudhomme: "I met [K Hinrichs] at the Maison Dupuy. She was a waitress. She was great at it. She was the only person in the dining room that would put up with what I considered normal stuff in terms of handling the customers and taking care of food and explaining food. I think what started the idea of K-Paul's was that we both wanted to have our own restaurant. We started going out, off and on. It wasn't serious, then it would get serious, then it wasn't serious. I wasn't the marrying kind, and she wasn't either."

Frank Brigtsen, chef-owner of Brigtsen's, first night chef at K-Paul's: "My feeling was that he opened K-Paul's for K, because they had fallen in love and he wanted to do something with her, [and because] he wanted a place that his family could come to town and eat at and feel comfortable. Commander's was too fancy."

Prudhomme: "K and I looked for three years, but we didn't have any money. I mean, the rent [at K-Paul's] was cheap [in 1979], fifty bucks a month.

That included the tables and the chairs and the counter and the bar and the refrigeration and the stove and everything in the kitchen."

Bourg: "It caused a stir, because the word was that the chef from Commander's Palace had opened this place where you could get dinner for $5 or $6. Plus, the menu changed every day. Some of it was quite good."

Brigtsen: "I would come in at ten in the morning. Chef and I would go over the lunch menu, then Chef would go over to Commander's and I'd cook lunch. I'd do dinner by myself with a dishwasher. And after dinner, Chef would come over from Commander's and we'd talk about dinner. . . . Back then, we had no recipes. None. Ever. No pieces of paper. It was all done by taste. He created sauces over the phone. He'd call in from Commander's: 'Do this, do that.' He created crabmeat hollandaise like that. He'd say, 'Do this, do that,' and he'd taste it. That's how I learned to cook, by taste. That's his magic to me. His palate is so incredible."

Prudhomme: "I pulled up and [K] was almost in tears. She said, 'I don't know what to do. The line's out the door, but we're not making any money.' I said, 'Well, what about if I join you?' She said, 'Would you do that?' I said, 'Yeah, if you're willing to take the chance that we gonna live with a lot less money,' because I made a good salary at Commander's. She said, 'I don't care about money.' I said, 'I'm gonna go give my notice.' I'd never seen [Ella] so upset."

Brennan: "I thought we were doing good for him. We were helping him and he was helping us. But [being angry] was a temporary thing. I guess I thought it was such a little restaurant—you can't make a living on that. He showed me. He stayed until we found the right guy. We kept looking and eventually found Emeril."

1979: A PLACE OF THEIR OWN

Brigtsen: "K had a lot of class. She also had a very clear vision, and it was a unique style. [The rules] were uncomfortable at times. No reservations. No credit cards. No wine list. If you wanted the food, you'd wait in line and pay cash for it. And if you didn't finish your plate, you were probably going to get yelled at."

Brennan: "I went, of course, and it was nice. But I thought he could do a lot better. I thought he could make it a more pleasant place to dine."

Mary Sonnier, co-owner of Gabrielle, former K-Paul's cook: "The community seating, just having the red and white wine, Cajun martinis, stars on the faces—that was all K. It was her restaurant, I don't care what anyone tells you. Chef loved her and listened to her. The kitchen was his, but the restaurant was hers."

Prudhomme: "You sat with whoever was there. People could be sitting four people to a table, two different couples and they've never met before. It was a real dump. The chairs was wobbly. The tables were uneven. [Laughs.] But I liked it."

Brigtsen: "Paul would do blue plate specials. Mondays were red beans and rice with ham hocks. Tuesday was garlic shrimp with oysters on pasta. Wednesday was Mexican. Paul was a wonderful cook of Mexican food. Fridays we'd do a sautéed seafood platter. Thursdays was lasagna. [Laughs.] This was the original K-Paul's menu. If we had any of those lunch specials left for dinner, Paul and K would argue about price. Let's say it was $4.95 at lunch. K would say, 'Well, let's charge $5.95 [at dinner].' He'd say, 'No, that's too much. How 'bout five and a quarter?' They'd really get into it."

Prudhomme: "I always knew that my food would work. I had the price right."

Brigtsen: "One of the interesting things about K-Paul's was the pickup window. We could peek out and watch people as they ate. And I'm telling you, people's reaction to this food was astounding."

Prudhomme: "You'd watch these four people [not] talking to each other. They take a bite of food and they put it in their mouth, maybe take a second bite. And then they go over to the person they weren't talking to: 'You won't believe this! Taste it!' [Community seating] was the customers' idea. They'd say, 'Man, I don't wanna be standing out there, you've got all these empty [chairs]. I'll sit with somebody else.'"

Greg Sonnier, chef-co-owner of Gabrielle, former K-Paul's cook: "It was definitely the hottest restaurant in the country at that time. They literally had a line of a hundred people outside to get in the place."

Alec Gifford, WDSU newsman: "One time I saw Lee Iacocca out in that line. He stood in line with everyone else to get a communal seat."

Prudhomme: "I did the restaurant because I wanted to do my own thing. I did the cookbook because we couldn't feed all the people I wanted. There were sixty-four seats."

Jack Leonardi, chef-owner of Crabby Jack's and Jacques-Imo's Café, former K-Paul's cook: "One day I just dropped by at lunch. I asked [Paul] if I could work for him for free. He wouldn't let me work for free. I wanted to learn. I didn't need the money. He was the Emeril of the time."

Brigtsen: "Here I am, just a kid, and just outside the pickup window is Vincent Price. He's saying, 'Hey, Frank, what do you think of that fettuccine? It was the best I've had in my life, better than any in Italy.'"

Prudhomme: "We were only open Monday through Friday. When it was vacation time, we'd put a sign on the door, 'Gone fishin'.' People loved that."

Greg Sonnier: "Nobody at Delgado [Community College] could believe that I had Saturdays and Sundays off. People used to call me 'the Banker' at school, because I had banker's hours."

Prudhomme: "[K and I] decided to get married. There was like ten people at the wedding, mostly [K's] family. They all came down [from her native Montana]. We got married in the restaurant, against the wall."

George Rhode, corporate chef for Outback Steakhouse, former Commander's Palace apprentice: "For his wedding I made a Cajun cottage out of chocolate. We filled it with fresh peaches, and a hot sauce was poured over it."

REINVENTING CAJUN CUISINE

Bourg: "The word *Cajun* was the hook he hung his cuisine on, and there were some very obvious Cajun elements in his cooking. But it wasn't traditional southwestern Louisiana cuisine. He didn't allow tradition to fetter his imagination."

Michael Batterberry, founding editor of *Food & Wine*, editor-in-chief and publisher of *Food Arts*: "People hadn't considered the idea of a regional cuisine being taken into the even playing grounds of haute cuisine. The French have long put a high premium on delicacy and subtlety. This was not without subtlety, but it was also a powerhouse."

Greg Sonnier: "One thing that I learned at K-Paul's is to keep everything fresh, nothing frozen. Dan [Crutchfield, a Mississippi farmer] used to come in every week at K-Paul's and drop off fresh rabbits. I remember poke salad. He used to grow peanuts. He used to bring in fresh flowers to sprinkle on the salads."

Mary Sonnier: "We butchered rabbits. We butchered legs of veal. We didn't order. We butchered just about anything."

Brigtsen: "I remember the first time Paul brought back tasso from the country. I can guarantee you that was the first time tasso crossed the parish line."

Paul Miller, executive chef of K-Paul's Louisiana Kitchen: "Upstairs [from K-Paul's] was called Louisiana Grocery. They had different sausages, tasso. They had meat pies, they had cakes, they had pâtés. They also had plate lunches and po' boys. We did seven different kinds of mayonnaise."

Bourg: "I don't think he could have [served crawfish] at Commander's, because that was not restaurant food. There was crawfish cardinale at Antoine's, but crawfish otherwise wasn't really found in restaurants until the late '70s, early '80s."

Brigtsen: "I remember when Chef was first invited on the *Today* show in New York. He chose to cook jambalaya. After that show, one of Paul's brothers called Paul and was furious: 'How could you cook that trash food?' To them, jambalaya was what poor people ate. It wasn't something that they were necessarily proud of. Paul changed all that."

Greg Sonnier: "Two things that were really brought from Cajun country were boudin and cracklins. [So was] cochon de lait. Also roast duck. [New Orleans restaurants] had duck à l'orange from France, but they didn't have roast duck with pecan gravy. It was something you couldn't see anywhere else besides K-Paul's."

THE DISH THAT ATE AMERICA

Prudhomme: "The beginning of [blackening was] at Commander's. In the old kitchen, we had what was known as the flat-top. It's where you put big pots to make soups. It's very hot, just a flat piece of iron. We'd throw a steak on there and just char it."

Brennan: "We were all sitting around. And someone said, 'You know what I'd really like some time? A piece of fish that's just come out of the water and just cook it right there, at the side of the water.' Paul went down to the kitchen and started."

Prudhomme: "Jay Blair was the broiler guy. I told him, 'Throw butter on a piece of fish and seasoning on it and throw it on the stove.' He did that. I went back upstairs; he brought [the fish] up. I thought it was the best thing I ever tasted in my entire life."

William Rice, food journalist: "That blackened redfish fad, it depopulated the Gulf of Mexico."

Prudhomme: "Ella liked it but wasn't that impressed by it. She didn't want to call it blackening. We put it on the menu at Mr. B's as a grilled redfish, but that was on an open fire. [At] K-Paul's, I started looking for another way to do it. I hit on a cast-iron skillet after several tries. The first night we did blackening was March of '80, for thirty or forty people. Within days the restaurant was full. And within weeks there were huge lines. People would come in, four to a table, and say, 'Four blackened redfish.'"

Lagasse: "I'll never forget. This was 1985. I went to a board meeting at Johnson & Wales [University, in Providence, Rhode Island]. These people were saying, 'We have to go to this amazing restaurant in Providence that has this amazing dish.' Blackened redfish."

Prudhomme: "We literally limited blackened redfish to one to a table. And we'd usually convince them to order one as an appetizer and everybody would taste it. I said 'K, if you give them good food, they're going to forget about the fact that you wouldn't give them blackening.' And it worked."

KNIGHTED IN NEW YORK

Prudhomme: "[In 1979] I cooked a dinner for the first anniversary of *Food & Wine*. I don't have any doubt that it was [a turning point]. To get the New York media to write about you is not easy."

Batterberry: "There had not been an event at which young rising chefs were cooking with their French equivalents, as peers."

The Washington Post, April 29, 1979: "The chefs came from three countries. Alain Dutournier and the brothers Henri and Gerard Charvet are French, Pier Angelo Cornaro is Italian, Paul Prudhomme and Alice Waters are American."

Batterberry: "There were a series of lunches and dinners, and each chef cooked one. It was part food community, but also people from the arts community, the international press, people from politics. It was like a New York party."

Bourg: "In the mid-'70s, every food magazine was looking for some kind of new authentic American cuisine to talk about. People didn't know about New Orleans at all. Nobody from New York came down to New Orleans to eat."

Batterberry: "Everybody [at the anniversary] thought, 'Well, the French will walk off with this.'"

Prudhomme: "We all had fresh stuff, which was a big deal back then. We cooked everything to order."

Batterberry: "Paul had done one of his seafood sausages, and he did his beef with debris sauce."

Alice Waters, chef-owner of Chez Panisse, Berkeley, California: "I will never forget the dessert. He constructed out of chocolate little Cajun cabins with little front porches. Each person had one, and under the roofs were little Louisiana strawberries. The waiters came around with a big bowl of warm crème anglaise. They poured it over the little Cajun cottages, and they all melted. I just thought, 'Who dreamed this up?'"

Prudhomme: "When it was over, I went into the room. When I came in, the room erupted. New Yorkers were standing on chairs screaming and hollerin'. It was like a fantasy. I heard a guy standing on his chair next to me saying to a person who had a French accent, 'This is real American food.'"

Waters: "The next day was my lunch. [Paul] had brought probably twenty people from New Orleans. I came with my sous chef Jean-Pierre. Paul comes over and says, 'Do you need some help?' I said, 'Oh, I don't think so.' He said, 'I think you do.' He was just like, 'OK, you three guys get a fire going for her. You two guys open oysters for her.' I tell you, he saved me. My whole reputation could have been ruined."

THE MEDIA TAKE NOTICE

Craig Claiborne, the *New York Times Magazine,* May 6, 1984: "Although a good many of the meals of my Mississippi childhood were Cajun, Creole, or soul food, I would have been hard put, until recently, to make an elaborate distinction between what is Cajun and what is Creole. But my solution was simple: Go to the undisputed pontiff and grand panjandrum of the Cajun and Creole cookstove, that genial genius of massive girth, Paul Prudhomme."

Prudhomme: "The print media was absolutely sure [the hype] about K-Paul's was absolute malarkey. [Writers] would come to write a bad story. Then they'd turn around and write a better one. That went on for years."

Rice: "The first time I ever talked to him at any length, I went to K-Paul's. It was early on. K was still alive, and I ordered the whole menu. He showed up a little while later to see who was doing it. We got along great."

Prudhomme: "Regis Philbin was a big, big influence on my career. He'd see me on the street in New York, and he'd tell me, 'You gotta come be on the show tomorrow.' That was just awesome for me."

Brennan: "Well, he looks like a Pillsbury Doughboy, and he has this magnificent smile. He has a warmth. People warmed up to him."

Brigtsen: "He didn't have a P.R. firm helping him out. This is stuff that happened to him. The media came to him."

Brennan: "The world had just been through nouvelle cuisine, and it didn't much like it. They liked what Paul was doing, the authenticity of it. We didn't have to worry about these French chefs, who at that time weren't very pleasant. Paul, being as sweet as he is, the media couldn't resist it."

THE DOWNSIDE OF BEING ON TOP

Prudhomme: "We started losing locals because they didn't want to stand in line. We even made medals, a get-in-front-of-the-line card, and we handed that out to the locals to try to get them to come. They would get harassed so much by people that had been waiting a long time that they didn't come. I went six years without seeing a card."

Bourg: "A lot of people came to New Orleans to eat at K-Paul's. It sort of made him a pariah in his own town."

Prudhomme: "It was very upsetting, because [locals] were the keystone of why we did what we did, because they knew the food. The greatest pleasure you can get is making someone happy. Elevating that pleasure is making someone happy that knows what they're eating."

Bourg: "He's also not from New Orleans. He's a Cajun boy, and that turned a lot of people off. There's a certain class that looks down on Cajuns, and I'm talking the older generation."

Rice: "[Prudhomme's success] was kind of hard on people who went to restaurants to study the furniture. All of a sudden people were eating with their hands."

Miller: "I hear people talking all the time in front: 'I used to go in there all the time, but now you can't get in. It's too busy. They don't take credit cards.' We've been taking reservations since '93."

Rice: "He was too successful. He was probably too downmarket for some of those folks that live in those big mansions. Out-of-towners really made his success, people that fell in love with the books and so on. There was always a bit of an edge when [local] foodies talked about Paul. It was always a little dismissive."

Waters: "At a certain point, the whole celebrity thing is a double-edged sword. Bigger is better, and more and more and more. Enough is enough. Stay home and run your restaurant."

Lagasse: "It's the American way. The more successful that you become the more people want to knock you down."

Greg Sonnier: "One of the things I learned from [K and Prudhomme] is not to let other people get to you. Their attitude was that if someone didn't have a good time, they did their best."

1993: A CRUSHING LOSS

The Times-Picayune, January 1, 1993: "K Hinrichs Prudhomme, the French Quarter restaurateur who ran the front of K-Paul's Louisiana Kitchen while her husband, Paul Prudhomme, turned out Cajun masterpieces in the kitchen, died Thursday of lung cancer at her New Orleans home. She was 48."

Lagasse: "That devastated him for a period of time."

Prudhomme: "It was probably just as much a business relationship as a husband-wife relationship. I admired her ability to run a dining room and she admired my ability to cook. That pretty much was what the relationship was based on."

Greg Sonnier: "One thing K did [was to] put stars on people's faces if they finished their food. They would have a second-line every now and again through the dining room."

Miller: "Customers came back because of her. I think in spirit she's still here."

Mary Sonnier: "She was his life. He loved her."

A NEW CHAPTER

Shawn McBride, president and CEO, Magic Seasoning Blends and Paul Prudhomme Enterprises: "It seems like from 1993 on, [K-Paul's] took on a whole new [personality]. It had to, because K wasn't there anymore in the front, and the restaurant scene kind of changed in New Orleans. K-Paul's had to make the decision to change some of the things it was doing too."

Prudhomme: "When it got crushingly busy, and I was doing a lot of thank-you, thank-you stuff with people and doing autographs, I could no longer do a [cooking] station."

McBride: "As we grew, we had to start realizing that people were coming almost as a destination to K-Paul's, and it was on a Saturday night, and we'd be closed. And we didn't take credit cards. So we started doing that to accommodate business people, because they didn't carry cash like they used to."

Miller: "In '96 we renovated. The building was built I think in the 1860s, and the more we dug, the worse we found out it was."

Prudhomme: "I remember going [to K-Paul's] one day, and they had bulldozers inside. They just left the walls up. I left very depressed, and I get home and I get a phone call. They said, 'The restaurant's sinking, and it's starting to crack.' The restaurant [is] still alive today because of the renovation. But it was the most horrible thing to go through on a day-to-day basis."

Miller: "The whole thing is pretty much new. We tripled in size."

McBride: "After we did the renovation, we started to develop the wine list a lot more, and we started getting a lot more questions from our customers about pairing the wines."

K-Paul's Louisiana Kitchen dinner menu, January 25, 2005: "Fresh Louisiana drum fillet seasoned, blackened in a cast-iron skillet and served with a chipotle compound butter. Served with potatoes & veggies. $31.95. Wonderful with Rombauer Chardonnay."

Prudhomme: "I guess [the food was mostly Cajun] in the beginning, but it's not totally true now. I've traveled all over the world. There's Asian stuff in my food now."

McBride: "We've been taking reservations now eight, nine years, and there are locals that still think you have to come wait in line."

Prudhomme: "We still have [staff] that resists. They just can't get into their head that it's just not the same restaurant anymore. They just can't seem to quite let loose of the way it was."

Miller: "Before it was a dump. People still miss that."

2005: THE LEGACY

Bourg: "A lot of young cooks in New Orleans decided to be restaurant cooks because of Paul Prudhomme. He liberated this city like no one before or since. He made it possible to make something besides trout meunière."

Rice: "Paul showed a way to make a culinary career more rewarding monetarily and socially, and as a result a better class of person has been drawn into the business."

Mary Sonnier: "You could say [his legacy] is the food, the blackened redfish. But I think it's all the people he taught."

Leonardi: "He's gone and done exactly what Ella did for him."

Brigtsen: "He asked me what I wanted out of life. I told him one day I'd like to have my own little restaurant. Seven years after I started, he and K decided I was ready to go out on my own. They got me a real estate agent. They lent me money out of their own pocket to open Brigtsen's. They hooked me up with an accountant and an attorney. They let me take staff members with me from K-Paul's. I really believe they wanted Brigtsen's to happen as much as I did."

Bourg: "[New Orleans cuisine] was a cuisine in confinement. Nobody really stretched the possibilities, and then Prudhomme came in and started using all these powerful seasonings, and he brought a lot of new depth to New Orleans cooking. Prudhomme is the one who really created New Orleans's restaurant reputation. I don't think there's any doubt about that."

Lagasse: "His aura, and I think his passion for cooking, tasting, seasoning, has really influenced a lot of people."

Miller: "When Cajun became popular it was because of him. New Orleans was always known for good food, but not in the way that he was."

Rice: "He's a pioneer in regional cuisine, he's a pioneer in seafood, he's a pioneer in not being embarrassed to use simple ingredients."

Brennan: "He was the pioneer in New Orleans of really going out to the farms [to] get the fresh products and get farmers to grow them for you."

Prudhomme: "If that culture wasn't there, if Mother hadn't handed me this stuff and my sisters and my cousins and my uncles and my aunts, if they hadn't shown me all this by putting it in my mouth and talking about it all the time, I wouldn't have done any of this. I don't kid myself. I wasn't born with it. I may have been born with the drive. But the food was taught to me by the family and the people around. It's their food as much as it is mine."

Louisiana and the Gulf Coast
After

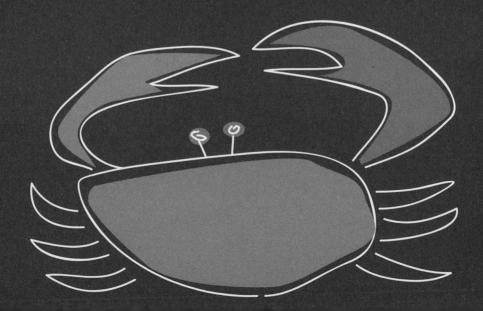

This Isn't the Last Dance

Rick Bragg

It has always had my heart in a box.

In the clip-joint souvenir shops in the gaudiest blocks of the Quarter, with canned Cajun music drilling rock-concert-loud into my ears, I could never resist opening the toy wooden coffins to see what was inside. I knew it would be just a cut-rate voodoo doll—a wad of rags, cheap plastic beads, and blind, button eyes. But every time, it made me smile. What a place, what a city, that can make you laugh at coffins and believe in magic—all the way to the cash register.

What a place, where old women sit beside you on outbound planes complaining about their diabetes while eating caramel-covered popcorn a fistful at a time. "It's hard, so hard, sweet baby," they will say of their disease, then go home and slick an iron skillet with bacon grease, because what good is there in a life without hot cornbread?

What a place, where in the poorest cemeteries the poorest men and women build tin-foil monuments to lost children in a potter's field, while just a few blocks over, the better-off lay out oyster po' boys and cold root beer and dine in the shade of the family crypt, doing lunch with their ancestors and the cement angels in cities of the dead.

What a place, so at ease here at the elbow of death, where I once marched and was almost compelled to dance in a jazz funeral for a street-corner conjurer named Chicken Man, who was carried to his resting place by a hot-stepping brass band and a procession of mourners who drank long-neck beers and laughed out loud as his hearse rolled past doorways filled with men and women who clapped in time.

Now, for those of us who borrowed that spirit and used that love and then moved away, these past few awful days have seemed like a hospital death watch—and, in fact, for so many people it has been. And we stare deep into the television screen, at the water that had always seemed like just one more witch, one more story to scare ourselves into a warmer, deeper sleep, and we wonder if there is just too much water and too much death this time.

Ever since I was barely in my twenties, I have loved this city the way some men love women, if that means unreasonably. I fell in love with it and a Louisiana State University sophomore on the same night, eating shrimp cooked seven ways in the Quarter, riding the ferry across the black, black river where fireworks burned the air at Algiers Point. I drank so much rum I could sleep standing up against a wall. The sophomore left me, smiling, but the city never did.

There is no way to explain to someone who has never lived here why every day seemed like parole. Every time I would swing my legs from under the quilt and ease my toes onto the pine floors of my shotgun double, I would think, I am getting away with something here.

How long now before the streetcar rattles down St. Charles Avenue and beads swing into the two-hundred-year-old trees? How long before Dunbar's puts the chicken and stewed cabbage on the stove, or the overworked ladies at Domilise's dress a po' boy on Annunciation Street, or the midday drinkers find their way back to Frankie and Johnny's on Arabella Street? Does my old house still stand on Joseph? It was high, high ground, on the lip of the bowl, and you could hit the Mississippi River with a silver dollar if you threw it twice.

I cannot stand the idea that it is broken, unfixable. I look at the men using axes to hack their way into hundred-year-old houses to save people trapped there by the suffocating water. I know there is life and death to be fought out for a long, long time. But I can't help but wonder what will come, later.

My wife, as wives do, voiced what most of us are afraid to say.

"I'm glad you took me there," she said. "Before."

We went there on our honeymoon.

Just a few weeks ago, I spent a week there, walking along Magazine, walking the Quarter, not minding the heat because that is what the devil sends, heat and water, to make you appreciate the smell of crushed cherries and whis-key on the balcony at the Columns Hotel, to make you savor the barbecued shrimp, to make you hear, really hear, the sound of a twelve-year-old boy blowing his own heart out into a battered trumpet by a ragged cardboard box full of pocket change.

How long, before that city reforms. Some people say it never will.

But I have seen these people dance, laughing, to the edge of a grave.

I believe that, now, they will dance back from it.

Letter from New Orleans

Lolis Eric Elie

I am writing to you from my usual desk, only now there is plywood to my right, covering the broken window. The ceiling above me is dry, though there is a stain where rainwater dripped through my 170-year-old roof. Behind me is a small patch of moldy sheetrock. I must preserve it as evidence to show the insurance adjuster, if he ever comes. . . .

As you have gathered, I'm lucky. My roof leaks, my fence is horizontal, my car is drowned, but in New Orleans as it exists since Hurricane Katrina, I am one of the fortunate ones.

I know that you are hungry for news of your favorite people and places. Much of the news is good, and I am anxious that you should know it. The French Quarter, the Garden District, and many of the other places you have probably visited escaped with relatively little damage. Mardi Gras will still take place at the end of February, though the planned eight-day celebration is four days shy of the usual duration. Jazz Fest will take place at the end of April, but with its fairgrounds so badly damaged, no one knows exactly what it will look like. The most devastating images you have seen were mostly from newer residential areas of the city, far from our historic architecture and legendary eateries. If you confine your movements to these older places, life can have that elusive quality we so long for these days, normality.

In those first days after the storm, when many of our people were stranded on floating rooftops and in rising waters, we waited patiently for our federal tax dollars to go to work. Then, those of us who were safe watched the televised scenes in horror. It seemed our government was on vacation or elsewhere engaged.

Far from Gabrielle, their celebrated restaurant, Greg and Mary Sonnier watched from a hotel room in Memphis. "In the beginning, I just felt like we were watching New Orleans go down, and nobody was coming to help. I was just blown away by that," Mary said. "The TV cameras were there, but where were the people to help? We were being flooded and it just seemed like nobody was there. 'Are we in the United States of America?'—that's what I kept thinking."

Our chefs were among our first responders. They worked like men and women on a mission. John Besh, the former Marine who commands the four-year-old kitchen at Restaurant August, secured his family in North Carolina, then made his way back to his home state. Unable to make or receive calls on local cell phones, he sent text messages to his former Marine buddies. Soon they were cooking red beans and rice in Slidell, across Lake Pontchartrain from the city.

"I don't think there was any point that we even mentioned the possibility that we weren't going to return as soon as we could," said Paul Prudhomme. Unable to cook at K-Paul's, his French Quarter restaurant, he set up his kitchen equipment in a tent outside his suburban spice factory. Nearly thirty thousand relief workers got their own relief from army-issue Meals, Ready-to-Eat, in the form of fresh salads, chicken Creole, and made-from-scratch desserts. "We're not firemen. We're not policemen. The best thing we could do is feed people," Prudhomme said.

Scott Boswell used to serve bold, multi-ingredient dishes at Stella!, his incongruously quaint French Quarter space: lobster-scented market fish with Gulf shrimp, jumbo lump crab pearl pasta, and micro green salad with lemon-chive butter, all on one plate in a room reminiscent of the south of France. He accelerated his plan to open Stanley! (a café named after the other main character of A Streetcar Named Desire). By September 21 he was serving cheeseburgers and sausage sandwiches cooked on an open pit and served with potato chips and a pickle.

Thanks to the storm, the water wasn't safe to drink or wash with. Small plastic bottles of hand sanitizer were everywhere. "I actually worked with the Louisiana Restaurant Association to write the regulations that the health department used to let us work without potable water," said Ralph Brennan, owner of Bacco, Redfish Grill, and Ralph's on the Park. "We were serving on plastic plates. We had those little packages of knives, forks, and spoons in plastic. That was a requirement of the health department, to use plastic, while we didn't have potable water. After the water came back we stayed on plastic for a while because we didn't have dishwashers."

In New Orleans food is identity. We are not fully ourselves in the company of picnic fare. Louis Armstrong performed "Struttin' with Some Barbecue" at a lot of his concerts, but he closed all of his letters "red beans and ricely yours." Emergency measures might have dictated a limited menu, but we were determined that such measures would endure for only a limited duration. By early October, very few New Orleanians had returned to the city, but chefs had a greatly expanded list of options.

"We didn't want to just open to open and serve the easy stuff like hamburgers and chicken fingers. We wanted to bring back the cuisine of New Orleans," said Dickie Brennan, Ralph's cousin and the owner of Bourbon House, Palace Café, and Dickie Brennan's Steak House. The opening-day menu at Bourbon House looked the way a New Orleans menu is supposed to look: Crab Fingers Bordelaise, Soft-Shell Crab Po' Boys, Shrimp Chippewa, Gulf Fish Pecan, Tournedos with Wild Mushrooms and Grits, and Bread Pudding.

Our food, which has long served as both our emblem and our sustenance, is one of the bedrocks on which we are building our recovery. It has been the local restaurants, not the national chains or even the deep-pocketed fast-food places, that have bounced back first. Even three months after the storm, it was a lot easier to find a po' boy than it was to find a Whopper or a piece of Popeye's fried chicken. That made me smile.

Jo Ann Clevenger is the philosopher queen of our restaurateurs. She routinely quotes old menus and old memories from long-ago places in order to put the modern scene into context. She was quick to understand the expanded mission our restaurants were forced to perform. "I really felt I had to open. If I didn't open because it was difficult and I couldn't find the staff, then it meant that other restaurants and other people might do the same thing. I think that one restaurant opening gives people hope and a sense of optimism. My optimism can be infectious. The people who are determined to make New Orleans work need to have it reinforced because when you get outside the part that's beautiful and you are reminded of the devastation, it's so disheartening."

Those owners who reopened have been heroic, in a way. Hindered by short staffs and abbreviated menus, they placed a bold bet that our population would return. (Mind you, nearly 100 percent of our people were ordered to evacuate.) The heroism of these owners was buttressed by the luck of geography. Most of the open restaurants dodged the raging floodwaters and falling trees. The owners at Gautreau's, Dooky Chase, Gabrielle, and Commander's Palace want to reopen, but they still face months of costly repairs.

Reopened restaurants got an unexpected boost from another phenomenon. As our people returned, they didn't dare open their refrigerators. The stench of rotting food was too strong. Folks simply taped the doors shut and placed the appliances on the sidewalk to be collected by the sanitation workers. In the absence of functioning home kitchens, people went out in search of food and fellowship.

"Restaurants have always had that nurturing part," says Jo Ann Clevenger.

"But now it's also a gathering place. It might sound Pollyanna to say it in a way that is so cheerful, but it is cheerful. I watch the people in here night after night get up and go to another table to someone they haven't seen since the storm, and they run to another table. They run! And they get up and hug each other. It's very luxurious for me because it gives me and the staff a feeling of creating that opportunity for people to be restored and to be joyous. . . .

"The other part of it, of course, is it creates the opportunity for them to remember," she says. "Proust was right. Having something to eat that you had before Katrina brings back that sense of normalcy. It can chase away sadness, but it can also enhance your determination to make it work."

Jay Nix has that determination. A carpenter by trade, he bought the Parkway Bakery in 1996 because it was next to his house and he feared that a liquor store or rowdy barroom might replace the business that had long baked bread and served po' boy sandwiches. Inspired by the legendary tales of the food the surly owner had served since the 1930s, Nix renovated the place and taught himself the restaurant trade. He had been serving nostalgia on French bread for less than two years when Hurricane Katrina inundated his place with several feet of water. In December, he was still cleaning up. But he was also plotting his return.

"I tell you what. New Orleans is coming back through people's stomachs and their appetites. New Orleans is coming back through restaurants. If you've been following it, it's the restaurants that are getting people excited and bringing people out. They're short-staffed. They have abbreviated menus. And the public is patient about it. You couldn't pull that off in regular times."

Willie Mae Seaton is determined too.

She had been cooking great soul food in relative obscurity until last year when her name was called at the James Beard Awards. An American Classic, they named her. Slowly, she walked. On eighty-eight-year-old legs she approached the stage. That audience, moved by the slow determination of her gait and the sincere sparseness of her acceptance speech, cheered and cried. She promised them then that she would still be cooking. Whenever they made their way south to the Crescent City, she would be there.

She is eighty-nine now. The shotgun double house that contains both her home and her restaurant was flooded. The furniture, the fixtures, all lost. Even after surveying the damage, she had a plan. Her son Charlie serves as waiter, purveyor, and handyman at the restaurant. She would call on him to clean up the place and get everything ready. It didn't seem to occur to her that, at seventy-one, Charlie wasn't the ideal candidate. She still hopes to reopen, but where will she find the money and manpower to do so?

All true New Orleanians, born or transplanted, have a Creole spirit. Our joie de vivre, we have long joked, marks us as redheaded stepchildren in the vanilla mainstream of our American siblings. But what was once a harmless joke is now a dreadful cloud. It seems as if, in the minds of many of our countrymen, we are distant relatives somehow unworthy of the sort of assistance that this nation has extended to other parts of the country devastated by disaster.

We have no doubt that we are worth saving. We live and we cook now with an intensity focused on reminding the world and ourselves of what will be lost if New Orleans is allowed to remain in ruins. John Besh used to take our local produce and spin it into dishes reminiscent not only of Creole traditions, but also of the food he cooked while apprenticing in Provence and the Black Forest of Germany. He hasn't abandoned his signature appetizer, a "BLT" of soft-shell crab, lettuce, and tomato over pain perdu. But the day he reopened, there were red beans and rice on his Monday lunch menu. His Friday lunch now boasts a downhome seafood and sausage gumbo, a dish that, while ubiquitous on New Orleans menus, was conspicuous in its absence from his decidedly nontraditionalist offerings.

"Instead of me trying to act and cook like a New York chef, I think we have a story to tell now. I've got something I've got to get off my chest and here it is. We might not be as suave and this and that. We're not going to be. But we will have a flavor that is undeniably Louisiana.

"It's taken this Katrina to shake us all up to say 'this is what I love.' You ask, culinarily speaking, what I dig about New Orleans; it's the tradition. All these crazy bloodlines that came in and created this culture here, and it is through that that we are able to really create one of the most interesting, heartfelt, soulful menus that you just really couldn't replicate anywhere else in the country. They have great food all over the place. But is it *their* food? I don't want to serve a damn thing here unless it has roots that stem from those cultures that built New Orleans."

To understand us now, you must learn the most popular phrase of our new lexicon. We speak now of "pre-K." It has nothing to do with early childhood education and everything to do with that long-ago period before the hurricane hit. This is the historical reference point that precedes the answers to such questions as "Do they serve lunch?" or "Do they have valet parking?"

In post-Katrina New Orleans, the hurricane is invariably the main topic of our conversations. But, as in pre-K days, breakfast talk is spiced with anticipatory statements about where one will dine for lunch or for dinner. No restaurant is more talked about than Donald Link's Herbsaint. Meatloaf remains on his lunch menu as a vestige of those days immediately after his October opening when he sought to serve comfort food to emergency workers. But it is his chile-glazed pork belly with beluga lentils and fresh mint, and his banana brown butter tart that dominate discussions of his restaurant now.

Fears were raised a year and a half ago when Tom Wolfe bought Peristyle from the popular Anne Kearney. Would the hearty fare from his self-named restaurant across town run roughshod over her meticulous, classic creations? The answer is that, both pre-K and post-K, Wolfe has proven himself adept at creating dishes as elegant as those Peristyle diners had come to expect.

But not everyone survived.

Perhaps the first and only jazz funeral ever held in Atlanta took place October 9 for Austin Leslie. The chef had come to fame in 1987 as the inspiration for the short-lived television show *Frank's Place*. His fortunes declined after that. In 1994 he closed his own restaurant, Chez Helene. But in 2004 he was starring at Pampy's Creole Kitchen, where his fried chicken garnished with fresh garlic, parsley, and pickles remained a favorite.

He stayed during the hurricane and had to be rescued from the attic of his home. Ultimately, he ended up with his family in Atlanta. When I talked to him after the storm, he was anxious to get back in the kitchen. "It's a new beginning for me," he said. "I'm seventy-one years old, but I've done it before. I'm willing to start over."

By the end of September, he was dead. The coroner said it was a heart attack, but we all know it was the heartbreak of seeing his city destroyed that killed him.

Joseph Casamento, who was born above his family's oyster bar in 1925, had only left the city a few times in his life before evacuating to Mississippi in advance of the storm. He died there on the day of the storm. The restaurant is once again serving raw oysters on the half-shell and fried oysters on pan bread, but the bivalves are no longer being opened by Mr. Joe.

There is still incredible optimism here. Two restaurants that were scheduled to open around the time of the hurricane simply altered their debut dates and moved forward. Uptown, Alberta serves elegant, French-accented bistro food. Across Lake Pontchartrain in Abita Springs, Slade and Alison Vines Rushing have transplanted the award-winning food they created at Jack's Luxury Oyster Bar in Manhattan to an environment closer to their Louisiana and Mississippi roots. At Longbranch, their bacon-topped reinvention of oysters Rockefeller may be the most exciting new dish I've tasted since the storm, though the smoked lamb rib served alongside the rack of lamb with wilted romaine and tomato jam has had my taste buds dreaming ever since I tasted it.

While the dining scene is vibrant here, once you leave the restaurants you are often confronted with the stark reality of life in New Orleans now. Many neighborhoods are still depopulated. Even though things may appear normal to the casual observer, Lakeview, the Lower Ninth Ward, eastern New Orleans—months after the storm they are still ghost towns.

"We want it to look normal. It's not normal," Prudhomme said. "The chefs and the cooks, the whole team in the kitchen are washing dishes. I wouldn't think that's normal."

This is already a long letter. I didn't intend it to be. But it has taken me this many words to explain to myself what I want you to understand about my hometown. Despite the pseudo-scientific pronouncements that our beloved city is too dangerous, too hurricane-prone for human habitation, we fully intend to build our city back to its former glory.

"New Orleans is truly different from everywhere else," Jay Nix says. "All the buildings look different and all the people look different. And if you think about it, most of the places you go, all the buildings look alike and all the people look alike. Nothing looks alike in New Orleans."

Put simply, this place, above all others, is where we wish to live.

Red beans and ricely yours,
Lolis

[Editors' note: Since this essay was originally published, a good bit of what Lolis Eric Elie describes has changed. What has remained the same is the determination of New Orleans residents to rebuild and revivify their city.]

From the Crescent City to the Bayou City

Peggy Grodinsky

What do you miss about New Orleans?

Harold Brown Jr., a salt-and-pepper-bearded, bespectacled gentleman now living in Houston, repeated my question, reworking it to mirror the title of the Louis Armstrong tune. The lyrics—with their moss-covered vines, tall sugar pines, Creole tunes, and magnolias in bloom—smack of Hollywood. But Brown's answer is as plain as the Garden District is ornate.

"What it means to miss New Orleans?" he repeated from a chair in the lobby of the Western Motel on the city's near north side, which he has called home since Hurricane Katrina leveled his.

"Everything. Red beans and rice on a Monday. Cabbage and cornbread on a Tuesday. Mustard greens and fried pork chops on a Wednesday, and on a Thursday meatballs and spaghetti. Friday, you go with anything seafood. Saturday is potluck. Sunday is gumbo, mirliton, roast beef."

Is that a song?

"No!" Brown was emphatic. "That's the way we live. That's the way we cook."

In a series of conversations, Brown referred to oyster po' boys, bread pudding, crawfish, and crab boils. But many of the dishes dear to his stomach and heart are not those that make tourists in the Crescent City wax romantic. He mentioned étouffée once, muffalettas and bananas Foster not at all. When I asked him about beignets, he scoffed.

"For you. Maybe for you. White. That's right. You come to New Orleans, you got to go get a beignet with the sugar all on it. When you get ready to eat, somebody going to say something to you, and when you say something back to them, they going to blow powder all on you. That's a trick. And the coffee is café au lait. That's not coffee! That's milk!

"I drink strong coffee because of my mama. My mama she drink Louisiana [brand]. Had the old black lady on the label with the Aunt Jemammy head rag on. That Louisiana, when you pour it in the cup, [it's so strong] you could write your name on the table. It was coffee! Ooooh! If you had that, you was up. You was ready to go. You get a cup of that and a piece of hoecake—hoecake is like a biscuit but made like a cake. You dip it in that coffee and you rolling."

Brown doesn't need strong coffee to roll. Just get him started on the subject of food.

Galatoire's and Commander's Palace, Arnaud's and Café du Monde—these are the restaurants that defined New Orleans eating and that seem equipped to survive in a post-hurricane city. But lovers of the city's singular food scene fear the loss of the countless, little-ballyhooed mom-and-pop joints that served oysters here, red beans and rice there.

Brown owned such a place, a "little greasy spoon," as he proudly calls it: Kingfish Seafood in the Ninth Ward, the low-lying, predominantly poor, predominantly black community where he was born, raised, and lived all of his sixty-one years. Until now.

"Kingfish Seafood. 2635 Desire. World-famous Desire. We boil crabs, shrimps, crawfish. We fried fish, oysters. We made gumbo. We did hamburger with cheese on French. Hot sausage with cheese on French. I was a one-man kitchen. From 6 o'clock in the morning to 12 o'clock at night. I did it all.

"My main dish is okra gumbo. Yes, indeed. Okra. We fried it. We boiled it. We made it [into] salad and we smothered it. You can do anything you want with an okra. Okra, when you cut it, it has a slime on it. You got to keep stirring and stirring and whipping it and flipping it. When I was cooking okra, everybody up and down the block knew Kingfish was cooking okra."

"He cooked some beautiful food," seconded Valerie Jeanmarie, a lifelong resident of the ward who used to eat at Kingfish. Like Brown, she's now living in a Houston hotel. "Make you lick your fingers. Make you run home and tell your mama. You could smell his food a block away. When you smell seafood, you knew it was coming from Kingfish."

Brown says he inherited the property twenty-six years ago from his father, who was a fisherman and a trapper. His father had inherited it from his brother, Brown's Uncle B'Boy, who sold fish.

"They called him B'Boy because he stuttered," Brown explained.

Brown, who lived above the business, hoped to pass the business on to his thirteen-year-old son, Harold Pierre Brown. That's not likely now. The building—long and narrow with a large lot in back, three stories, five apartments, eighty-five years old—was uninsured and now is unsalvageable. Brown visited the wreckage in late November when the city allowed residents to return, "to look and leave."

"That old neighborhood that was full of life reminded me of a graveyard. Didn't even see a bird. Not even a pigeon.

"I was in it when it went down. A gush of wind came and moved the whole building, moved it about fifteen feet. Jesus! I couldn't believe it! I started counting. One potato. One foot. Two potato. Two foot. I counted to six potatoes. The water was six foot high in six minutes."

Brown and his companion, April Bowie, had a harrowing night and a narrow escape. Four days later, bedraggled, hungry, and beyond exhausted, they reached Houston. It was another three months before Brown located his son.

When Brown talks, the Ninth Ward lives on, a community of characters that could have stepped out of an August Wilson play. Tangle Eye—"We called him Tangle Eye 'cause he got cross eyes"—who occasionally fetched Brown fresh figs that grew in the neighborhood.

Big Tyrone. "Tyrone was a demolition man. Guess he got plenty business now. Big Tyrone wanted three fried fish with a big plate of potato salad and Texas toast. He would have an eat-a-thon. He was a man about that wide," Brown held his arms apart as far as they would go.

Big Eddie, a train engineer, taught Brown to fry turkey wings. "When he was off the train, he would eat. Yes, ma'am. Eat. Anything I cooked, anything to be cooked, he wanted it."

Brown's Uncle Melvin grew cotton in his backyard, in the city. "I don't know what the man did with it, but the man had a green thumb."

Robert Carsen sold rabbit (Brown called it "lapin"), possum, and raccoon, all of which Brown served at Kingfish on occasion. "He would go outdoors and kill this or drown that."

You eat raccoon?

"Suuuuure." Brown stretched the word to several syllables. "Nutri-rat, too. A coon got maybe thirty-one, thirty-two muscles in different parts of his body, but once you get those out, then you got a good coon. It's not that big an animal, but the meat is unique. Sort of chickeny. Sort of gatory. Sort of coony."

He gave me detailed cooking instructions, should I ever need them.

"Possum," he added, "you do it the same way. They say possum eat dead people 'cause he hang out around graveyards."

That got Brown thinking about turtles. He's not a connoisseur, but his mother is.

"He got about four or five different meats in him. You got to get him out of the shell. Once you get him out of the shell, you got to boil him. Once you boil him, you got to put everything in the kitchen in that pot. Plus wine. And you cook him for maybe four or five hours.

"And his heart don't ever die. You put the heart in the pot while it's"— Brown paused and tapped his chest to show a heartbeat. "Never dies. His head don't die till maybe nightfall. Chop his head off—his head still looking, still able to snap."

I ascribed this unlikely observation to New Orleans–style voodoo. Nonetheless, the conversation stopped.

We picked up again with Thanksgiving, which was approaching. How did he celebrate at Kingfish? Brown said he fed everybody in the neighborhood, including "all the bums, all the hookers. If you didn't come to Kingfish on the holiday, you wasn't no way.

"See, I was the who's the who. Who came? Who brought what? Who is with who? Who was hitting on who over at the radiator? Who met who round the corner? Who slipped who a couple of bucks?

"All that went on in the neighborhood. See, in the 2600 block, you had Delta Supermarket, Q. Lee's—the Oriental store across the street—and Kingfish was in the middle. If you didn't go to one, two, or three, you didn't go nowhere."

In Houston, Brown and Bowie were befriended by Houstonian and Louisiana native Quealy Antin, an attorney who supplied them with basics—including pots, pans, and spices—and has tried to help them find a more permanent address.

Not long ago, she volunteered the kitchen of her Heights home so that Brown could cook a meal for me and several of her friends. At the hotel, Brown cooks on a Coleman stove.

At first, he planned to make gumbo and stuffed mirlitons, but when we got to the Fiesta Mart to buy groceries, his enthusiasm grew. It had been a brutal three months, and the thought of cooking cheered him up.

He brushed aside my attempts to keep the meal simple: "Gumbo ain't nothing but a soup," he assured me. "Mirliton ain't nothing but a vegetable."

Eventually, he "jacked up" the evening's menu with boiled crabs, potato salad, sweet potato pie, and bread pudding. He purchased the groceries as carefully as if he were cooking for Sam Cooke or Otis Redding—singers whose shoes he had shined as a boy—sniffing this, squeezing that, rejecting the other, comparing prices, and grilling the fish clerk.

It was late afternoon when we arrived at Antin's house. There was a lot of food to make, and Brown is neither as young nor as nimble as he once was. In the year before the storm, he had suffered from a heart murmur and "sugar" (diabetes), and business had been off. His restaurant license lapsed in 2000, according to city records.

Now, Brown bustled and fussed around the kitchen—unself-conscious in the bunny apron that Antin lent him—tenderly supervising Bowie and sending Antin out for whiskey for the bread pudding.

He gave Antin's pots the once over before selecting one for rice. "You need you a pot. You got to know your pot. A jive pot is a pot that got hot spots. It stick. I know you have one of them at home."

He started the trinity (the chopped celery, onion, and bell pepper mixture that underpins Creole and Cajun cooking). He set the crabs to purge, the fish stock to simmer, and the potatoes, eggs, and sweet potatoes to boil. The mirlitons were boiled too, then hollowed, stuffed, and baked, with a big "lob" of butter on each. Most everything got a hit of cayenne—"the ruler of New Orleans," as Brown puts it.

Gradually, Antin's guests arrived, and the hour grew later, then late. It was 10:30 p.m. before we ate. Brown settled down on a stool in the kitchen and declined to join the party in the dining room.

"I tasted a little. I been tasting it since the start," he protested.

"Look, the average cook is humongous. Ever seen some of them cooks in New Orleans? I'm not getting like that. No, no, no. I used to be big. I got that way because [of] sipping this, eating that. Eating that grits and egg in the morning, eating them sausages in the morning with syrup on them. Pancakes. Oh, man. Big ol' gallon of milk. That much of crawfish. Everything that was left, I had to eat it. I'm not going to pile myself back up again."

The group insisted. Worn out but elated, Brown quietly took a chair at the table.

Within minutes, he was spinning tales and arguing New Orleans reconstruction policy over bowls of steaming gumbo and slices of eggless, milkless pumpkin pie.

Brown doesn't think much of the food in Houston. He complains about the barbecue, the fish, and the beans. "I don't know why they can't cook no bean in here. Terrible. Where are all the bean people?"

Despite my skepticism, he claims that the fast food, the Coca-Cola, and even the sugar taste different here. He is a man who is far from home. But Brown can't say enough good things about Fiesta. He rides the bus to buy groceries there each week. He praises the store's roasted corn, honey buns, and "barbecue bird."

"Whatever your heart desires that's edible, they have it," he told me. As Antin's guests toasted "the chef," I lifted my glass to Brown and made a silent wish for the man without a ward: "Whatever your heart desires that's edible, whatever your heart desires."

A Meal to Remember

Judy Walker

Forget the fireworks. Justin Lundgren has a plan to commemorate the events of last year in a respectful, positive, and moving way. It's a ritual Katrina dinner.

"How powerful would it be if every New Orleanian currently living in Houston, Dallas, Atlanta, and every other town across the country sat down at the same time to recognize the losses of the last year and to reaffirm their connection to the city?" Lundgren writes on his website. "The entire New Orleans diaspora could sit down simultaneously, fork in hand, to tell the world that this was a special place, a special community, one worth fighting to restore."

Within a versatile framework, he invites "the lost tribe of New Orleans" to participate in a dinner with symbolic foods, readings, a candle blessing, and more. Lundgren, a rehabilitation doctor at East Jefferson General Hospital, based his ritual on the Passover seder, with a little voodoo thrown in. "I just wanted to focus on New Orleans and healing and rebuilding," he said.

And he emphasized that his ritual is flexible, so we invited a few food gurus to share their thoughts on how they would make it more personal. For instance, to symbolize the bitterness of life, Jessica Harris suggested substituting pickled okra for Lundgren's dill pickle. And she and Poppy Tooker both said gumbo is a must.

Lundgren's wife, Kiersta Kurtz-Burke, is also a rehab doctor and was working at Charity Hospital for six days during the storm. Lundgren, who had evacuated to Baton Rouge, came back to the flooded city with a SWAT team to deliver supplies and helped evacuate her fifth-floor rehab ward.

The couple lost their Mid-City home and are living in an apartment. And they consider themselves lucky. "We have a place to live and we still have jobs. Overall, I still feel very blessed," Lundgren said. "All day long, my job is talking to people, and I have a good sense of what people have gone through. Every one of my patients had some loss related to Katrina. A lot of patients are from St. Bernard and New Orleans East."

The Katrina dinner that Lundgren details on his website consists of twenty to twenty-five minutes of ritual before a group meal. He has tried to get his idea out to as many people as possible, and overall the reaction has been positive. Lundgren's suggested recipes are from Emeril's website, but you can use your own, or make it a potluck.

The ritual starts with a candle blessing, then proceeds to five questions asked by the youngest person and answered by the oldest. Adults then take turns with the readings, selections from Lafcadio Hearn, John Kennedy Toole, Louis Armstrong, Charles Dudley Warner, Andrei Codrescu, Jed Horne, and Martin Luther King Jr.

Next up is ritual tasting of very small bites of symbolic foods, and Lundgren suggests that the person who has attended the most Mardi Gras parades should read the text for it. Sips of wine clear the palate between bites, and "if this ritual is performed correctly, everyone should be a tad drunk by the end," Lundgren writes.

Cane syrup reminds attendees of the sweetness of life, and dill pickle symbolizes its bitterness. Oysters symbolically link us to the sea and wetlands. A chocolate reminds us "that in New Orleans it's sometimes OK to eat dessert first," and grits symbolize the grit and determination of the people as they rebuild their lives along the Gulf Coast. Lastly, Lundgren said, "borrow your neighbor's spoon and feed him or her a few kernels of corn: This is to remind us of one of Katrina's greatest lessons, that we depend on each other."

Everyone who attends is asked to bring a small object of personal value that symbolizes Katrina or the year following. In a quasi-voodoo ritual, the meaning of each item is revealed as it is put into a bag; after a poem is recited over it, the bag is put under the table while dinner is eaten. Then there is a moment of silence for those who died in the storm. Finally, there is the feast, and Lundgren also gives an extensive list of suggested New Orleans music to play as it unfolds.

This Saturday, Lundgren will have fifteen to twenty people attending his Katrina dinner, he said. "The idea is not for it to be a rigid ritual. I provide an outline, some ideas of what I would do, what I would say, like the Q-and-A part," Lundgren said. "But you can say whatever you want to say." In that spirit, several people suggested how they would make the Katrina dinner their own.

Poppy Tooker of Slow Food sent her version of "diaspora gumbo" as the most important addition to the plate and the meal, with symbolic directions for the cook: "Cook the roux until it reaches the color of the muddy Mississippi River, and give thanks that levee held, while invoking its strength in the future." The gumbo preparation ends with the "greening of the gumbo," a sprinkle of filé powder. Tooker also suggested that dried red beans could become the Katrina dinner "gris-gris," like the dried fava beans that are part of the St. Joseph Day altars.

Fava beans are more to the taste of Poppy Z. Brite, author of *Liquor*, *Prime*, and *Soul Kitchen*, popular novels set in the New Orleans restaurant scene. "I think it's so personal for everyone involved, how they would observe the anniversary" of the storm, Brite said. "For me, personally, if I was going to do something to commemorate [the date] I would do a miniature St. Joseph altar" because she loves the altars and has always felt that, in a way, St. Joseph "is looking out for New Orleans, too." She would keep it simple, with "seed cookies from Nor-Joe's, and the pasta with red gravy and sawdust crumbs. And fava beans, the bread, and a St. Joseph statue, of course," Brite said.

Jessica Harris, known as the expert on food and foodways of the African diaspora, lives in New York City, where she is an English professor, and at her house in the Marigny. She met Lundgren at Martha's Vineyard in July, and she immediately took to the notion of a Katrina dinner. "I love the idea," Harris said. And she had ideas galore to customize the ritual foods, such as substituting pickled okra for the dill pickle. "There has to be an okra pod somewhere," she said. Instead of sips of wine between the foods, she suggested New Orleans drinks—a Sazerac or brandy milk punch or a hurricane—since New Orleans is the home of the cocktail. And she pointed out that oysters are totemic but that redfish or shrimp would be equally appropriate and symbolic of the sea connection for those who don't eat oysters. And a praline as well as chocolate could symbolize "dessert first."

"I think on that plate there needs to be some gumbo," Harris said. "You could feed gumbo to each other with the spoon. That works all the way around. Gumbo is so totemic, and people could make their gumbo, whatever their family gumbo is, so it's a way of sharing food and their family recipe and themselves." Somewhere, Harris said, there should be a little piece of king cake to represent our joy in life, which is different from sweetness. And the ritual plate should be placed in a circle of Mardi Gras beads, she added.

"You need pepper for the heat, a dab of Crystal Hot Sauce or Tabasco for the fire of life that moves in folks," Harris said. And she had suggestions for the meal. "I would think about Leah Chase's fried chicken, and Ken Smith's duck, with both of the sauces, please. And crabmeat or shrimp should definitely be part of the meal. Maybe Galatoire's Godchaux salad, or the garlic salad. And a good shrimp Creole says it all.

"There should be something Cajun, too, maybe some maquechou. And a little Vietnamese spring roll. And something Croatian, maybe from the Uglesich cookbook." The meal should end with café brûlot "for the coffee and heat and sweet," Harris said. "Black as the devil and sweet as love."

Diaspora Gumbo

Serves 10 to 12.

½ cup vegetable oil, plus about
   ½ cup for frying
2 pounds okra, thinly sliced
   (⅛ inch thick)
1 cup flour
1 onion, chopped
3 ribs celery, chopped
1 bell pepper, cored and chopped

1 (1-pound) can whole peeled
   tomatoes
2 teaspoons dried thyme
1 bay leaf (ideally from neighbor's
   backyard)
1 gallon shrimp, chicken, or
   vegetable stock
1 clove garlic

One or more of the following diaspora ingredients, depending on personal preference and availability at your evacuation site: 4 gumbo crabs (hard-shell crabs with the top half removed, claws and legs attached), 2 pounds raw shrimp, 1 pint raw oysters, 1 pound sliced and browned smoked sausage (first choice: andouille), 2 cups chopped cooked chicken meat, pinch of filé powder

1 bunch green onions, thinly sliced
Salt, freshly ground black pepper,
   and hot sauce to taste

Cooked rice, ¼ cup per serving

Cover the bottom of a 10- to 12-inch skillet with oil (about ¼ cup) and place over high heat. In several batches, fry the okra in the very hot oil until lightly browned. Set aside.

In a 10- to 12-quart Dutch oven–type pot, make a dark roux by combining ½ cup of the oil with the flour, cooking until it is the color of milk chocolate. Add the onion, stirring until the roux darkens to a bittersweet chocolate brown. Add the celery and bell pepper. Cook for 5 minutes over medium-high heat. Add the tomatoes, thyme, and bay leaf and continue to cook for another 5 minutes. Add the stock, garlic, and diaspora ingredients, *except for the shrimp and oysters, which must be added in the last 5 minutes before serving, and filé powder, which must be added at the end.*

Bring to a boil, reduce the heat to a simmer, and cover. Cook for 45 minutes or so, stirring periodically to be sure there's no sticking. In the last 5 minutes, add shrimp or oysters if desired, along with the green onions. Season with salt, pepper, and hot sauce and serve over rice with a sprinkle of the filé powder stirred in if desired.

Adapted from "A Culinary Survival Kit for New Orleans Citizens in Exile," by Poppy Tooker. Used with permission.

Comforting Food
Recapturing Recipes Katrina Took Away

Rick Brooks

For her husband's thirtieth birthday in February, Amy Cyrex Sins had her heart set on baking a doberge cake—a traditional New Orleans dessert piled eight layers high and slathered with chocolate ganache. Flooded out of her dream house by Hurricane Katrina, she could make do with two cake pans and the galley kitchen in the couple's temporary French Quarter apartment. But the most critical element—the family recipe for the frosting George Sins grew up craving—had been lost in the storm.

Ms. Sins, a twenty-nine-year-old pharmaceutical sales representative, could recall only two ingredients: chocolate chips and Karo syrup—a light sweetener ubiquitous in Louisiana kitchens. She and her mother-in-law worked up a best-guess version over the phone and she popped it in the oven.

"It's good, baby," Mr. Sins told his wife, when the cake was done.

But not as good it used to be.

A year after Katrina, a lot of people on the devastated Gulf Coast are slowly rebuilding cherished collections of handwritten recipe cards, dog-eared cookbooks, and yellowed newspaper clippings that were wrecked by wind, water, and mold. They search through ravaged homes, send pleas to newspapers and websites, and struggle to pin down the recollections of loved ones. The effort for many is just as daunting as dealing with insurance claims, finding a building contractor, and all the other perpetual battles of post-Katrina life.

"Could you PLEASE, PLEASE send me your bread-pudding recipe from your original book—my husband gave it to me years ago with a wonderful message comparing our marriage as a mixture of 'spices,'" wrote Elaine Acosta in an email message to Paul Prudhomme, owner of K-Paul's Louisiana Kitchen in the French Quarter and author of eight cookbooks. "My house blew or floated down Hwy. 11 and I lost everything. I'm living with my daughter and son-in-law and their family and they want bread pudding, NOW!"

The next day, one of the chef's employees posted on a message board the recipe for New Orleans bread pudding with lemon sauce and chantilly cream—promising "a magnificent pudding." Mr. Prudhomme himself was forced to flee with employees and their families to Pine Bluff, Arkansas, as Katrina zeroed in on New Orleans. They returned with a caravan of trucks to cook thousands of meals for the National Guard, firefighters, police, volunteers, and other rescuers. Mr. Prudhomme's house was untouched, and K-Paul's sustained only minor damage. His recipes were spared.

The determination to recover recipes that Katrina took away runs as deep as the region's famous love affair with food. Shannon Gustafson, thirty-eight, spent dozens of late-night hours searching online for replacement copies of her favorite recipes left behind when she fled her home on Marshall Foch Street in the Lakeview neighborhood of New Orleans.

But as Christmas approached last year, with the family relocated to Orlando, Florida, she still hadn't found a sweet-potato casserole recipe made with orange juice, raisins, and a chopped pecan streusel topping. "I wanted to provide something of normality for my kids and my husband and to feel like we're not on the road anymore," she says. Ms. Gustafson posted a request for help on the "Recipe Swap" site of *Home Cooking* magazine. Just in time for Christmas, two readers responded with casserole recipes, and she found a version online "that tasted pretty much the same." She has received fifty more responses since then.

The family is still trying to adjust to a new Florida home. Ms. Gustafson's three-year-old daughter asks about once a week whether it will be flooded. Her five-year-old brother started kindergarten this month. The stay-at-home mom has yet to locate a certain paella recipe, but a woman in Phoenix who recently remodeled her own kitchen has offered to ship the Gustafsons all the cookbooks and recipe cards she no longer has room for.

"People are trying to keep that culture alive," says Kathy Broussard, forty-eight, of Maryville, Tennessee. She has offered on the "FoodFest!" section of neworleans.com to share with those who lost recipes her collection of more than two hundred cookbooks—including *River Road Recipes*, a 1959 primer on Creole cooking by the Junior League of Baton Rouge.

Some dishes, of course, are such mainstays that recipes don't have to be written down. Pauline Troxclair, sixty-five, lost a handwritten journal of family recipes when Katrina destroyed her Chalmette, Louisiana, house. But the recipe for her mother's anchovy gravy with fedelini, a skinny spaghetti, was committed to memory. Ms. Troxclair remembered every step. Now, at her new house in Covington, Louisiana, she is having Sunday dinners again and serving the dish. "I used to never miss a Sunday. It'll get back to that," she says.

Other cooks write forlornly to the food section of local papers. "William Schram Jr. wants a recipe for banana-nut bread. He, too, lost all his old recipes in Katrina," the *Sun Herald* in Biloxi wrote earlier this month. "Readers, check your files and cookbooks and send me your best banana-nut bread recipes." The paper then published three sent in by readers. In New Orleans, the *Times-Picayune* prints recipe requests every Thursday and keeps an online archive.

Mississippi's Department of Marine Resources has given away about seven thousand copies of its oyster, shrimp, and seafood cookbooks since April, says Irvin Jackson, director of the state seafood-marketing program. He personally contributed an eggplant-casserole recipe with shrimp, diced ham, and Ritz crackers. Locals quickly snapped up hundreds of copies from the agency's Biloxi office.

Last month, Rodney Thomas, eighteen, and his parents decided they had waited long enough to cook the gumbo that was a staple at their New Orleans East house before Katrina. Now living in a Federal Emergency Management Agency trailer park next to a shuttered public-housing complex, they spent one Sunday last month chopping vegetables, peeling shrimp, and cooking down the okra on the propane stove in the trailer. It was good, Mr. Thomas says, but what was missing was the rich hue imparted by the family's old cast-iron gumbo pot.

"We all wanted it so bad," he says. "Just to look at it reminded you of your past life and what it could be."

Since moving out of a FEMA trailer in May and back into her renovated house with a brand-new kitchen and whirlpool tub, Geraldine Bankston, fifty-five, has begun working her way through *From Woodstoves to Microwaves*, a compilation of thirteen hundred local classics like oyster gumbo filé and red velvet cake. The recipes originally were sent out with electric bills by Louisiana Power and Light and New Orleans Public Service Inc. and later were compiled in a book now sold as a fund-raiser by the United Way for the Greater New Orleans Area. It has been reprinted from a computer disk rescued from the agency's flooded building. More than eighteen hundred have been sold.

Ms. Bankston says the cookbook brings back memories of Sunday afternoons when she pitched a tent in the front yard, setting out macaroni and cheese, cake, and other goodies for family and neighbors. "It helps me remember the good times," she says. She's sad, though, that many of those people in New Orleans East haven't come back since the storm. "Normally, everything would be gone in one day," she says. "Now I have leftovers."

Even as so many struggle to reassemble their lost food routines, the cuisine of south Louisiana and Mississippi is also adapting to privation. Recipes are emerging, especially for the tiny kitchens that are standard in FEMA trailers, where burners pump out lots of heat and sometimes set off smoke detectors.

Cooks are also giving more thought now to future hurricanes. The Crescent City Farmers Market in New Orleans marked the anniversary of Katrina with an "early Thanksgiving" community picnic where people could pick up a new three-postcard "survival kit" of "essential" recipes—diaspora gumbo, for instance—for use during a hurricane evacuation.

So far, Ms. Sins—the wife of the doberge-cake lover—has rebuilt her cookbook collection to about fifty titles. That's nowhere near what was ruined when Lake Pontchartrain poured into her living room and double-oven kitchen through a levee breach ten houses up Bellaire Drive in the Lakeview section of New Orleans. Ms. Sins's only copy of a jambalaya recipe from her father, who died in 1996, was unsalvageable. And locating the original seemed hopeless, since her uncle George Mayer's nearby house was also flooded. But a few of Mr. Mayer's handwritten recipes had survived, including the jambalaya. He laid the recipe out to dry in the sun, then gave it to Ms. Sins.

Ms. Sins's mother-in-law, also in Lakeview, was able to save some of her recipe cards, but they smell so moldy that she keeps them in a plastic binder and washes her hands after touching them.

After new drywall was installed in Ms. Sins's house in late July, it got easier to see past the Viking range rusting near the swimming pool and a brown waterline still obvious on a first-floor window. She hopes to be home again in October.

Ms. Sins says she will be ready for the next hurricane. She has written a self-published cookbook called *Ruby Slippers Cookbook* that puts many of her favorites in one place.

And the doberge cake? She has tried making it three times since her husband's birthday, altering the recipe slightly each time. The icing still is too firm and not glossy enough, but she isn't giving up.

"We're just going to keep making it," Ms. Sins says.

Easy Birthday Doberge Cake

2 cakes made with Betty Crocker Butter Recipe Yellow Cake mix

For the filling:

1 cup sugar

½ cup all-purpose flour

3 cups milk

1 (3½-ounce) Lindt dark
   chocolate bar, chopped

4 large egg yolks

2 tablespoons unsalted butter

1½ teaspoons vanilla extract

For the ganache:

1 cup finely chopped semisweet
   or bittersweet chocolate

¾ cup heavy cream

2 tablespoons unsalted butter

1 tablespoon corn syrup

Cut the cakes into a total of 6 to 8 layers and set aside.

Make the filling: In a medium-sized saucepan over medium-high heat, combine the sugar and flour, then gradually stir in the milk and chocolate. Heat until thick and bubbly, then reduce the heat and cook for 2 minutes more. Remove from the heat. Temper the egg yolks in a cup of the chocolate mixture, then return it to the saucepan and bring to a gentle boil. Stir in the butter and vanilla. Let cool in the fridge, and cover with plastic wrap so it doesn't form a skin. Smooth filling between layers of the cake and stack them. You may hold it together with a wooden skewer, removing the skewer before serving.

Make the ganache: Put the chocolate in a heatproof bowl. In a saucepan, combine the cream, butter, and corn syrup. Over medium heat, bring the cream mixture just to a simmer, then pour it over the chocolate and stir until the chocolate melts.

Pour the ganache over the top of the cake to cover the entire cake with chocolate. Let cool before serving. The icing will harden.

Adapted from Ruby Slippers Cookbook: Life, Culture, Family, and Food after Katrina, *by Amy Cyrex Sins. Used with permission.*

Willie Mae's Scotch House

Jim Auchmutey

Willie Mae Seaton didn't have time to gather many of her belongings before the flood. She grabbed a change of clothes and scooped up some family photos, then secured her most prized possession: a bronze medallion attached to a loop of ribbon like an Olympic medal. She wrapped it in a napkin, sealed it in a plastic bag and put it in her purse. Only then did she join two carloads of loved ones as they fled the city ahead of Hurricane Katrina.

The medallion came from the James Beard Foundation. Seaton had never heard of the group that sponsors the prestigious food awards, but she was overjoyed last spring when it named her little soul food restaurant one of "America's Classics." At the awards banquet in New York, she limped to the ballroom podium on bunioned feet and broke down crying as she tried to express her gratitude.

It was the high point of her life.

Four months later, Katrina brought the low point. After the levees failed, four to five feet of water inundated her street in the Tremé neighborhood of New Orleans and soaked the double shotgun house where her residence and restaurant sit side by side under the same roof.

"I lost everything," Seaton says.

Not quite.

The storm couldn't destroy her reputation for cooking some of the best Southern food around. In recent weeks, that reputation has drawn an unlikely group of food enthusiasts from across the nation to help rebuild Seaton's restaurant in a Habitat for Humanity–style construction project that has given a devastated city a hopeful scene of rebirth.

At eighty-nine, it seems, Willie Mae Seaton hasn't fried her last drumstick.

In a city of famous restaurants, Seaton's is not one of them. Visitors to New

Orleans know about Antoine's, Galatoire's, Commander's Palace, Emeril's. Willie Mae's Scotch House—the name refers to its 1957 origins as a bar—isn't even the best-known restaurant in her neighborhood; just two blocks away is Dooky Chase, a black Creole landmark, which also was flooded out.

It was the locals who knew about Willie Mae's. For decades, an interracial crowd including judges and lawyers and several mayors has gone there for lunch in an eight-table dining room decorated with religious art and a portrait of Martin Luther King Jr. The menu is as downhome as Seaton, a gray-headed Mississippi native who smiles under big glasses and calls everyone "baby." She serves country vegetables and old favorites like pork chops and smothered veal and fried chicken, her specialty.

"Nobody fries chicken like I fries chicken," she says, refusing to divulge any secrets except to say that she uses a wet batter and a deep-fryer. "You couldn't pan-fry as much chicken as I've got to fry."

Seaton's following broadened in recent years as New Orleans journalists like Lolis Eric Elie, a *Times-Picayune* columnist, started to champion her restaurant. Influential food writers like *Vogue*'s Jeffrey Steingarten and the *New Yorker*'s Calvin Trillin dropped by. The James Beard Foundation, which stages the food world's equivalent of the Oscars, took note.

Elie accompanied Seaton to Manhattan last May to accept the prize. "She was the belle of the ball," he says, remembering how she charmed the food glitterati and kept her stamina during the swirl of cocktail parties.

After the award, New Orleans leaders threw Seaton a birthday gala. Tourists flocked to her corner café and sang her praises on Internet food sites.

"I just proposed marriage to Willie Mae after eating her fried chicken," wrote Diner Girl on eGullet.org. "I love this woman, and if there was ever a reason to approve stem cell research legislation for cloning, this is it."

Then came Katrina.

On the last Sunday in August, Seaton heeded the city's evacuation order and drove with her family to Shreveport, a trip that usually takes six hours but lasted fifteen because of the exodus of traffic. Over the next few days, she watched on TV as her hometown descended into chaos.

Even then, she was itching to return.

"She kept saying we need to get back to New Orleans," says Kerry Seaton Blackmon, a great-granddaughter who worked in the restaurant. "And I'd say, What are you going to do in New Orleans? Look at the TV. People are screaming to get out of there."

Seaton tried to return several times but was stopped at roadblocks. She moved from motel to motel in Mississippi and Louisiana before ending up in Houston with her son Charles, who also works in the restaurant. One day she overheard someone say that flights to New Orleans had resumed. She took one on the spur of the moment without telling her family, who were understandably alarmed, and hired a cab to drive her to her place on the corner of Tonti and St. Ann.

The neighborhood was deserted. Downed trees blocked the sidewalks. Abandoned cars lined the streets. The air reeked of sewage and decay.

Seaton stood in front of her property and stared at the water stain circling the building four feet above the ground. It looked like a scummy ring on a bathtub. She didn't bother going in.

A police cruiser pulled up. The officers asked what she was doing.

"This is my place," she told them. "I was in Houston, and I had to come back and see about my business."

They said they couldn't leave her alone, so they picked her up and arranged for emergency lodging. Seaton eventually moved into an apartment across the Mississippi River in Algiers. She returned to her neighborhood in January, moving in with an old friend whose home sat above the floodwaters.

"She wanted to keep a closer eye on things," says Seaton Blackmon, who also returned, from Atlanta, where she and her husband had rented an apartment after the hurricane. At twenty-six, she wants to run the restaurant whenever her great-grandmother decides to step aside.

Seaton's home and business were uninhabitable after Katrina. The deluge ruined the interior. Like so many others on the Gulf Coast, she had no flood insurance and little in the way of savings.

As word of her plight spread, two organizations united to get her back on her feet.

The Heritage Conservation Network, a preservation group based in Colorado, proposed a work project to repair the 1890s structure. The Southern Foodways Alliance at the University of Mississippi put out a call for volunteers to work a series of weekends in January and February. Some 120 people responded, three times the number that could be accommodated.

But the job is proving more expensive than anyone expected. The cost is estimated at more than $100,000, says alliance director John T. Edge. So far, his group has raised about $10,000 through the sale of pickles on its website.

"Mrs. Seaton wants to cook again," he says, "and we want to help her."

It's an overcast Friday morning as the work project enters its second weekend. Heaps of lath board and plaster have already been removed from the building, along with a sodden jukebox and a grease-encrusted stove hood that still smelled of chicken. On the sidewalk out front, a dozen volunteers gather over coffee and Mardi Gras king cake to get their assignments. The workers include two graduate students from North Carolina, an Episcopal priest from New Mexico, a couple who ran a bakery in northern California, and one Beard award–nominated chef, John Currence of City Grocery in Oxford, Mississippi.

For at least two of the laborers, this dank scene of destruction is all too familiar. "We were doing this kind of work in our home last fall," says Becky Feder, whose bottom floor was flooded by Katrina's storm surge in Ocean Springs, Mississippi.

Suited up in white coveralls and respirators that make them look like hazmat technicians, she and her husband, Ron, get busy gutting Seaton's kitchen. Becky takes a whack at a partially rotted two-by-four and laughs. "This is a good way to take out our frustration."

At lunchtime, someone goes down the street to fetch Seaton. For the next hour, she sits outside the restaurant in a lawn chair—an elderly peacock in red sweater, white kerchief, and burgundy slacks—and holds court.

"Y'all didn't throw away my skillets, did you?" she says. "You know I can clean those up."

Seaton is so cheerful, it hardly seems possible she was washed out of her home and business less than five months before.

The reason? The volunteers.

"These people have put me up on a golden platter and carried me around," she says. "And I want to do something for them. I haven't got any money. But when I'm up and running, I want everyone to come back so I can fix them a big dinner. Pork chops, smothered veal, limey beans, string beans . . ."

She rises up in her chair, excited by the mere sound of her menu.

"Baby, it isn't just going to be chicken."

[Editors' note: The SFA eventually raised about $200,000 for the project, and Willie Mae's Scotch House reopened in the spring of 2007.]

Although southwestern Louisiana and the Texas Gulf Coast were spared by Katrina, shortly afterwards they got hammered by Hurricane Rita, which for some reason got less literary and journalistic attention. This story isn't about Rita, but the storm figures as a major presence in the background, which is why it's in this section.

Crab Man

Robb Walsh

A cute waitress dropped off a plate of six barbecued crabs, hot out of the deep fryer. I picked one up and juggled it, trying not to burn my fingers. All that stood between me and a whole lot of luscious crabmeat was a little bit of hot shell. And I was hungry.

When you order barbecued crabs at Sartin's, the top shells and the messy innards are removed in the kitchen—what's left are spicy, meaty crab bodies with two claws attached. I removed the claws from the one I'd grabbed, cracked the body into two halves, and dropped them on my plate. The crunchy barbecue spices that coated the shell stuck to my fingers. I licked some off as an appetizer.

The crab pieces were still too hot to handle, but using paper towels as oven mitts, I gripped a half-body with both hands and snapped it. The shell broke open to reveal a nice chunk of steaming meat, bright white and freckled with crispy seasoning. I took a bite, burning my lips and tongue.

The rich marine flavor of the spicy crabmeat, slightly greasy from the deep fryer, was sensational. Barbecued crab is Maine lobster and drawn butter's roughneck cousin from Beaumont. Invented in the corner of Texas that borders Louisiana and the Gulf of Mexico, it tastes like a cross between barbecue and Cajun deep-fried seafood. People who don't even like crab love barbecued crab.

It was Sartin's Seafood restaurants that made barbecued crabs famous. The legendary Sartin's now has three locations, all of them family-owned. Kelli Sartin, the daughter of the founders, opened the Clear Lake Sartin's near NASA after the old one in Beaumont was destroyed by Hurricane Rita. The owners of the ones in Beaumont and Nederland are Kim Lynch and Emily Summers.

When asked how she's related to Kim and Emily, Kelli said, "In my family we put it this way, 'Every time my brother meets a nice girl, he gives her a restaurant.'" Then she mumbled something about some other words they might use instead of "nice girl."

I'd been hearing about Sartin's for decades, but I wanted the whole story of Texas barbecued crabs. So I asked Kelli if she could hook me up with a crabber who could take me out on his boat and explain the business. And that's how I met her Miller Lite–loving brother, Charles Douglas Sartin Jr.

"You want a beer?" Doug asked me when I sat down in his johnboat. He was dressed in white shorts, a pink T-shirt, and a tan gimme cap with a sailfish on it. He also wore a shark's-tooth necklace, a silver bracelet, and a conspiratorial grin.

"Why not?" I said.

He fished me a Miller Lite out of an eighteen-pack in the ice chest and grabbed one for himself. I noticed there was a second eighteen-pack in the bottom of the cooler.

"Thirty-six beers? I thought this was just a three-hour tour," I joked.

"The other one's for my dad," Sartin said. "There isn't any place to buy beer in Sabine Pass anymore, so I always get some extra."

Sartin's parents' house, and most of the rest of Sabine Pass, was under eight feet of water when Rita's storm surge hit. The town was nearly wiped off the map. The little five-store shopping center that used to greet you as soon as you crossed the causeway looks like somebody smashed down squarely on top of it with an enormous cast-iron skillet. The high school is about the only building still standing. But the senior Sartins have no intention of moving.

Doug throttled up the little Evinrude 40 outboard as we cruised out of the canal that leads to Keith Lake, just east of Port Arthur. We both scanned the horizon as we entered the wide part of the lake, but there were no crab boats in sight yet. So we drank beer and talked.

"That was my parents in the truck," Doug said. When I first arrived, he was saying good-bye to a gray-haired couple in a big white pickup truck who waved at me as they sped off.

"Don't let him drown you," the woman yelled as the back wheels of the truck sprayed gravel across the parking lot. Charles Douglas Sartin Sr. and Jeri Sartin founded Sartin's first location, in Sabine Pass.

"Too bad they took off; I would love to interview them," I said.

"They don't talk to the press anymore," he said. "They aren't good at talking."

Doug, on the other hand, spoke freely. In fact, he didn't seem to know when to shut up.

"I'm the crazy one in the family," he said. I asked him about his two former wives. His estranged wife, Emily, looks just like his ex-wife Kim, he said. People think they're sisters. Having seen a photo of Kim Lynch on her website, I said she was a good-looking woman.

Doug laughed and said he bought those titties—and his second wife's, too—four titties total. I reminded Doug that I was a reporter and we were on the record. He said he was just a commercial fisherman and he could say whatever he wanted.

Doug Sartin Jr. started not only the Beaumont and Nederland restaurants, which he ended up giving away, but also several other Sartin's locations—all of which are gone now. There have been a total of fourteen over the years, counting the three that are still in business. But it wasn't Doug's partying that caused all the business failures. Hurricanes did most of the dirty work.

The first Sartin's opened in 1972. "My daddy was a pipe fitter at the Texaco refinery," said Doug. "He fished for crab and shrimp on the side." Doug Senior set up wife Jeri in a fish market on the dock at Sabine Pass. But Jeri, who grew up in a family that owned several restaurants, decided that she would rather sell cooked seafood. And anyway, there was nothing else to eat in Sabine Pass. So she started a little restaurant in front of the family's trailer with four tables inside and four outside. Things took off quickly.

As the business expanded, Jeri hired a fry cook, who brought along a recipe for a dish called barbecued crabs that was invented at a restaurant called Granger's, which was popular in Sabine Pass in the '40s and '50s. It burned down in 1958.

The barbecued crab tradition was continued at a Port Arthur restaurant called Mama's in the '60s. These days, besides Sartin's, Stingaree Restaurant in Crystal Beach on the Bolivar Peninsula also specializes in barbecued crabs. They are also a summer special at Floyd's, Ragin' Cajun, and a few other seafood restaurants.

Charles Douglas Sartin Sr. left his job at the refinery to devote more time to catching seafood for the restaurant. It has been reported that he actually didn't want to quit that job, but Jeri went down there and quit it for him. She told the foreman she needed her husband to catch more crabs.

The Cajun crabs you get in Louisiana are boiled whole in highly spiced water with corn and potatoes, just like crawfish. On the East Coast, Maryland-style crabs are sprinkled with Old Bay seasoning and then steamed. Both Cajun crabs and Maryland-style crabs come to the table whole—the diner cracks the shell and cleans out the guts.

Texas barbecued crabs are much more civilized—at least for the diner. The crab has its top shell and guts removed while it's still alive. It is then dipped into a barbecue spice blend that is the Sartins' re-creation of Sexton's Alamo Zestful Seasoning, dropped into a deep fryer, and brought to the table piping hot and crusted with caramelized barbecue spices.

All-you-can-eat barbecued crabs at Sartin's became a tradition for beach lovers from Beaumont, Port Arthur, and Orange. Texas 87, the highway that used to run the length of the beach-lined Bolivar Peninsula, went right through Sabine Pass before it turned inland. Sandy, sunburned diners clad in their bathing suits stopped at Sartin's on the way home from the beach—and it didn't matter much that barbecued crabs were messy to eat.

The original Sartin's became enormously successful. They added dining rooms several times, until the capacity of the restaurant eventually reached five hundred. On weekends, the lines were so long that the restaurant started setting out tubs of free beer for those who had to wait. Free beer remains a Sartin's family tradition. Kim Lynch sells beer for a penny when there's a line outside her door.

But the original Sartin's was open for only eight years before it developed a hurricane problem. In 1980, it was Hurricane Allen. In 1983, it was Alicia. The storms did some damage to the restaurant, but what devastated Sartin's business was the closure of Highway 87 between High Island and Sabine Pass. Beachgoers were forced to use other routes. The road was finally reopened in 1985, and Sartin's began to make a comeback.

Three years later, in 1988, Hurricane Gilbert's storm surge took out the road again. In 1989, after Hurricane Jerry hit the Texas coast, plans to repair the highway were abandoned. On most highway maps, Texas 87 between High Island and Sabine Pass looks just fine. But don't try to drive it. The road has been closed for seventeen years now.

The senior Sartins relocated to Beaumont. Doug Sartin and his wife, Kim, opened a second location in Nederland. Doug lost the Nederland restaurant in his divorce. Then he and his second wife, Emily, opened the Highway 90 Sartin's in Beaumont a few years ago. The Highway 90 and Nederland locations survived Rita, but the storm destroyed the Sartin's that had belonged to Doug's parents.

"Where did you go when Rita hit?" I asked Doug.

"Me and my buddy Ricky got fifteen cases of beer and rode out the storm in China," Sartin said. China is a small rice-growing town twenty-five miles or so inland. "In four days, we drank all fifteen cases," he said. "Then we went around giving away food to volunteers. We had six hundred pounds of shrimp at the restaurant that was going to go bad anyway, so we cooked it all up and gave it away."

Ahead of us, the crab boat we were looking for was chugging along the horizon. "You ready for a beer?" Doug asked his buddy, crabber Craig Ray, as we pulled up alongside. Craig already had a tallboy going, but he took another one anyway, and Doug and I got ourselves fresh ones too. Then we climbed on board and checked out the crabs.

Craig Ray is a burly bear with a crew cut and an anchor and ship's wheel tattooed on his enormous upper arm. The day I met him, he might have been intimidating, except that he was wearing shorts and goofy-looking white rubber boots and was grinning from ear to ear. In fact, he never stopped smiling the whole time I was on his crab boat.

His bright white twenty-one-foot Carolina skiff is a shallow-draft design built on a flotation hull that draws a mere six inches of water. The day we went out, the deck was shaded by a piece of bright blue vinyl stretched across a metal frame.

Ray has been crabbing for twenty-seven years. He fishes exclusively for blue crabs. The blue crab's scientific name, *Callinectes sapidus*, translates to "savory beautiful swimmer." It is the only crab species of any commercial significance in Texas.

Most of the crabbers on Keith Lake use smaller boats, Ray said. The big skiff has made his life easy. He steered the boat while his deckhand pulled up the traps, marked by colored plastic floats. The first trap held fourteen crabs of various sizes.

"Is that normal?" I asked.

"If they all had that many crabs, I would be home already," Ray chuckled.

Strangely enough, Hurricane Rita improved the fishing. "This is one of the best seasons I have ever seen," Ray said. "Hurricane Rita stirred things up. The oxygen level of the water is way up. And so is the salt. I've heard that those dead zones out in the Gulf of Mexico were all shook up. It sure cleaned this area out. There used to be an oyster reef in the middle of the lake that I couldn't get my boat over. It's gone now. The oysters are spread out all over. All the sand bars and debris were washed out too. The crabs sure like it. I'm seeing more sponge crabs [egg-bearing females] than ever before."

Not that Ray was making a lot of money. The storm put the local restaurants that bought crabs out of business. It also closed down the distributors, who needed electricity for refrigeration. There wasn't any reason to go crabbing for a while because there was no one buying.

Ray also talked about the cycles of the crab season. The crabs hibernate under the mud when the water gets cold, he said. They get active when the water warms up, usually around April. That's when they spawn. The peak of crab season is from May to August. Then there's a second spawning season in August. If you parboil the crabs and then freeze them carefully, you can stockpile them during the summer and use them when crabs are scarce in the winter, he said.

A light bulb went on over my head. The first time I visited Sartin's was in March, and I was disappointed. Half the crabs I got were disgustingly mushy. Evidently the restaurant serves frozen crabs in the winter.

Add crabs to a long list of foods whose seasonality Americans have lost track of. Sure, you can get oysters on the half-shell, crawfish, and barbecued crab all year. But you'll enjoy them a lot more if you only order them in season. Oysters are sweet and plump in the winter, but tasteless and loaded with the *Vibrio* virus in the summer. The big tasty local crawfish are harvested in the spring. And crabs are at their peak in the summer.

As the traps came on board the skiff, we drank our beers and watched. The crabs were dumped out of the traps and sorted according to size. If one measured less than five inches point to point (from the end of the spiky point that sticks out from one side of the crab's shell to the same point on the other side), then the crab went overboard. If the crab measured between five and six inches, it went into the wooden crate with the No. 2's.

A crab that measured over six inches went into the box with the rest of the prized No. 1's.

"Most of these crabs will go to Massachusetts, where they sell for $60 a dozen," Ray said, admiring the largest ones. "Here they sell for $15 a dozen." As a result, although lots of premium crabs are taken in Texas, few are eaten here. The way around this frustrating dilemma is simple: do your own crabbing. It's pretty easy. You can catch all the crabs you want with a chicken neck, a string, and a fishing net. Or you can get more sophisticated with an umbrella trap.

I told Ray I planned to go crabbing near East Beach on Galveston Island. He didn't think that was such a great idea. "The best-tasting crabs come from brackish water," he said, picking up one of the biggest No. 1's. "We call them sweetwater crabs." He turned the crab over and pointed to a fuzzy dark scum that stuck to the shell. "You want to see this black rusty color on the bottom; that's the sign of a really sweet crab."

"I always thought that was mud," I admitted, thinking about making barbecued crabs at home. I already had a fryer, and surely I could find some "zestful seasoning." "So if I wanted to eat the ultimate barbecued crabs, I would start out by catching some No. 1 sweetwater crabs," I said.

"Here, let me get a bucket," he said. "I'll give you some of the best crabs you'll ever eat." I wondered whether to take them. I was afraid they'd die before I could get them back to Houston, and I didn't want to ruin such awesome crabs.

"I'll get them," Doug said, slipping Ray some folded bills. "We'll cook them at Emily's restaurant." So we headed back with a dozen No. 1 crabs in a bucket in the middle of Doug's little boat.

"What a nice guy," I said. "He sure smiles a lot."

"Yeah, he sure does," said Doug. He went on to tell me that he'd seen Ray out there with crabs hanging all over him, and he didn't even notice. Then he offered me another beer for the road.

I turned down the third beer. But I was beginning to think I was in the wrong business.

Before accepting Doug's invitation to go crabbing, I'd already made a date with his ex-wife, Kim Lynch. I was supposed to stop by her restaurant around three in the afternoon. But now things were getting complicated. Doug Sartin was carrying around that bucket of sweetwater No. 1's. What if he got pissed off and I missed out on the ultimate plate of barbecued crabs?

But as I was getting in my car, Doug told me he'd promised Kim he'd get me to her place at three. Then he gave me directions to the Sartin's in Nederland and said he'd give me a while to talk to her and then come by, and I could follow him over to Emily's place.

I was dumbfounded. Doug Sartin may not own any of his namesake restaurants, but he sure seems to know everything that goes on in them.

I ordered some crabs and sat down at a table with Kim Lynch. She was a big good-looking blonde. I tried hard to look her in the eyes at all times.

"Doug and I are still friends," said Kim, who once cleared tables at the Sartin's in Sabine Pass. But she made clear that being married to a Sartin was no picnic.

"It's an interesting family," she said. "I could write a book."

"Well, Doug calls himself the crazy one in the family," I said with a shrug.

"The crazy spoiled one," she replied. Their parents made things too easy for Doug and his sister Kelli, according to Kim. Doug never stops partying. "His best friend says that being with Doug is like being held captive," she said. "But he doesn't have to go back to the real world, and you do."

I asked Kim what Hurricane Rita did to business.

"After the storm, I quit offering all-you-can-eat," she told me. "What a difference that made!" At first, there just weren't enough crabs, she explained. The supply has come back now, but the all-you-can-eat policy has not. When Sartin's first started serving all-you-can-eat crabs at the original restaurant in the '70s, you could buy a dozen crabs for $3, she told me. Today they cost anywhere from $8 to $15 a dozen.

"I called Emily and we talked about it. She isn't doing all-you-can-eat anymore either," Lynch said. "The problem is human nature. When they're all-you-can-eat, people just eat the easy parts and throw the rest of the crab away," she said. "We used to go through two hundred dozen crabs a night. Now we're making more money selling a hundred dozen."

Kelli Sartin's location near Clear Lake is the last one offering the all-you-can-eat option. "She's just getting started," Lynch said. "She has to do it for now." But Lynch is convinced that the days of all-you-can-eat barbecued crabs are coming to an end. And she isn't going to miss them.

"You want something to drink?" Doug Sartin asked me. We were in the kitchen of Emily Summers's Sartin's location on Highway 90 in Beaumont, cleaning our giant crabs. If I wanted to eat the ultimate barbecued crab, then I was going to have to work for it.

"Yeah, I'll take an ice tea," I said. Doug set down a Miller Lite on the work table in front of me.

"We call these ice teas here," he said with a laugh.

Cleaning the live crabs is the most difficult part of making barbecued crabs. If Doug hadn't shown me how to do it, I probably never would have figured it out.

First you have to plunge the crab into ice water to stun it enough so it stops fighting. Then, with the crab upright on a flat surface, you hold down a flipper on the bottom left side of the crab with your left thumb and then rip off the shell from left to right with your right hand. It takes considerable force to get it started. Then you clean out the exposed guts under running water.

When we were finished, we handed our crabs to the kitchen manager, a Vietnamese woman who's been with Sartin's since the early days in Sabine Pass. She would dip the crabs in the spice mix, drop them in the fryer, and bring them to us when they were ready.

We waited in the dining room, where a few of Doug's friends had gathered. Emily Summers's Sartin's location is by far the most comfortable of the three. The dining room is furnished with wooden tables and lit naturally by large windows looking out on a tree-shaded patio.

The subject turned to Rita, and I told the group I was shocked by all the damage I'd seen driving around Beaumont and Port Arthur all day. You didn't hear anything about this devastation from the national media, I remarked.

"You guys must be pretty tired of seeing New Orleans and Katrina coverage on television," I said. The table suddenly went silent.

After a few seconds, somebody said, "You mean they had a hurricane in New Orleans, too?" And then everybody had a good laugh.

Then the ultimate plate of barbecued crabs arrived, and it was my turn to be silent for a while. There were six of them on the plate, and they were indeed the best I've ever eaten. I could barely believe the huge gobs of meat I was getting out of those sea monsters. The meat was sweeter than crabmeat usually tastes and very juicy. I sucked each body cavity clean and washed the spicy crabmeat down with one last beer.

Since I had just been to all three Sartin's locations, Doug's friends asked me what I thought.

I said it was a novelty to have a Sartin's in Houston, and Kelli seemed like quite a character.

"Kelli is a fruit loop," said Doug Sartin.

"That's the nicest thing I've ever heard Doug call his sister," said one of his friends, laughing. They were drinking Coronas now; I lost track of how many beers Doug drank in the few hours we were together, but it was more than six.

"Sartin's has a new image," I said. "There's three good-looking women running the restaurants now—"

"And one dumbass named Doug running around in the background," interrupted Doug Sartin.

It is indeed a bizarre situation. Doug Sartin is the only thing the owners of the three Sartin's restaurants have in common—and not one of them wants him around.

Kelli, Kim, and Emily aren't terribly fond of one another, either. Each Sartin's restaurant prints its own T-shirts, runs its own website, and generally acts as if the other two don't exist. It all sounds kind of like a William Faulkner plot—a proud family dynasty battered by booze, bad marriages, and incessant hurricanes, but still hanging on.

Of course, none of the Sartin family melodrama matters much if you're hungry. In that case, you'll want to know that crabs are in season right now. And that the new generation of Sartin's Seafood Restaurants is serving bona fide Sabine Pass barbecued crabs—and keeping an old Texas food tradition alive.

Interlude
The Lowcountry

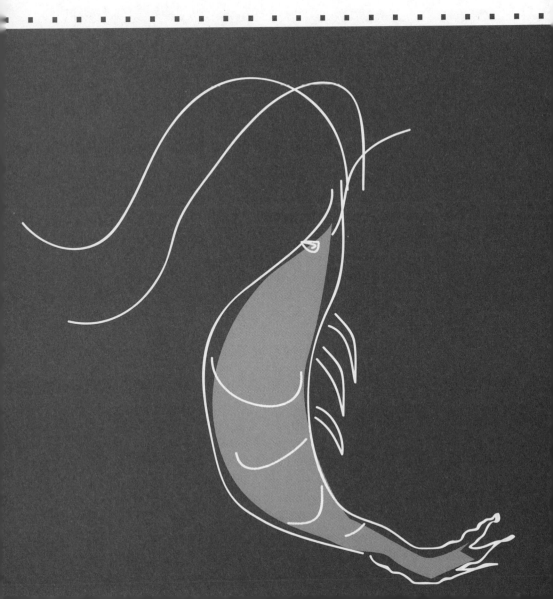

Lowcountry Lowdown

Jack Hitt

To celebrate my mother's seventy-fifth birthday, my brother and sisters and I took her to one of the elegant new restaurants in our hometown, Charleston, South Carolina. It wasn't easy. Going out to eat was a violation of her food aesthetic, which was always just to throw something together at home.

But there we were, marveling at an appetizer called "shrimp and grits." It arrived on one of those absurdly wide plates in an arrangement that looked like a 3-D military map. The grits had been molded into a pillbox. Over the top, a creamy sauce flowed out onto the plate like the ragged shore of our intracoastal waterway. Five shrimp were set like bunkers against an army of infantry-green cilantro flecks marching to the sea. Flying high above it all was a sprig of rosemary, planted there like the ensign of an invading force out to vanquish the Lowcountry.

"Just how I make them," noted Mom, the family master of deadpan, who wanted to go home now. Actually, we weren't marveling so much as hooting—to the point where a waiter skittered to our table hoping (in vain) that a face full of panic might persuade us to lower the volume of the howls that were gusting from our table.

Only now, when the laughter has almost died out—that dinner took place thirteen years ago—can I start to fathom how my beloved shrimp and grits became a congealed puck of fusion gunk. Shrimp and grits are, arguably, the signal dish of Lowcountry, or Gullah, cuisine—the food of my youth, which, since that youth, has become famous and, as a result, is undergoing the changes that keep any dynamic cuisine alive. But this was such a violation on so many levels: the silly portion size, for starters. This dish has always been about getting down with a heap of small, tender shrimp that have made the journey from their pluff-mud creek bed to your plate with almost no interference other than a little heat and butter. So a sauce just catapults the whole meal into some other time zone. And recasting grits to look all fussy and haute is like putting a Victoria's Secret teddy on the family dog. Funny to somebody, but wrong.

Lowcountry cuisine comprises a handful of recipes—mostly seafood dishes (crab, shrimp, oysters) and wild game gumbos (duck, deer), as well as the usual Southern standards (rice, collards, local beans)—prepared and improved upon by slaves over the centuries with ideas and ingredients tossed in by the European plantation owners.

This food is born of our history, so much of it tragic and difficult to discuss outright. But all Southerners love to talk, and the talking is easy when we're talking (and arguing) about food. The kitchen is where race relations have always been at their best, a place where many of the good things that can be reaped from our past come together like fine flavors.

So I set off on a philosophical mission last winter to find the best cooks in homes or restaurants and, not incidentally, to determine what keeps Low-country food alive and what kills it off—a search for, as they say in the movie *Spinal Tap*, that "fine line between stupid and clever."

I called my childhood friend Preston Wilson, who has spent the past decade fixing up the old Claussen Plantation house near Florence, and by the time I got there, two guys from down the road, Dickie Reynolds and Alan Turner, were in the vast set of meadows that constitute Preston's backyard, ready to talk their way through a venison mustard fry, grilled dove breasts, smoked venison tenderloin, and wild duck purloo.

The purloo (often spelled "perloo" or "pilau," it's pronounced "pur-LOW") quickly became the focus of the afternoon because it took the longest to cook, and Dickie and Alan were their own reality show. "For a good purloo, you need some wild meat," Dickie explained. "Alan has brought us two wood ducks and two mallards. Alan likes to age his ducks by tying them to the hood of his car and driving them around town to show off in front of folks for a few days."

Nobody tried to out-story Dickie. The guy worked Preston's back forty like Seinfeld in a nightclub. He owned the afternoon, especially after we got to talking about his dog, a Lab with a noticeable limp. As a puppy, the dog had run under Dickie's pickup and gotten his hip crushed. The howls of pain were too much for Dickie, so he fetched his shotgun. Taking aim at the screaming pup in his backyard, Dickie was steadying himself to pull the trigger when his other dog marched up and stood in front of the gun. Shooing him away, Dickie aimed. Again the older dog marched right in front of the gun barrel, protecting the suffering puppy.

So Dickie put the gun down and spent the next few days and nights nursing this little boy, and he grew up into a fine and friendly dog. "And that's the story of my dog Speed Bump," Dickie explained.

Dickie is the kind of guy who's very good at explaining. When he got to talking about purloo, he and Alan burned up most of the afternoon arguing about the proper way to get it going (andouille sausage to get some fat in the pan, peppers and onions to follow), as well as the proper amount of liquid that the meat and vegetables should cook in before the rice gets added. Purloo's danger is like paella's; it all comes down to that liquid-rice magic toward the end. When Dickie poured in a half can of beer without Alan's approval (or, at the very least, fireside consult), a chaos of creative name-calling erupted until Dickie wound up saying that maybe he was cooking a duck bog and not a duck purloo.

"A bog is what you get when you don't have enough rice to take up the liquid in your purloo," Dickie explained, looking nervously at the huge pot bubbling away.

The early dishes got eaten as soon as they finished cooking. The dove breasts, toothpicked with good greasy bacon to fatten up that lean dark meat, were perfect. And the mustard fry—chunks of venison dipped in a mustard goop—required a long marinade in some Madeira. Preston had found a bottle tucked away in his father's antebellum home back in Charleston and had brought it along. I peered at the odd bottle and informed my old friend that our venison was soaking in Portugal's finest from 1863. We all took a shot, and somebody claimed to detect the smoke of Gettysburg in the bouquet.

"Here's the secret to spicing a purloo," Dickie said, confident again now that the rice looked like it was doing its work. "You look down the driveway and see how many cars are coming. The more you see, the more pepper you add." But it seemed clear to everyone, after various repetitions of the punch lines and revisiting the details, that the key ingredient to the purloo was the biography of Speed Bump.

The next day I found myself in McClellanville, sitting on a stool at T. W. Graham & Company, where Claudia Kornack started to tell me the secret of her legendarily fragrant grits, but the morning soon veered into the story of when her mother trusted her, at age twelve, to bake her sister's birthday cake all by herself. She's been behind the stove ever since. And I visited Fred Scott at The Wreck of the Richard & Charlene, in Mount Pleasant, to discuss his red rice secrets, but we got sidetracked by the story of the old woman who bequeathed the recipe to him and all the attendant mysteries that went with it. By the time I'd left, it was my secrets that had been spilled.

Red rice is a Lowcountry staple, but it can be tricky. After I began hanging out with my godmother's son Thomas Barnes, a fantastic cook who died way too young, my own version of the general recipe started to come together:

You cook enough bacon in a cast-iron skillet to get a few tablespoons of fat, and in that you cook down a chopped onion and bell pepper, also adding a little salt and pepper as it cooks. Add a large can of crushed tomatoes and then throw in a can and a half's worth of chicken broth or water. Add a cup and a half of long-grain rice. Cook for five or ten minutes to get it going. Then cover the skillet with a lid or tin foil and put it in a 350-degree oven for thirty minutes. Pull it out and—this is imperative—don't touch the foil for fifteen minutes. Some alchemy happens here that, if messed with, will result in slightly crunchy rice. As Thomas said, "It's best not even to look at it."

Because Lowcountry food is both white and black (and mostly black), it's most easily marketed along the new segregationist lines (a.k.a. "demographic niches"). Go into any Charleston bookstore and you'll see dozens of cookbooks, ranging from *Charleston Entertains: Season by Season*—filled with nostalgic pictures of dinner tables laden with old family silver and pitched to Southern white parvenus—to one with the subtitle *Smokin' Joe Butter Beans, Ol' 'Fuskie Fried Crab Rice, Sticky-Bush Blackberry Dumpling, & Other Sea Island Favorites,* marketed for middle-class African Americans. Open them both, though, and you'll find the same recipes, by and large.

Lowcountry menus nowadays make repeated use of words like "authentic" and "traditional." It's understandable. Charleston is growing really fast, and folks want to feel that in the midst of so much change they can clutch something original. After a week on the road, I wasn't certain which was more crucial to this food, the recipes or the stories and arguments and secret-trading that poured forth in every kitchen. If I were a Zen master, I might well claim that you can't eat Lowcountry food, you can only cook it.

My sister's friend called me one morning with a hot tip. Just north of Charleston off Highway 17 is a place (it's not on any map) called Tibwin. Folks who live near it say that if you're talking about good food, then you're talking about Buckshot Colleton, a black man who cooked his meals in a shack and sold them right out of the kitchen. You had to eat in your car. But when I called, the number was out of service and he wasn't listed. Here's how I found him:

411: "This is information, what city please?"
Me: "Tibwin."
411: "There is no such place."
Me: "Try the next town, Awendaw. Listing for Colleton."
411: "First name?"
Me: "Doesn't matter."
411: "Excuse me?"
Me: "Pick a Colleton, any Colleton."
411: "If you say so, sir. Please hold while I dial that number at no extra charge."

Random Colleton: "Hello?"
Me: "Hello, is Buckshot home?"
Random Colleton: "My cousin Buckshot? Call his sister Miriam Green. She's a councilwoman for Awendaw."

Investigative journalism, the Lowcountry way. Five minutes later, the Colleton family has invited me over for a day of cooking and insisted that I bring my family with me. All the Colletons, men and women, cook, and it's obvious when you enter Miriam's house that cooking is at the center of this family. When my two sisters and brother-in-law and I arrive we are led into a kitchen that is practically a Martha Stewart set—multiple counters and ovens set around the object of honor: their grandmother's wood-burning stove, from which all of them had had their first meals.

Buckshot, a big man with the devil's own sultry smile, introduces his brother Bernard, tall and fit with an easy tranquility that commands the room, and his niece April, who has a killer dimple and studied culinary arts at Johnson & Wales University. "She's making the food pretty for us now," needles Buckshot. The whole family is hoping next month to reopen Buckshot's restaurant, this time with tables and chairs and a good location right on Highway 17. Until then, Miriam and her brothers practice here in her kitchen. Buckshot calls me over to the sink, where he wants to show me how he prepares crab.

"First, you got to clean them live," Buckshot says in the lilt of his Gullah accent. I have never seen it before, but Buckshot just pops off the top shell, so the crab is instantly killed. Clean out the dead man's meat and split the body in half: what you're left with is a handy crab bouquet you can grasp by those useless flippers. After the crabs are sautéed in garlic butter by Bernard, the meat is easy to suck out of those little bony chambers, making the dining experience one that more resembles eating than laparoscopic surgery.

April makes the family's she-crab soup, a rich delicacy involving crabmeat, crab roe, and a capful of sherry placed in each bowl before ladling. But she-crab soup is not really, um, an "authentic" dish. It's said to have been invented in the early twentieth century by a Charleston butler or a chef at Henry's, an old local restaurant that no longer exists. Put in perspective, she-crab soup is really the beta-test of capitalizing on Lowcountry cooking's deep African American roots.

"This here is the roe," Buckshot remarks, as he pops open another crab. "We sometimes call that the cheese." I dutifully write down this colorful Gullahism; then I ask about that yellow stuff in there that's troubled me since I was a kid.

"That's the fat of the crab," Buckshot says. With my pen poised, I ask him, what do you call that in Gullah?

Buckshot's trademark smile curls onto his face. "We call that the fat of the crab," he replies.

The Colletons have the hot plates out and it is beginning to look like a church social. We have red rice, she-crab soup, butter beans, chicken purloo, fried blue crab, garlic crab, oysters and grits. Neighbors are just somehow drifting over and soon the house is humming with forty people.

"The Colletons can make food dance," says a cousin named Ascue, who confesses he never misses a chance to eat here. By the middle of the evening, we all start talking about what we ate growing up. We trade some stories, and I notice how hard it is here in the Colleton house to say "Lowcountry" instead of "Gullah" cuisine. I can claim this food, but we all know who invented it. Fancy terms like *purloo* might come from Europe, but you don't need to be a linguist to guess the continent responsible for the words *gumbo, goober, benne seed, okra,* or *yam.*

Ascue wants to know if I've ever had chitlins, which are the business end of a pig's small intestine. I confess I've never had them. Right away it's clear we have ventured into a breach—on the other side are foods that didn't cross over from the kitchens of the field hands to the tables in the house. It's a slightly awkward moment, at least until we start talking secrets.

"It's washing the chitlins that makes them so hard," Ascue says.

"I scrape them with a knife," reveals Bernard.

"You know what I do," says Ascue. "I buy a two-gallon bucket of chitlins from the Bi-Lo, and I put them in the washing machine." Ascue's wife sends up a howl of disbelief that he is saying this, which only encourages him. "And I set it to cold wash."

Another howl goes up. Someone mentions the notoriously lasting smell that chitlins impart to their surroundings.

"You have to remember to put a little bleach in the machine afterward," Ascue notes, "and run it for a few hours before you put your clothes back in." Ascue's wife apparently has found Jesus a second time; she looks back and forth in mock horror between her husband and my scribbling pen.

"What are you thinking?" she wails. I have no idea what Ascue is thinking. But on my mind is the critical issue of timing for my newest story—that is, whether I'm going to tell my wife what's happened to our washing machine before or after I serve her dinner.

Carolina Comfort, out of Africa

Matt Lee and Ted Lee

In the '80s, when Robert Stehling was cooking at Crook's Corner in Chapel Hill, his boss and mentor, Bill Neal, changed the menu from Continental-eclectic to Southern classic. Overnight, or so it seemed, Stehling went from cooking Spanish paella to Charleston purloo.

A purloo, which in the Lowcountry also goes by "pilau" and "perlo," is a baked pot of rice, vegetables, stock, and poultry. A dish with roots in the Middle East, purloo most likely arrived in Charleston with the rice plant itself, by way of northwestern Africa and the slave trade. The marshy Lowcountry became the cradle of rice cultivation in North America in the 1800s, and even today the region retains a deep affinity for the starch.

On reflection, Stehling now acknowledges that the transformation at Crook's Corner took place over a longer period, because between the paella and the purloo he remembers an important detour to the Creole rice dish jambalaya. "It gave me a lot of confidence to see how all three food traditions were connected underneath," he said, as he transferred browned thighs and breast quarters from skillet to plate and scattered a few handfuls of chopped onion into the grease in the skillet.

From jambalaya Stehling borrowed an ingredient, eggplant, that is scarce in Lowcountry recipes for purloo but has become the secret ingredient in the version he cooks at his Charleston restaurant, the Hominy Grill. "The eggplant adds so much to this dish," he said. "It melts, gets almost creamy and helps keep moisture in."

Once the onions had browned, Stehling added chopped celery to the skillet and let it sauté a few minutes before adding chopped green pepper, four minced cloves of garlic, pinches of red pepper flakes, dried thyme, basil, a couple of bay leaves, and the diced eggplant. He stirred, sautéing the mixture for a few minutes before transferring it to a four-quart stainless-steel pot. "There are four main layers in the dish," he said. "Vegetables on bottom and then the rice. Then ham, okra and tomatoes together, and then the chicken and stock on top of that."

Stehling returned the empty skillet to the burner and added just a little peanut oil. He shook long-grain white rice from a plastic container into the skillet and gently tossed the rice around with a spoon until all the grains were glistening with oil. When the rice had turned slightly golden, he added it to the pot in a layer over the vegetables.

"Since you do a lot of sautéing in this recipe you need to be careful not to get too much oil in the purloo," he said as he poured a touch more peanut oil into the skillet. "You need barely enough to get the job done each time."

He added chopped tasso—a smoked ham from Louisiana—to the oil, along with sliced okra. He stirred them until they released a sweetly smoky fragrance, then added about a quarter cup of red wine and let it nearly simmer away before adding more than two cups of canned whole tomatoes that he had chopped.

"That's the flavor of the South, right there: okra, tomatoes, and smoked pork," he said. The mixture bubbled, the tomatoes and their liquid thickening. He layered the contents of the skillet over the rice in the stew pot.

He reached for the plate of seared chicken and nestled the pieces into the top layer. "You want to put the thicker, darker meat toward the outside of the pot, closer to where the heat's coming in quicker," he said, adding the chicken juices that had pooled on the plate as they rested. From a small saucepan of boiling stock, he poured about two cups, which percolated to the bottom of the layered pot, nearly filling it.

Stehling crimped a double sheet of foil over the top of the pot. "I make sure it's good and tight 'cause I really don't want any steam to get out," he said. He then transferred it to his oven, which had been heated to 375 degrees.

After an hour he removed the purloo and let it rest for ten minutes before peeling back the foil. A glorious head of steam escaped from the pot, filling the kitchen with the aroma of chicken on the bone, stewed onion, herbs, and smoke.

He tossed the rice and vegetables in the pot before tasting them. Each grain of rice remained distinct, without the pastiness of overcooking. The rice was firm but creamy-textured, and infused with the flavors of the pot. The chicken was moist and tender, with skin that was not crisp, but not limp or fatty either.

He added a final touch, two good shakes of red pepper sauce, to the pot before stirring it up again. "Purloo is like gumbo," he said. "It doesn't just happen."

Chicken Purloo
Serves 4.

1 (4- to 5-pound) chicken, cut into
   serving pieces
Kosher salt
3 tablespoons peanut oil
2 cups diced yellow onion
1 cup diced celery
2 tablespoons chopped garlic
1½ cups diced green bell pepper
⅛ teaspoon crushed red pepper
   flakes
⅛ teaspoon dried basil
⅛ teaspoon dried thyme
2 bay leaves

1 cup peeled diced eggplant
2 cups long-grain white rice
¼ teaspoon freshly ground black
   pepper
½ cup diced tasso or other
   smoked ham
2 cups okra, sliced ⅓-inch thick
¼ cup red wine
2½ cups canned whole peeled
   tomatoes, chopped
2 cups chicken stock or canned
   broth
Tabasco sauce (optional)

Preheat the oven to 375 degrees. Season the chicken with salt to taste. Place 1 tablespoon of the oil in a large sauté pan over medium-high heat, and brown the chicken pieces. Transfer to a medium bowl and set aside.

Add the onion (and 1 teaspoon oil, if necessary) to the pan, and sauté until golden brown, about 6 minutes. Add the celery (and 1 teaspoon oil, if necessary) and cook until slightly softened, about 4 minutes. Add the garlic, bell pepper, red pepper flakes, basil, thyme, and bay leaves; sauté for 2 minutes. Add the eggplant (and 1 teaspoon oil, if necessary) and sauté until the eggplant is tender, about 4 minutes more. Transfer all the vegetables and pan juices to a wide 3- to 4-quart ovenproof casserole dish and spread them in an even layer.

Heat 2 teaspoons oil in the sauté pan and add the rice. Sauté until the rice is lightly golden, 2 to 3 minutes. Spread the rice in an even layer over the vegetables in the casserole. Sprinkle 1 teaspoon salt and the black pepper over the rice.

Add 1 teaspoon oil to the sauté pan. When hot, add the tasso, stirring until it is fragrant. Add the okra and sauté until lightly browned, 6 to 8 minutes. Add the wine and cook until the pan is almost dry. Add the tomatoes; simmer vigorously until the mixture has thickened, about 6 minutes. In a small saucepan, bring the stock to a boil, then remove from the heat and set aside.

Layer the okra and tomato mixture over the rice in the casserole. Arrange the chicken pieces on top, placing the thigh and leg portions near the edge of the pan and the breast pieces in the center. Top with any juices from the bowl of chicken. Pour the hot stock into the casserole and cover the dish tightly with a lid or aluminum foil. Bake until the rice has absorbed all the liquid, about 1 hour.

Transfer the chicken pieces to a platter. Toss the rice and vegetables in the dish and season to taste with salt, black pepper, and Tabasco sauce. On each of 4 plates, place a portion of chicken and a serving of rice and vegetables. Serve hot.

Adapted from Robert Stehling.

Sweet Things

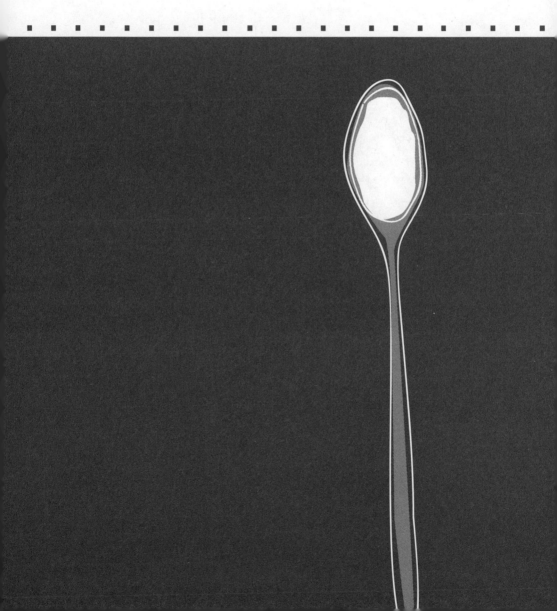

Sugar
Savior or Satan?

Molly O'Neill

For the past three years, I've been writing a memoir about my family and I've been thinking a lot about sugar. A lot of my story is about sugar. At first, it is a story about wanting it and not being allowed to have it. Once I am on foot and capable of lying, conniving, sneaking, babysitting, and, ultimately, baking, however, my story is about getting sugar. Ultimately, I end up chafing under the bondage of sugar. (*Chafing* is, of course, the operative word.)

To understand how sucrose shaped my worldview, it was necessary to drill down, down, down through layers of sugar memory. Past those amber-hued recollections of childish sweets. Past the nostalgia for simpler times and the pie-cooling-on-windowsill society. Down to the cellular level where good and evil do battle for possession of the soul. I have made this journey.

Is sugar a little piece of heaven or is it Satan in disguise?

Salvation: RED VELVET CAKE. LEMON CHESS PIE. COCONUT CAKE. BANANA CREAM PIE. BANANA PUDDING. BREAD PUDDING WITH WHISKEY SAUCE. In the first year of writing this book, sweets saved me. When self-doubt became my own personal Katrina, I reminded myself of the passage from Eudora Welty's *Delta Wedding*—"They all sat down on two facing sofas and had a plate of banana ice cream and some hot fresh cake and felt better"—and I left my desk and went to the kitchen to bake. MOLASSES GINGER BREAD. BURNT SUGAR CUSTARD. BLACK BOTTOM TOFFEE PIE. The intoxicating combination of sugar and fat sheathed the frayed and exposed nerves. Perhaps it would be more accurate to say, swaddled.

Or damnation: According to the Centers for Disease Control and Prevention in Atlanta, more than 20 percent of Americans are obese. America's fattest state is Mississippi (29.5 percent of adults), followed by Alabama (28.9 percent) and West Virginia (27.6 percent).

In A.D. 1000 few Europeans knew about sugar, which is thought to have originated in New Guinea, but by 1650 the British had become inveterate sugar eaters and sugar had become the keystone of the slave-based plantation economy in their Caribbean colonies. In the final decades of the eighteenth century, church-based European abolitionists became anti-saccharists. "Every person who habitually consumes an article of West Indian produce raised by slaves is guilty of murder," reads one of the movement's pamphlets, adding: "Every pound of sugar used is considered the same as consuming two ounces of human blood." Sugar's bad effects were also seen at home: another eighteenth-century commentator warned that "SUGAR . . . not only inflames the poor man's expenses but his blood and his vitals, also." (It's better than Viagra. Here, honey, have another piece of that pie . . .)

These debates accompanied the colonists into the New World. For several centuries, sweetness was most often next to Godliness in the American South. (Think of your average church supper. Which table groans loudest under its load? Here's a hint: not the salad table.) When a bright light was shone on the dark side of sugar, until recently it tended to happen north of the Mason-Dixon line. Historically, Southerners stood to profit from singing sugar's praises, because virtually all the cane sugar grown in the United States comes from Southern soil. Long before anybody thought of producing recipe pamphlets to promote the use of a product, generations of Southern ladies stood by their men by turning white sugar into the stuff of dreams.

PRALINES. COCONUT CAKE. RED VELVET CAKE. DIVINITY. PENU-CHE. PEANUT BRITTLE. PRALINES. SWEET POTATO PIE.

In addition to being masters of the obvious, these steel magnolias had a genius for concealing sugar—glazed yams, sugared pecans, pig candy, ice tea. For quite a few generations, Southerners were far too busy hiding sugar in their food supply to have time to worry about its moral implications. Until recently, only a Yankee could say the words "sugar" and "sin" in the same sentence. Unless, of course, "sin" was meant as a compliment.

The Southern way with sweets may, in fact, have been the original viral marketing campaign. I offer a part of my story as evidence. I grew up in Ohio, but my images of heaven list to the south.

HUMMINGBIRD CAKE. BREAD PUDDING WITH WHISKEY SAUCE. PECAN PIE. BOURBON PECAN PIE. CHOCOLATE PECAN PIE. BLACK BOTTOM PECAN PIE.

I believe that I caught these tastes from my mother's mother, who married a Southerner. My Virginia grandfather was convinced that there were fortunes to be made in yellow cake mix. He was sure, moreover, that the most logical market for this invention lay south of Ohio, so he moved his young family to San Antonio. In his effort to put yellow cake mix in every cupboard, my grandfather traveled constantly. While he was gone, my grandmother developed a terrible thirst and the habit of leaving her three young children unattended in their beds while she wandered from bar to bar in downtown San Antonio, frequently losing certain items of clothing along the way.

My grandmother also developed the habit of remorse. "Give me sugar," she would purr drunkenly at dawn when she returned to her babies.

By the time my mother was six, she had been removed from her home and sent back to Columbus to live with her mother's family. There, in an attempt to offset any tendencies she might have inherited from her mother, my mother was given lessons in self-control. These involved dainty eating and sitting in a chair without moving for ten-minute stretches. I was her firstborn child and my mother attempted to impart similar lessons to me within days of my birth. Concerned that my roly-poly newborn thighs might indicate a future fatso, she limited my caloric intake and strictly prohibited sugar ingestion.

Her mother, having long since exhausted all cures and dry-outs, to say nothing of her family's patience, was, by then, living in the state mental institution in Columbus, Ohio. When I was born, my father's mother came to help. She was a farm woman from Nebraska, a baker. She had an innate distrust of any woman who had not strangled and gutted a chicken, and having raised eight children of her own, she was not impressed by my mother's dietary restrictions. She mixed sugar and heavy cream in my formula and announced my weight gains as if each ounce were a rise on the NASDAQ index.

People who study taste claim that sweetness is an innate preference. Sweetness elicits gummy smiles and greedy grasping in infants. It can calm. It can soothe. It can seduce. Within days of her arrival, I preferred Grandmother O'Neill to my mother.

My grandmother stayed for a few months. Long enough, it seems, to establish a connection in my mind between sweetness and safety, sweetness and love. But of course, Grandmother O'Neill did eventually return to Nebraska and perhaps this was my own personal Paradise Lost.

Having been thoroughly indoctrinated in self-control, my mother's greatest concern in life is "being all set." Being all set requires discipline and organization, so life was less cozy after Grandma O'Neill went home.

There was no shortage of sweets—my mother is a superb baker—but there were significant regulations governing their dispersal, particularly to me.

When I was a toddler, my mother made a pie every day. She usually began at 11 a.m. by locking me in my high chair and preheating the oven to 350 degrees.

"Watch me, honey," she said, as she poured flour into her sifter and held it over the smooth white hills of Crisco in the bottom of her mixing bowl. Watch her? I couldn't take my eyes off of her! It was lunchtime and I was famished for the carefully weighed and measured portions that my mother served me daily: one carrot stick and one celery stick, two ounces of canned tuna fish, one half slice of Hollywood diet bread, and one quarter of an apple or pear. But I also relished the slow and careful torture of pastry taking shape under my mother's hands.

By the time I could walk, sugar had taught me that longing is a higher good. Satisfaction was embodied by my mother's pie. It was always at a distance, it was never enough. Achieving it was a perpetual aspiration that burned like cinnamon on the roof of the mouth.

My sense of the forbidden nature of sweetness was soon reinforced.

In addition to daily pie-baking, being all set demanded that my mother wash and iron the bed sheets daily and maintain linoleum floors that were, at all times, sanitary enough to become an operating arena should the need for open heart surgery unexpectedly arise. To maintain this required single-minded diligence. Therefore, as a toddler, I spent most of my time outside playing alone.

My best friend was a mermaid named Karen. We played together in the front yard. During one of our heart-to-hearts we were, one day, approached by a Fairy Godmother.

She was very tall, and her gray hair was pulled back in a bun. I was especially fascinated by her large crocodile purse, which boasted two miniature crocodile heads at the clasp.

"This is my friend, Karen. She is a mermaid," I said gravely, patting the air next to me.

I invited her to join us in my castle under the pine tree. Once inside the tree, we were completely hidden from the house.

I had used pine needles, dirt, and stones to build various rooms in my castle. I used the same materials—plus clover, grass, leaves, flowers, or the purslane that grew between the line of stones that led to the front door—to make pies for Karen.

"Hmmm," said Fairy Godmother, when I offered her a taste, "that smells delicious. Why don't we let that finish cooking, darling, and have us a little sweet."

From beneath the crocodile heads, she extracted a glassine bag of pastilles. They were small, slightly rounded discs with a delicate pink candy coating that was, initially, as sweet as a birthday cake on the tongue. But the candies had beads of licorice liqueur in their center, bitter and black and a terrible surprise. I gagged and Fairy Godmother took me into her lap. "Shhh, just wait," she said, rocking me. "Don't spit it out."

Her dress smelled like lavender. Her breath smelled like malt whiskey. Pressed next to her, I drifted, probably as drunk as she was, through the fear and revulsion of the harsh taste in my mouth, the visions of mud and swamps and pirates, the feeling of being lost in the dark, of being paralyzed and incapable of calling for help. But somehow I felt safe enough to wait for the sugar coating to triumph.

My mother had not, as I said, seen her own mother since she was six years old. As she campaigned against domestic dirt and disorder, she was blissfully unaware that her mother was out of the nut house. She had no idea that her mother was living in a residential hotel downtown and making friends with her daughter. I knew better than to mention my meetings with Fairy Godmother. Instinctively, I understood that the woman, like the candy she brought me, was something dangerous and forbidden. Sugar made me a liar.

"Who were you talking to under the pine tree?" my mother would ask.

"Karen the mermaid!" I would say.

"What have you been eating?" she would say, sniffing my mouth.

"Nothing, Mommy!" I would say.

When she greeted me and when she left me, my grandmother always said the same thing. "Give me sugar," she said. The words still make me tingle and flush.

Salvation: BROWN SUGAR, STRAIGHT FROM THE BOX.

When I was old enough to begin to buck my mother's anti-saccharist policies, I stole sweets from her pantry. Recently, waking as if from a blackout to find myself not at my desk but standing in the kitchen with a box of brown sugar in one hand, I had the same thrill I'd had as a child. "Stolen sweets are," as Colley Cibber wrote in *Revival of Fools*, "the best." I was also surprised by my behavior, because I would have said that as an adult, I have little taste for sweet things.

Devil: There is reason to believe that the human response to sweetness is right up there with the desire to sustain and perpetuate life. Like crack, the desire is immediate and all consuming. "I wondered," writes Michael Pollan after observing his infant son's ecstatic response to his first taste of sugar, "could sweetness be the prototype for all desire?"

Salvation: STRIPED PEPPERMINT CANDY. PEANUT BRITTLE. BUTTERSCOTCH DROPS. GOO GOO CLUSTERS.

As I pondered my origins as a cook, I remembered my first cooking lesson. It was from a woman at the Ohio Power and Electric Company who demonstrated, for my brownie troop, how to make *GLAZED CARROTS*. It probably goes without saying that this woman had a Southern accent. I thought of her as my own personal Betty Crocker. I remembered how thrillingly subversive that had felt to me, as a little girl, sugaring a vegetable. This was my Helen-Keller-at-the-well moment, the moment when I understood how truly revolutionary the art of cooking is. Forty years later, after a day of writing my memoir, I began glazing anything I could lay hands on.

A month later, when I'd reached driving age in my memoir, I was, in real life, beginning to leave my desk in the afternoons, leaving the house in upstate New York where I was sequestered and driving ten miles to buy candy bars.

PLANTERS PEANUT BARS. REECES PEANUT BUTTER CUPS. ALMOND JOY. M&M'S. YORK PEPPERMINT PATTIES.

Like LSD, the sugar seemed to burn away the barriers that normally order time and corral memory. As the wrappers piled up and my car began to look like the floor of a general store in the South, I was fifteen years old and I was on fire.

Devil: Do you remember that experiment that teachers used to do in elementary school? They'd take some kid's baby tooth and drop it into a glass of Coca-Cola. It would fizz up and a couple days later, when the teacher fished it out, the former pearly white was this black corroded rock?

I had repressed this memory, but under the influence of candy bars it came flooding back. I couldn't shake the horror of that image, even with sugar. Or perhaps, especially with sugar. I began investigating this scare tactic. This was, of course, not the first time I'd begun reading and seeking expert opinion on the topic of sugar.

From 2002 to 2003, as I wrote about my early childhood lust for the stuff, I'd alternated between eating sugar and learning more about sugar. I'd found that the United States is the world's fifth largest producer of sugar and its fourth largest consumer. USDA data indicate that in the United States sugar consumption rose through 1925 and then remained stable at about one hundred pounds per person a year until 1970, when high-fructose corn syrup came on the scene. Since then, the consumption of added sugars has increased by sixty-five pounds per person.

Everyone agrees that people who live in the South eat more sugar than people in any other region of the United States, but in several weeks of phone calling I was unable to establish the Southern mouth as evidence of the dangers of sugar. Bob Kusak, who heads dental research at the National Institutes of Health, shared my frustration. In the case of the South, he said, "We all know their decay rate should be higher than it is."

"How do you explain this?" I asked.

"They tend to eat their sugar with fat," explained Mr. Kusak. "Dietary fat seems to offset the effect of sugar on dental enamel."

Salvation: CREAM-FILLED KRISPY KREME DOUGHNUTS WITH CHOCOLATE FROSTING.

I developed a policy of eating fat and sugar in equal measure. Then I found that I'd gained fifty pounds in two years of writing about sugar.

The answer seemed simple. A diet. Of course, I am not one to go on some regime without thorough research into its history, efficacy, chemistry, and, of course, the recipes involved. I also believe in starting at the top, so I set up telephone interviews with the Duke Diet Center and Structure House, fat clinics in North Carolina that have been around for over thirty years. The South Beach Diet and Protein Power regimes came up repeatedly in these discussions, so soon I was interviewing the founders of each of these plans, one in Florida, the other in Kentucky. Weeks passed, however, before I realized that every diet call I made was answered by someone with a Southern accent.

"Well, what did you expect?" asked Dr. Louis Ballard, a physician at the University of Southern Louisiana who, along with three other Southerners, founded Sugar Busters, the spiritual ancestor of all low-carb regimes. "When I listened to what my patients ate, the typical Southern diet, all I had to do was the math. I stopped eating sugar and carbs and dropped four pounds in a week. I got a few patients to try it. The results were amazing."

"Great," I said, "so I just follow one of these and I'll fit into my clothes in no time."

My results were, initially, spectacular. The pounds came tumbling off. But in short order, I was falling off the low-carb wagon. Always with sugar.

"The data are not conclusive," said Dr. Ballard, "but there is some pretty compelling anecdotal evidence that suggests addictive properties associated with sugar."

So if sugar is addictive, I asked, how does one recover from it? Just as the premier medically based diet centers were concentrated in the South, and the early sugar recovery literature sprang from Southern writers, the nation's first sugar rehabs are—you guessed it—in the South. The karmic justice of this will remain a topic for another day.

As I began once again to write pieces for magazines, assignments brought me close to one place in Orlando, Florida. Like headquarters in a spy movie, this day-treatment clinic is simply called "the Center." It is a counseling facility based on the twelve-step model. People attend three to four meetings a day and they tend to cry once a day.

Observing, with the promise of anonymity, I heard men and women sob about lives ruined by sugar, jobs, marriages, dental enamel, waistlines, and dreams lost.

"The Twinkie defense is no joke," sobbed one middle-aged woman with terribly expensive blond hair. "I feel like I got here just in time. I was starting to behave irrationally behind sugar."

In the five years since it opened, the Center has treated about six thousand people. Most are Southerners. Two hundred patients have found that they could not maintain their abstinence from sugar after their initial stay at the Center and have moved to Orlando to live in community. Which is to say, they bought condos in Orlando and continue to go to daily meetings and, most importantly, they say, to eat together. The group I observed had twenty-two women and thirteen men. The men eat together and the women eat together. Not since the Shakers has gender segregation at the table been so thoroughly enforced as it is at the Center. But the Shakers, unlike clients of the Center, had lemon pie.

The people I interviewed were proud of what they called "their mood stability," which seemed to me flat and beaten.

"I can't afford to get excited," said the woman who was assigned to squire me around. "I could lose my abstinence if I get excited," she said. In addition to abjuring sugar, people at the Center do not eat flour or wheat products. These products are referred to as "substances" and never called by name in meetings at the Center.

"If I have to sit and listen to people romance one of my substances, I may start desiring it," one guide told me. "If you want to live a holy life, you don't swear. If you want to live an abstinent life, you don't name substances."

This, I realized, could pose significant problems to me in my chosen subject. Nevertheless, I pushed on.

Hallelujah Acres, in Shelby, North Carolina, was, in a way, a logical extension of the program of physical and spiritual recovery advocated in Orlando. Founded by Reverend George Malkmus, Hallelujah Acres espouses the Garden of Eden Diet. Rev. Malkmus was just another pentecostal minister in upstate New York until thirty years ago when he was diagnosed with cancer and turned to God for medical advice. God prescribed the perfect human diet in the book of Genesis.

"He gave us all we needed to eat, brothers and sisters. All the plants and nuts and fruits in the Garden of Eden." Rev. Malkmus claims that there was no sugar cane or sugar beets in the Garden of Eden. There was also, he says, no cooking. He claims that a sugar-free raw food diet cured him of cancer. At his center he teaches classes to support his Bible-based food plan.

The classes have a tent-revival aspect. Sugar, he says, "opens pathways to other worldly diversion, and to illness." The audience when I visited looked like a crowd of Wal-Mart shoppers, although in subsequent interviews, I've spoken to about a dozen highly educated people in upper income brackets. One described his sugar-free odyssey as "a spiritual awakening." Another said she felt as if she had shaken off the shackles. "I'm free at last!" she said. I believed her and I envied her.

To date, 250,000 people have studied with Rev. Malkmus. In the past year, he has opened four additional Hallelujah Acres lifestyle centers, which offer week-long retreats for a spiritual recovery from sugar and other cooked food.

I have not yet signed up for sugar rehab. I still want to go away someplace and wake up thin. But I'm not through with my research yet. I started saying No to sugar about a year ago and I lost about a pound a week. If this continues, I should be able to do television spots on shows other than *The Biggest Loser* by the time my memoir is published.

I'm still not convinced that just because sugar looks like cocaine, it has a similar affect on the moral soul. Of course, this view is gaining momentum—helped along by things like the increasing rate of obesity, the rapid growth of diabetes, the rise of all-natural chic, and class. Food is always about class. If you don't believe me, close your eyes and summon a mental picture of two different women eating dessert:

The first is eating a dish of wild raspberries. The raspberries are as tiny as rubies and they are flanked by slices from a fresh white peach. There is a small dollop of unpasteurized, organic clabbered cream—a genteel sufficiency, my mother would say. There is no sugar in sight.

The second woman is eating a fried pie. It's unwieldy and the filling, which is sweet potato, is dripping off her mouth. The pie itself is greasy and it leaves a sheen on her fingers. Whoops, there it goes, right down the front of her blouse. Jesus, it looks like she put powdered sugar on it too, look at that white stuff all over her nose.

Now that you have that picture, let me ask you one more question: Which woman is carrying a Prada handbag?

Addiction is the twenty-first century's word for Satan. We need a demon to blame for the increasing disparity between the haves and the have-nots, an "Axis of Evil" that is within our control. Life seems safer, simpler, more directly a cause-and-effect sort of deal, when it can be found in your sugar bowl.

Molasses-Colored Glasses

Frederick Douglass Opie

Molasses has been one of the three M's of the diet of Southern common folks, along with meat (salt pork) and meal (cornmeal). It has served as a baking ingredient, condiment, and cold remedy, and it was central to special-occasion meals in the South. We can draw on a range of sources including travelers' accounts, autobiography, community studies, WPA narratives, and interviews conducted for the Origins of Soul Food Oral History Project to examine its importance and its changing role in Southern foodways.

Molasses is made from sugar cane. Sorghum syrup, also referred to as molasses, comes from sweet sorghum grass. Both crops were probably introduced to the New World during the Atlantic slave trade. Travel accounts tell us that West Africans were familiar with both because women merchants made and sold sweets from these plants. Describing a coastal market in Guinea in 1602, the Dutch traveler Pieter de Marees writes, "Very early in the morning, at daybreak, the Peasants come to the Market, carrying on their heads two or three bundles of Sugar-cane, like Faggots. They untie the bundles of Sugar-cane and spread them out on the Market-place. Then the Inhabitants of the place come and buy Sugar-cane from the Peasants there, one buying two Canes, another three, according to their needs. Thus these Peasants quickly dispose of their Sugar-cane, for people are accustomed to eat a great deal of it."

In the sixteenth century the Portuguese established sugar plantations in Brazil, and the Spanish, French, Dutch, and English soon followed suit, in the Caribbean and then in the South. English planters in the Caribbean sold molasses along with sugar and rum to Africans, Indians, and the English working class. White colonists in Virginia and the Carolinas also traded for Caribbean molasses, using it in a variety of ways. An anonymous observer wrote around 1730, "Molasses is generally used throughout all the Northern

Colonies, and at our Fisheries, in brewing their Beer, and the poorer Sort, who are very numerous, eat it with their Bread, and make Puddings of it, Ec [*sic*]." One common use was as a sweetener in "hasty pudding"—oatmeal porridge or cornmeal mush served with butter, milk, and molasses. In many places molasses was also used as feed for both livestock and enslaved Africans.

After the Louisiana Purchase, sugar cultivation for national and international markets became gradually limited to Florida and Louisiana, but sugar cane was still grown for local consumption in states like Virginia and Alabama. Sweet sorghum, grown primarily in the Midwest in the mid-nineteenth century, had also become a predominantly Southern crop by the 1890s. A U.S. Department of Agriculture study done in 1895 and 1896 found that African American farmers in Tuskegee County, Alabama, for example, dedicated some of their fields to raising sugar cane and sweet sorghum, which they "used to make molasses for home consumption," although "only a part of the molasses used by the farmer is made on the farms, the rest is bought at the stores with other commodities."

Others obtained molasses through various systems of barter. Joyce White remembers that in her Choctaw County, Alabama, hometown African American men would go to the local white-owned sugar mill in November to help with the long, hard, "hot and tedious" task of making molasses: "The work began at daybreak and lasted until nightfall. The stalks of cane were fed through a hand-operated press to extract the sugar-sweet juice, which was poured into large vats. A fire was set and the juice was boiled until the sugar caramelized. Daddy would arrive home dead tired. In those days black families bartered services for goods and produce, and his earnings were several gallon cans of molasses, which Mama cooked with throughout the winter."

Entrepreneurs with mobile equipment provided syrup-making services in communities without commercial sugar mills. To make molasses, the juice of the sugar cane must first be extracted with a grinder or press, then heated, clarified, and boiled until it condenses into a thick mixture called massecuite. Once the massecuite is separated into sugar crystals, a thick dark syrup forms during the condensation process and creates molasses. Ninety-year-old Ella "Gold" Baker told me how it was done in the Chesapeake region of Virginia. Born in 1915, she remembered growing up in the predominantly African American farming hamlet of Cloverdale. Every autumn, a one-legged man named Henry Lewis went from house to house with a portable sugar cane grinder and a vat on a horse-drawn wagon, converting cane growers' small harvests into molasses for a share of the product (typically a third).

Other Virginia subsistence farmers had to buy their molasses. Virginia Banks, for example, remembers from the 1920s that her family and others in Middlesex County raised most of what they ate, but bought blackstrap molasses from local merchants who imported it by the barrel from as far away as Puerto Rico. She remembers carrying quart jars with her to the store. (Blackstrap molasses is produced from the third boiling of the sugar syrup and is the most concentrated type of molasses left over after the sugar's sucrose has turned to crystal. Its rather bitter taste has almost no sweetness, but it has a high nutritional value. After the Spanish-American War cheap Puerto Rican molasses became widely available in the United States.) The molasses barrel "with flies buzzing around the wooden spigot" was "ever-present" in most general stores in the South, writes Erwin Stephens of Harnett County, North Carolina.

Molasses, like cornbread, was considered by most to be among the "roughest of food," suitable primarily for slaves and poor whites. Travelers in the antebellum South observed that slaveholders included niggardly allotments of molasses among the rations distributed to their slaves. During a mid-nineteenth-century trip, Frederick Law Olmsted observed that slaves on a plantation somewhere in Georgia or the Carolinas "commence work at sunrise, and at about eight o'clock have breakfast brought to them in the field. The provisions furnished them consist mainly of meal, rice, and vegetables, with salt and molasses, and occasionally bacon, fish, and coffee."

Charles Ball was born a slave in Calvert County, Maryland, around 1781. Between the harvest and Christmas, slaves on his plantation survived on a diet of "corn bread, sweet potatoes, some garden vegetables, with a little molasses and salt, assisted by the other accidental supplies that a thrifty slave is able to procure on a plantation." Many "hunted rabbits, opossums or fished," said Maryland slave Silas Jackson. South Carolina's Henry Brown remembered receiving molasses as a part of his meager weekly rations. "A peck o' co'n, t'ree pound o' bacon, quart o' molasses, a quart o' salt, an' a pack o' tobacco was given the men. The wife got the same thing but chillun accordin' to age."

Some slaves were able to supplement their rations with food grown in truck gardens and domestic animals raised around their quarters, and some could sell any surplus on market days. In 1850 the Swedish traveler Frederika Bremer observed enslaved Africans in Charleston selling chickens and eggs to buy "treacle or molasses (of which they are very fond), biscuits and other eatables."

Although upper-class whites in colonial America considered molasses fit only for slaves and preferred refined sugar for themselves, the irony is that sugar is full of empty calories while molasses is rich in minerals and vitamins. A tablespoon of blackstrap molasses, for example, provides about a fifth of the recommended daily intake (RDI) of iron and copper, over a quarter of the RDI of manganese, and a seventh of the RDI for potassium. Growing children and menstruating, pregnant, or lactating women all need increased levels of iron, and blackstrap molasses provides more iron for fewer calories than red meat—and it is fat-free. Copper promotes the development of bone and connective tissue, manganese is essential to the functioning of the nervous system, and potassium is necessary for muscle contraction and nerve transmission. Molasses is also high in calcium, which is required for strong bones and teeth, aids blood clotting and the transmission of nerve impulses to and from the brain, and reduces the risk of colon cancer. Finally, molasses is rich in vitamins B1, B2, B6, and E.

Black cooks eventually changed upper-class whites' views of molasses, just as they had with the greens, sweet potatoes, and yams that whites had also spurned. Cooked foods and candies made with molasses would find their way into local markets and the kitchens of inns and plantation big houses soon enough. Enslaved Africans bent "the taste of the Big House toward that of the quarters," argues historian Eugene D. Genovese, "because the slaves as a class, including the rudest field hands, had quietly been making a life for themselves that included a healthy concern with cooking."

Similarly, according to Sidney Mintz, markets "enabled the slave to produce what they (or the markets to which they sold) desired and thus influenced both the breadth and the stability of cuisine." He adds that "the markets made both slave cultivators and slave cooks familiar with a wide range of foods—creating demand and stimulating supply at the same time." We know, for example, that in sugar-producing regions of Cuba and Brazil, all classes of people enjoyed hard treacle candies. Treacle, made from the drippings accumulated from the vats used in sugar refining, looked and tasted like molasses and sold very well when combined with chopped coconut, nuts, and fruit.

In the United States, poor white and black Southerners ate molasses in some form with almost every meal, but it was most often eaten at the breakfast table with cornbread and fatback bacon. The cornbread served as a "sop" for the greasy gravy and molasses. When Olmsted visited a small farm on the Red River in Louisiana, he was served a breakfast of cold salt fat pork, stale cornbread, "a jug of molasses, and a pitcher of milk." On another Louisiana farm, a bowl of molasses stood at the center of a breakfast table surrounded by bacon, bread, fried eggs, and sweet potatoes. Olmsted was "pressed to partake" of the molasses as family members poured some on their plates and then sopped it up with the bread. In central Mississippi, he joined a white family for a breakfast of "fried ham and eggs, sweet potatoes, apple-pie, corn bread, and molasses." Olmstead wrote, "This last article I declined, and passed it to the young lady opposite, looking to see how it was used." (It was poured between the items on one's plate, and most likely sopped up with the cornbread.) It seems that white women served molasses at every breakfast meal, unlike most enslaved Africans in Mississippi, who apparently enjoyed molasses with their breakfast only on holidays like Christmas, when masters usually distributed it along with coffee and tobacco as a gift.

Many Southern recipes that call for molasses originated during the Civil War, when sugar was rationed, particularly in non-sugar-producing states where the Union blockade prevented the importation of sugar from Louisiana, Florida, and the Caribbean. To meet the challenge of cooking during the Civil War— and later, during World Wars I and II—many recipes substituted molasses for sugar. "Long sweetening," as some call molasses, was used to make cookies, pudding, pie, and "stickies." Molasses stickies, according to WPA writer Wendell B. Phillips, "were made of a rich biscuit dough, rolled thin, spread with molasses and butter, rolled up like a jelly roll, then sliced thin, placed on a biscuit tin and baked. This does not sound like it would be so good, but try them!" Bell Irvin Wiley in *The Life of Johnny Reb: The Common Soldier of the Confederacy* writes that by the end of the war "many soldiers who previously had no cooking experience became experts at creating Southern delicacies" like molasses custard. I suspect that molasses pudding, which, according to Reginald Ward of North Carolina and Nettie Banks of Virginia, was "made like a cake," also dates back to the Civil War and sugar shortages in those states. Banks also remembered her mother making gingerbread with molasses.

The use of molasses was not limited to puddings and baked goods. Wilkes County, North Carolina, is famous throughout the South for its country ham, particularly those from the smokehouse of Clayton Long. From his family comes a cider and molasses recipe for cooking ham:

Country Ham Cooked in Cider and Molasses
For a 14- to 16-pound cured country ham.

Soak for 4 to 12 hours in the refrigerator, then simmer for 20 to 25 minutes per pound in a mixture of:

1 cup molasses

1 cup firmly packed light brown sugar

1 gallon apple cider

3 medium onions, chopped

3 medium carrots, peeled and chopped

Remove skin and excess fat and coat with:
2 cups dry bread crumbs mixed with 2 cups firmly packed light brown sugar

Roast at 400 degrees for 15 minutes to brown.

Southern cooks also use molasses to season baked beans. Born in 1872 in Christiansburg, Virginia, Mattie Fletcher Shafer grew up in Virginia and moved to Harlem in 1908. She raised her son Adam Clayton Powell Jr. on Southern cooking, including Southern-style baked beans with molasses. The New York congressman remembered that her beans "cooked all night long on the back of the stove with plenty of black molasses on top and hunks of salt pork inside."

After the Civil War, access to sweets like molasses became one of many indicators of social and economic status. Many tenant farmers, like slaves before them, received food rations from white planters, and for some cornbread and molasses were the only food during hard times. A 1928 Mississippi Agricultural Experiment Station report, by Dorothy Dickins of the black college Mississippi A & M, studied African American tenant farmers in nine counties of the Yazoo-Mississippi Delta, where they made up the overwhelming majority of the farm population. Dickins found that most blacks (and whites as well) got the better part of their calories from sweets. African Americans, says the report, "like molasses and eat a great deal of it especially in fall, winter, and early spring."

A 1941 study of tenant farms in the Deep South reported that a family of six or seven people typically received two gallons of molasses per month as rations. In addition, they received one hundred pounds of cornmeal, twenty-five pounds of flour, two pounds of coffee, twelve pounds of sugar, eighteen pounds of shortening, twenty-two pounds of salt pork, and two boxes of salt. "The meat and flour rations were so small that workers were compelled to live chiefly upon a diet of corn bread and molasses until they could obtain vegetables from their gardens in late may [sic]." In urban settings, poor Southern folk ate a similar diet. Louis Armstrong recalled living for six months on a "supper of black molasses and a big hunk of bread" at the Colored Waifs' Home for Boys in New Orleans. He said after six months he got used to it; that molasses and bread "seemed just as good as a home cooked chicken dinner." (A similar description of molasses and bread sandwiches comes from Prince Edward County, Virginia, in the 1940s.)

Independent farmers in the South had more choice than tenant farmers about what they ate. For example, the staple food of African American farm owners in Tuskegee, Alabama, in the late nineteenth century included molasses as often as possible. Black women added molasses to fatback to make a gravy for sopping cornbread. They also served a beverage made from hot water sweetened with molasses three times a day throughout the year. With collards, turnips, sweet potatoes, and an occasional cooked opossum, molasses and fatback sopped with cornbread was "the bill of fare of most of the cabins on the plantations" in the Black Belt South. Historically, poor white Southerners ate the same three M's as blacks. White Southerner Erwin Stephens recalled that "molasses, biscuits, fried white sowbelly or side meat, and white gravy was a staple diet on many tables" in Harnett County, North Carolina.

My interviews with whites and blacks raised in the South or by Southern parents show that molasses sopped with cornbread or served as a condiment remained a prevalent tradition in many parts of the South until at least the 1960s. Edward Williamson's father was born in 1918 in Atkins, South Carolina. Williamson remembers that his father, who did not like maple syrup, referred to molasses as "mule blood" and used to take grease "from fatback, which he would then pour in the middle of molasses and then sop the molasses and grease with bread, cornbread, or something like that." Marcellas C. D. Barksdale remembers molasses from the cafeteria at the segregated public school in Amityville, South Carolina. At the "Harrisburg Street elementary school . . . they served molasses at the lunch time to use in our blackeyed peas." Barksdale also wrote that "one of the delightful breakfast meals, I recall, was a combination of hot biscuits, molasses, and fatback. Fatback bacon fried! Fried fatback." Alexander Smalls's grandfather from Spartanburg, South Carolina, argued that a Sunday breakfast should be a banquet. He would cook catfish, sage sausage, rice, grits, "and maybe gravy from the previous night's veal or beef stew. But no matter the menu, Grandpa's breakfast was not complete without biscuits and sorghum or molasses."

Folks in North Carolina felt the same way as Grandpa Smalls. In the small farming town of Windsor, in eastern North Carolina, Hattie Outlaw regularly served molasses and biscuits to her children. Her son Benjamin, born in 1921, recalls, "Mama would also make a pan of biscuits, and fry a slice of ham or some bacon, and you would sop molasses with biscuits." The best cook my mother, Margaret Opie, knew from her childhood was her aunt, Maggie. Born in Windsor in 1903, Aunt Maggie was famous for serving a large black skillet of fresh-baked spoonbread and molasses. My mother and her four cousins, a girl and three boys, would sop the spoonbread with molasses until they were full. As young men, Aunt Maggie's three sons were big enough to be NFL linebackers, and molasses-sopped spoonbread served with a main course of fried chicken, green beans, and baked sweet potatoes was an economical way to satisfy their hefty appetites. Similarly, Reginald T. Ward, born in 1944, grew up in Robinsonville, also in eastern North Carolina, on hoecakes and molasses. His mother used molasses to sweeten coffee as well.

Further north, black residents of Virginia also remember molasses at the breakfast table. Eugene Watts from Charlottesville remembers his mother serving biscuits and molasses at breakfast, and Nettie Banks of Middlesex

County recalls that her mother always served molasses in the wintertime for breakfast, serving it with fry fatback or some other kind of meat. In Prince Edward County, Lamenta Crouch grew up with molasses as syrup on pancakes and to "sweeten our oatmeal." Young children in Virginia often used molasses to sweeten their mush, which was generally bread or cornbread mixed with milk or buttermilk.

Southern cooks also incorporated molasses into their special occasions, particularly in the fall of the year. The family hosting a hog killing in Alabama would serve up sweet potatoes, cracklings, pans full of fresh-baked cornbread, and molasses to those who helped with the hard work of butchering the hog. Joyce White of Choctaw County, Alabama, remembers her mother's cutting up the hog's skin and frying the pieces in washing tubs of hot oil until they became crisp cracklings. "The cracklings were passed out to the workers, along with a couple of pans of hot cornbread, roasted sweet potatoes, and a can of molasses that Daddy earned from helping Mr. Ras, who owned the sugar cane mill," she writes.

Molasses figured in other community events as well. Gertha Couric of Barbour County, Alabama, told a WPA writer that in November, there was no better place to get all tangled up than at "an old-fashioned cane grinding and candy pulling." At the center of the event were elderly African American women from the community who knew how to turn raw sugar cane into the essential ingredient needed to make highly prized peanut brittle and candied popcorn balls: "An old Negro mammy usually stirs the boiling syrup candy. In another pot is peanut candy. The peanuts are put into the boiling syrup, and when cooked it is poured into the tin plates to cool. Into another pot of boiling syrup, popcorn is dropped, and is then taken out quickly with long handled spoons, and put on large platters. When cool, it is rolled into balls." At these events courting couples, dressed in "clothing that will stand a tubbing or may be discarded," made candy together for a small fee.

Erwin Stephens tells how the community of Hickory Grove, North Carolina, raised funds for books for the local library. "On the designated night a crowd gathered around a large iron pot full of molasses." While the molasses was cooking to the proper consistency, folks played games, adults sat around and talked, and there was generally a "short program of recitations and declamations" lighted by lanterns hanging from trees and people's porches. Once the molasses was ready, the cook ladled it out onto paper to cool. Stephens recalls: "Getting a wad of the sticky molasses, the hands first being covered with flour to prevent sticking, the couple would begin pulling the gooey molasses away from each other, double it back and pull it out again. Flouring the hands from time to time, the couple would continue the process until the candy was stiff.

Then they would eat it or give it to the smaller children. Some times there would be a couple dozen couples pulling candy, touching hands, chatting, or courting. It was lots of fun. I don't recall how the money was raised, but I think each couple paid a nickel or a dime for enough molasses to pull. Anyway we raised enough money to buy a considerable amount of books and I was in my second heaven when I could get my hands on one to read."

In many parts of the South, people without access to affordable medical care did what they could on their own to maintain their health and cure ailments. Many Southerners had a good knowledge of herbs, and some apparently learned from Native Americans that molasses, in addition to the vitamins and minerals it provides, had other medicinal qualities.

Since sugar cane was introduced to the Western Hemisphere by Europeans, Native Americans must have learned of its medicinal properties after 1492 (how and when is not recorded), but Native Americans in the Carolinas used turnips and molasses to cure coughs and colds. "Just take sorghum molasses and a turnip, and put them in a pot and boil it until the turnip is good and tender," writes Southern herbalist Thomas A. L. Bass. Native Americans would eat the turnip and drink the syrup. Molasses, argued Bass, is a "good tonic" that will cure almost any cold or cough.

Similarly, North Carolinian Hattie Outlaw used to make a tea out of molasses. She would put molasses "in a jar with some hot water and wait until it became illuminated" says her son Benjamin. "It taste good, and they tell me it's good for the bones."

Like sopping molasses and fatback with cornbread, using molasses as a cure became associated with a person's regional origins, lower class status, and ethnicity. Upper-class whites avoided the practice, and maintained that only poor folk, blacks, and Indians believed in such remedies.

The love affair between Southerners and molasses dates back to the colonial period when settlers in Virginia imported it from the Caribbean for puddings and custards. Because of the prominent place given to molasses in the rations of slaves, it came to be viewed as fit primarily for them, and for poor whites. Although some uses of molasses—to sop with cornbread, or as a tonic—are still stigmatized, the exigencies of wartime sugar-rationing and the talents of African American cooks eventually reintroduced molasses to the diets of upper- and middle-class white Southerners, paralleling other adaptations, in music, dance, religion, and so on. And so a humble liquid serves to illustrate an important process of cultural diffusion in which enslaved Africans not only adapted to the life imposed on them by their masters, but influenced their masters' lifestyle as well.

The Genie in the Bottle of Red Food Coloring

Beth Ann Fennelly

The first time I came to the South, I was twenty-four and heading to the University of Arkansas for graduate school. My family in Chicago kept talking about my move to the "Deep South" with wonder and trepidation—to them, yuppified Fayetteville was just down the river from *Deliverance* country.

While I was making my trip south, my future husband, Tom Franklin, was leaving his home in Alabama to head to the same university on his first trip "way up north," as his family called it, also with wonder and trepidation—for them, Fayetteville was just down the road from the gang warfare of St. Louis.

Here's the short version of what happened next: we met the first day of school, and we fell in love, and I never really went back north again.

Understanding my new home in the South meant, of course, coming to understand its foods. I easily adopted grits, fried okra, and sweet potatoes. But these were rather superficial adoptions; mostly I ate and cooked what I have always eaten and cooked. That's not acculturation. Acculturation, as acculturated folks know, involves pain. My story of acculturation begins with an innocent offer: What type of cake would Tommy like for his birthday? Here I will brag that I make wonderful cakes, probably because I have a determined sweet tooth so I've grown cagey about gratifying it. Invite me to a dinner party, for example, and I'll not ask, "Can I bring something?" but "Can I bring dessert?" which prevents the postprandial surprise of the host passing sliced strawberries at the table. Friends—strawberries, unless dipped in white chocolate, are not a dessert, they're a *garnish*. Dessert means chocolate, preferably dark, what someone with a less distinguished palate might call "too rich." So would Tommy perhaps enjoy my chocolate almond ganache with crème anglaise? My bitter chocolate hazelnut torte? Dacquoise? Génoise? Anything that rhymes with "awes"?

"Um, how about red velvet?" he asked.

"Um, sure," I replied. But not only had I never heard of this concoction, I couldn't find it in either my batter-splattered *Elegant Desserts* or *The Cake Bible*. Finally I went to the Source: my future mother-in-law, who was glad to share the recipe. Now that I think of it, perhaps it was that phone call that began our deep friendship, because Betty saw her son's Yankee girlfriend wanted to make him happy.

But there was a *problem* with the recipe. More than one, in fact. First, when I sprinkled the vinegar on top of the baking soda, it hissed at me. The cakes I baked did not require safety goggles. The cakes I baked did not talk back. I discovered the second, bigger problem when the batter was almost finished and I realized just how much red food coloring was in the four-ounce bottle the recipe called for. Should I phone again and ask my potential mother-in-law to recheck her recipe? "The cake's supposed to be dark red," Tommy said.

"How red?" I asked.

"You know, like a dead armadillo on the roadside." And I'd been in the South *exactly* long enough to know how red that was.

All my sweet husband-to-be wanted for his birthday was a red velvet cake, but, I confess, he didn't get one. I tried—Lord knows I tried. But as the bottle of food coloring hovered over the batter, my hand just couldn't commit to tilting. What was in this stuff anyway? I brought the bottle close: propylene glycol, propylparaben, and FD&C Red #40. I let three fat drops fall into the batter, stirred it to a lovely cherry-blossom pink, then shoved the pans in the oven.

And so July 7, 1995, the pink velvet cake was born. I have made it each July 7 since for Tommy's birthday. The last three years, I've also made it May 19, our daughter's birthday. Claire, unlike her mama, has never known anything but Southern cuisine. Her first solid food was sweet potatoes, and her favorite vegetable is "fried Oprah." Claire enjoyed her first dessert, like most babies, at her one-year birthday party. At that point, Claire's little rosebud palate was pure of processed sugars, not to mention FD&C Red #40. When the moment for her debauchery arrived, I held up the baby fork with a crumb of the cake on it. She stuck out a tentative tongue, touched the icing, then slipped her tongue back in her mouth. An expectant hush overtook the solemn party guests wearing conical hats. Then, as if the glorious gates of sugar-rush paradise trumpeted open before her, Claire leaned forward in her high chair and, with both hands, yanked the fork into her mouth. Next she was tearing into the cake with both fists, smearing cake up her nostrils and into her eyelashes. The following morning, as I got Claire ready for the day, I was reliving the memory of a party so successful that its clean-up involved swabbing Q-tips in my daughter's ears. But as I began to change her diaper, I felt a panicked sickness at finding a bloody mess inside of it. I was heading for the car to take Claire to the doctor before I realized it was just the red food coloring.

Of course, all of this brings up a thorny question—by adapting Southern food and foodways for my New South family, am I merely diluting them, bleaching them, producing pale pink when crimson is called for? Perhaps. But I also know that healthy traditions can accept adaptations, in the same way that healthy animals and plant systems do, and in the same way language does, for we think of language as a closed system, but it is no fossil, it is an organic, seething marvel, continuously created and re-created, tumbling into the future with its bundle of blanks and redundancies. The only languages that are perfected are those that are dead. And if I've learned one thing living in the South, it's that Southern cuisine is anything but dead.

Back to my story now: Girl meets boy. Girl meets delicious Southern Boy, and they have themselves a delicious Southern Child. Well, where does that leave the Girl? I know, as much as I'd like to call myself one, I'm not a Southerner. But I'm also no longer a Yankee, at least not the kind my husband was warned against. Oh, I don't claim to admire everything about the South, or understand it—I still think the term "Fry Daddy" sounds more like a rapper's handle than a kitchen appliance. And my thighs hope it stays that way. But I'm learning where I fit in the South, and where the South fits in me. Learning what to adopt, and what to adapt. And learning that, sometimes, one moves through the pain of acculturation to come out on the other side in a rainbow of pleasure. If you don't believe me, stop by my house May 19 or July 7 for what I guarantee is the best pink velvet cake you've ever had.

Corndog Nation

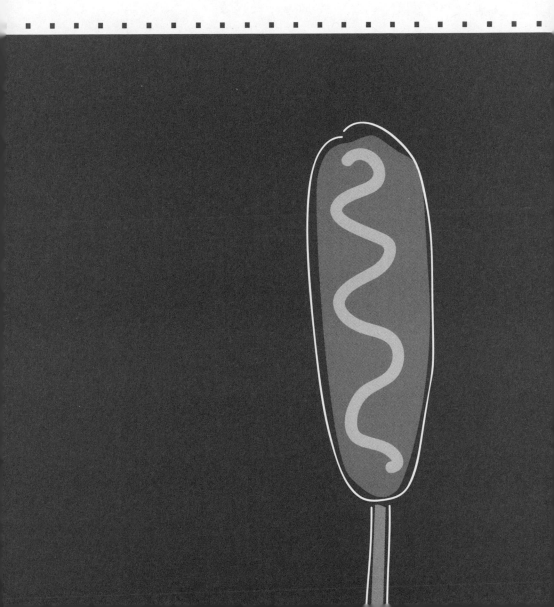

Store Lunch

Jerry Leath Mills

Throughout the rural South, men with regular business in the country—hunters, fishermen, farmers, surveyors, and traveling agents of various trades—traditionally enjoy a repast known as the Store Lunch. I say "men" advisedly, for this tends to be a gender-specific ceremony seldom enjoyed by women. The beauty of this meal lies partly in its simplicity—a knife blade and a knee to balance cans on suffice for a place setting—and partly in its comprehensive nutrition, combining as it does the four major food groups: fat, sodium, sugar, and dirt. It may be eaten in the country store where it is purchased, or on the front steps thereof, or off the tailgate of a truck somewhere beside a dirt road.

The following list is for the full complement, the High Store Lunch. Items may be omitted or recombined at will.

1 (8-ounce) can pork and beans

1 small can Vienna sausages (the real ones, with various pork scraps, not the effete low-fat chicken variety)

1 small tin potted meat or deviled ham

1 tin sardines packed in soybean oil and sprinkled liberally with Texas Pete or other hot stuff

1 pickled egg, preferably a pink one that has had beet juice added to the marinade

1 wedge yellow hoop cheese

1 large box saltines

1 pickled pig foot (known variously as "trotters" or "mudgrips")

1 can (size optional) mixed fruit packed in heavy syrup

1 cellophane-wrapped creme-filled oatmeal cookie or raisin cake

In these modern times, most of the cans will have easy-open ring tops. If not, they may be pried open with any heavy, pointed tool from the tool box in the back of the truck. To eat, remove knife from pocket and lick thoroughly to remove any residual fish scales or rabbit hairs; then use blade as an all-purpose implement to ladle food into mouth.

The South's Love Affair with Soft Drinks

Tom Hanchett

"What kind of coke you gonna have? Orange? Grape? Dr. Pepper?"

For a kid growing up in Troutville, Virginia, in the early 1960s, pure pleasure came out of the drink box in front of the Texaco station. On a hot summer evening, you'd plunk a pair of nickels into the slot, then plunge a hand down into that icy water to slide out a cold glass bottle.

Even though it was a blue box with the name of the Pepsi-Cola company ("Hits the Spot!") clearly emblazoned on the side, we called everything in it a coke. When I was ten we moved up to New York State, and in later years, whenever I thought back, I figured that "coke" was just a childish imprecision. Turns out that pretty much the whole South talked the same way when it came to soft drinks.

Researchers Matthew Campbell and Greg Plumb at East Central University in Oklahoma have gone to the trouble to map regional names for soft drinks. In the Northeast, from New England down to the Mason-Dixon line, people say "soda." In the Midwest and Great Plains, the preferred name switches to "pop." Out in California it reverts to "soda"—maybe a legacy of an influx of sun-seeking newcomers from cold New England in the early twentieth century. But look down to the lower right-hand quadrant of the U.S. map, and Campbell and Plumb show us the "coke" zone. From Texas to north Florida, upwards into western Virginia and Kentucky, most folks said "coke" for all soft drinks, just the way our family and our neighbors did in Troutville.

Having its own peculiar name for soft drinks is just one manifestation of the South's deep love affair with carbonated beverages. Most of today's leading brands sprang from Southern roots, including Coca-Cola, Pepsi, Mountain

Dew, and Dr. Pepper. Regional flavors continue to inspire fierce local loyalty, among them Cheerwine and Sundrop, Buffalo Rock and Blenheim, Ale-8-One and Dr. Enuf. Southerners consume almost sixty gallons of soft drinks per capita per year, much more than when I was a boy. As "snowbirds" flood into the Sunbelt the region may be becoming less distinctive, but the love affair shows no signs of ebbing, as immigrants from around the world add a bevy of new sugary beverages to the Southern drink box.

Any survey of Southern soft drinks has to start with Coca-Cola, the world's dominant brand. Concocted in 1886 by Dr. John Pemberton in his Atlanta drugstore, the pick-me-up tonic took its name from extract of coca leaves and caffeine-rich kola nuts. The real genius in the story, though, was the marketing man Asa Candler. Building America's first nationwide network of franchised bottlers, he made Coke a household name first in the South (hence the linguistic regionalism of my youth) and then throughout North America. In the 1920s his successor, Robert Woodruff, took Coca-Cola to the global market. Today that history is enshrined in the World of Coke, a museum and tourist attraction close to company headquarters in downtown Atlanta.

Smart as they were, Pemberton and Candler were just a small part of a wave of beverage entrepreneurs who tasted success in the 1890s and 1900s. The reason lay in two modest inventions. In 1892 a Maryland tinkerer named William Painter patented the cheap and reliable crimped metal "crown" bottlecap. And by the decade's end, machinery existed to mass-produce glass bottles. Both innovations were probably devised with beer-making in mind, but they opened the way for a new industry: carbonated nonalcoholic ("soft") drinks.

In 1885, a year before Pemberton, a Virginia druggist who had moved to Waco, Texas, swirled together a cocktail of flavorings to create Dr. Pepper. The drink won strong regional loyalty but without Asa Candler's marketing drive it remained a Southern brand well into the 1960s. I can recall cradling two precious six-packs of Dr. Pepper in the backseat of our Rambler American as we left Troutville, Virginia, for the foreign lands of upstate New York.

In 1898 a New Bern, North Carolina, pharmacist named Caleb Bradham mixed up a tonic of pepsin and kola nut extract that he initially called "Brad's Drink." He patented it in 1903 and began franchising bottling rights under the name "Pepsi-Cola." First to buy a franchise, in 1905, was Henry Fowler, in the fast-growing textile town of Charlotte, North Carolina. Fowler already bottled his own ginger ale and fruit drinks; Pepsi nicely rounded out the flavor menu.

Indeed by the middle of the first decade of the 1900s nearly every American town had at least one soft drink entrepreneur. Beginning in 1905, Columbus, Georgia, with fewer than twenty thousand people, supported bustling bottler (and former druggist) Claud A. Hatcher and his new drink Chero-Cola.

Hatcher added a line of fruit flavors in 1924, which he called Nehi, and in 1934 to avoid a lawsuit from Coca-Cola he reformulated his cola as Royal Crown; by 1940 Royal Crown and Nehi reached customers nationwide. Southerners, though, felt a special affinity for "RC" and eventually their nickname became the brand's official moniker.

While Nehi and RC live on as part of the Dr. Pepper/7-Up empire (now owned by Cadbury-Schweppes), literally hundreds of other small-town brands are remembered only by bottle collectors (an impressive social network with its own accomplished historians). My own small Southern collection includes Tom's, distributed by the route salesmen who brought Tom's snack foods to groceries and gas stations in South Carolina; Tom's self-effacing slogan "It's better" modestly avoided any claim to be "the best." I also have a bottle of Dixie Grape from Charlotte, touted as "The Hospitality Drink" by the demure, hoop-skirted Southern Belle on the bottle. There's nothing self-effacing or demure about my most recent purchase, from a junk store in Staunton, Virginia: the James E. Crass Bottling Company controlled the Coca-Cola franchise for the Richmond area and offered a line of fruit flavors and ginger ale as well, under the fearless brand name Crass.

A handful of regional brands hang on in the South, braving the homogenizing tendencies of corporate America:

Barq's root beer is officially recognized by the Mississippi legislature as the state soft drink. It is now nationally available through Coke bottlers, but it is still controlled by the Biloxi descendants of 1890s inventor Edward Barq.

Dr. Enuf, launched by Tri-City Beverage of Johnson City, Tennessee, in 1949, harks back to soft drinks' pharmacy roots. It boasts 240 percent of the minimum daily requirement of vitamin B1, 80 percent of daily B3, and 120 percent of potassium.

Buffalo Rock Ginger Ale, with a spicy ginger kick, can be found around Birmingham, Alabama, produced by the local Pepsi bottler, which also offers a regional grape flavor called Grapico.

For really spicy ginger ale, try Blenheim's, now owned by the promoter of South Carolina's famed tourist complex South of the Border, on Interstate 95. Water still comes from the Artesian Mineral Springs in the nearby village of Blenheim, as it has since the drink originated in the 1890s, and colored caps on the clear glass bottles still warn drinkers of the degree of hotness: red = #5 Hot; gold = #3 Not As Hot.

If spicy is not your thing, get some Ale-8-One ginger ale, available since 1926 only in Kentucky and a few counties of contiguous states. Say the name out loud and you'll get the pun—perhaps a reference to the fact that it is caffeine-free.

Several Southern regionals are anything but caffeine-free. Cheerwine, for example, hails from Salisbury, North Carolina, where the great-grandfather of its current CEO first made the drink in 1917. The cherry-flavored non-alcoholic beverage is now trying to leap from regional to national distribution. Double Cola comes out of Chattanooga, Tennessee, where an enterprising bottler debuted a twelve-ounce bottle in 1933, countering the six-ounce industry standard. It once went head-to-head with Coke and Pepsi nationally, but pulled back to serve just the South. Double Cola Bottling Company of Gastonia, North Carolina (now CHOICE Beverage), gave it a try in 1953 and it immediately caught on in the area's cotton mill communities. Gastonia ranked as America's top textile town throughout much of the twentieth century, the buckle on a textile and furniture manufacturing belt that extended through the piedmont Carolinas and into eastern Tennessee, western Virginia, and northern Georgia. The mills were notorious for long hours and hot, humid working conditions, and millhands already slurped gallons of cola drinks in order to keep working through the day. In fact they had their own name for soda pop, more common than "coke" in some places: a "dope" was millhand slang for a soft drink, perhaps linked to Coca-Cola's early alleged use of a cocaine derivative, but more likely referring to the stimulant effect of caffeine. Many mills had a "dope wagon" that rolled through the work floor each shift selling snacks and soft drinks.

Caffeine is also a key ingredient in Sundrop, a Southern regional concoction that inaugurated an entire soft drink sales category. St. Louis flavor chemist C. P. Lazier came up with the citrus flavor, tinged with orange and jacked up generously on caffeine. In that environment, Sundrop ("The Golden Cola— Refreshing as a cup of coffee") became a swift seller and other Southeastern bottlers rushed to get on board. Up in Chattanooga, for instance, Double Cola added citrus Ski in 1956. In nearby Johnson City, local Tri-City Beverage reformulated a marginal brand called Mountain Dew (hillbilly slang for moonshine). It had debuted in 1948 as a lackluster lemon-lime drink. Reborn about 1960 as today's familiar caffeinated citrus beverage, Mountain Dew positively flew off storekeepers' shelves. In short order Cheerwine introduced Cool Moon, a Highlands, North Carolina, maker offered White Light·nin', and Atlanta's Monarch company rolled out Kickapoo Joy Juice featuring hillbilly characters from the comic strip *Li'l Abner*.

Corporate giant Pepsi took notice of all the fuss stirred up by Sundrop and its followers. On September 2, 1964, Pepsi purchased the Mountain Dew formula and trademark, and within months introduced the flavor to consumers coast to coast. Today Mountain Dew ranks just behind Coke, Pepsi, and Diet Coke on the list of America's most popular soft drink brands nationwide.

Enough. I'll not give recipes for Coca-Cola cake, a Dixie tradition at least since the sugar-rationing era of World War II, nor will I mention the immortal 1951 song "RC Cola and Moon Pie," by hillbilly stars Lonzo and Oscar. I won't tell you how Royal Crown kicked off the national low-calorie craze in 1958 with its Diet Rite brand. And we won't get into the controversy over the substitution of high-fructose corn syrup for sugar in soda pop since the 1970s (except to note that the top health expert warning of the dangers of HFCS and obesity is a North Carolinian, Dr. Barry Popkin, and that a high-profile holdout against the trend is a bottler in Dublin, Texas, who still resolutely offers only sugar-formula Dr. Pepper).

Instead, let's talk about the impact of newcomers on the Southern drink scene. Americans today are moving more and more freely between regions. Northerners have streamed into the Southeast in large numbers for the first time. The South is no longer nearly so poor and isolated as when I was a boy. What is the impact of all that on Southern distinctiveness?

Statistics from the trade journal *Beverage World* indicate that back in the 1970s, the South unquestionably was distinct in soft drink consumption. Southerners led the nation in thirst for carbonated beverages. The first published gallons-per-capita data, for 1977, showed the South (Alabama, Arkansas, Florida, Georgia, Louisiana, Mississippi, North and South Carolina, Tennessee, and Virginia) drinking 38.3 gallons annually—far ahead of any other region. Climate did not seem to be the deciding variable, interestingly. The desert-hot states of Arizona, New Mexico, Oklahoma, and Utah each drank less than the national average of 32.9 gallons, almost identical to amounts in cold Maine, New Hampshire, and Massachusetts. For whatever reason, the South was the epicenter of soft drink culture.

Today the South is still a strong consumer but regional differences are blurring. All Americans are buying more soda pop, 51.5 gallons each in 2005, compared with 32.9 in 1977. In that time the South's figures have grown impressively, but its rate of growth has dipped below that of several other regions. Today, surprisingly, the "West Central" states (just west of the Mississippi River from Missouri up to the Dakotas) actually consume more pop per person than the South. Folks down in Dixie remain pretty thirsty, though, now ranking second in the nation in gallons gulped.

And there is evidence that some of the South's newest arrivals are renewing the region's liquid love affair. During the 1990s and 2000s, the once isolated Southeast began attracting foreign immigrants in large numbers. A 2004 Brookings Institution study identified Atlanta, Raleigh, Greensboro, and Charlotte as the nation's four fastest growing Hispanic cities—and Latin Americans are only the most visible members of a wave arriving from around the globe. As a result, international soft drinks are becoming a familiar part of the Southern scene, if you know where to look.

Many immigrants come from Mexico, the only place on the face of the earth where per-capita consumption of soft drinks has traditionally exceeded that of the American South. Check out the hundreds of corner tiendas popping up not only in Southern cities but also in the smallest country towns. You're sure to see Jarritos fruit drinks, Mexico's biggest brand, in half a dozen flavors from toronja (grapefruit) to tamarindo (tamarind). The well-stocked tienda may also have rival Barrilitos, or the apple soda Sidral Mundet, or an orange drink called Boing! or the wonderful nonalcoholic sangria by Senorial—my personal favorite. There'll probably also be heavy glass bottles of Coca-Cola and Pepsi imported from Mexico. Why bring in foreign Coke and Pepsi? Well, it is said that bottlers south of the border still use sugar, rather than high-fructose corn syrup, and to Latino customers those Mexican sodas taste like home.

It is not just Mexican immigrants who are remaking the South. My daughter and I enjoy exploring the beverage coolers of multinational Central Avenue just around the corner from us in Charlotte. We sample glass bottles of Country Club sodas at the Dominican restaurant, LaCascada pineapple pop at the Salvadoran deli, and beerlike Malta India and Thums-Up cola at the Indian grocery. We join Middle Eastern and North African customers crowding the store that sells Fayrouz lemonade from Egypt and the English soft drink Vimto, a favorite in former outposts of British colonial rule. At the Bosnian grocery we taste Cockta sodas in cola or orange. The oddest drinks show up at the two Asian groceries. There are unfamiliar flavors such as coconut and pink guava, and other beverages with jelly globules in them. Our current passion is a Vietnamese pop made from dragonfruit, a beautiful red and green fruit with tiny black seeds—which float suspended in the soft drink.

Today young Southerners no longer refer to all carbonated beverages as "coke." That's yet another indication of the transformations this region is going through. The South my daughter is experiencing is very different from the one I knew in Troutville. We've gained so much in economic growth and cultural connectivity, but are we losing the regionalisms that made the South a beloved place? Will this newest New South create a distinctive blend of old and new traditions that my daughter's children will consider "Southern"?

Let's reach into the soft drink cooler, pour us something cold, and ponder that question.

The Moon Pie
A Southern Journey

William Ferris

When I began to explore the Moon Pie, I little imagined the journey that lay ahead. Sugar plums haunted me as I remembered how I made brandy with wild plums as a child. I covered each layer of plums with a layer of sugar, then put the sealed jar on a shelf. Several months later the potent concoction was ready for consumption. There were names for loved ones like "Sugar," "Sugar Plum," "Sugar Pie," and "Sugar Britches." There were cubes of Domino sugar that I fed my horse to gentle him. There were dreaded trips to the dentist to fill cavities caused by eating too much sugar. And there was the thought that life without sugar was the lowest life imaginable, like Scarlett reduced to eating a turnip.

To understand the Moon Pie, we should consider the words *moon* and *pie* that form its name. The moon is a satellite of earth long associated with love and dreams, and the pie is a pastry with a sweet filling. Each word has a long, rich history in the English language, and their convergence in the Moon Pie was clearly a historic moment for the food world.

If we Google Moon Pies, 3,060,000 references appear on subjects that range from art and literature to festivals, recipes, and astrology. Before entering the turbulent waters of the Internet, I opened my trusted resource for all things Southern, the *Encyclopedia of Southern Culture*, and read its "Moon Pies" entry, written by Tom Rankin. Tom explains that the Chattanooga Bakery in Chattanooga, Tennessee, marketed the Moon Pie as "the original marshmallow sandwich." The delicacy was invented in 1919 and consists, according to the *Encyclopedia*, of "one quarter inch of marshmallow sandwiched between two cookies about four inches in diameter." The sandwich is then coated with chocolate, banana, coconut, or vanilla frosting.

Earl Mitchell Jr. claims that his father, Earl Mitchell Sr., invented the Moon Pie. Mr. Mitchell Sr. worked for the Chattanooga Bakery, and while visiting a company store in Kentucky, he asked coal miners what kind of cookie they would like in their lunch pails. They said they preferred a big one. When Mr. Mitchell asked what size the cookie should be, the miners pointed to the moon. His son recalls: "Moon Pie was a big seller especially in the coal fields where they didn't make much money. And when they bought something, they wanted to get the best bargain. And there they were getting a great big pie for a nickel. I'm sorry Dad didn't patent that thing. I'd have a Cadillac on each foot." (These and many more details about the history of the Moon Pie are included in a film entitled *How Chattanooga Mooned America: An Affectionate Look at the History of the Moon Pie* by Emily Ley-Sheley.)

No history of the Moon Pie is complete without mention of its soul mate, Royal Crown Cola, which was invented in 1895 by a young pharmacist named Claud Hatcher in the basement of his family's wholesale grocery business in Columbus, Georgia. For more than a century the tastes of RC Colas—which Southerners pronounce "arah see" Cola—and Moon Pies have been intimately linked in the Southern palate. Like a good Beaujolais and steak frites, RC Cola and the Moon Pie should be consumed together to achieve the full impact of regional memory exploding on the tongue.

Moon Pie and RC Cola are intimately linked with the country store. Together, they are among the most powerful icons in Southern culture. Along with the courthouse on the square and the columned Georgian mansion, they are mythic symbols of the region. Within the country store Southerners first discovered the Moon Pie and its liquid companion, RC Cola.

Thomas Clark argues that the country store was the heart of every Southern community. The store "was far more symbolic of the Southern way of rural life than were other institutions. Even the church and school were often administered as much from the store as from their own buildings. The storekeeper was all things to his community. He served as school trustee, deacon or steward, railway agent, fertilizer salesman, social adviser, character reference, politician, lodge master, and general community 'obliger.' His store was the hub of the local universe."

The country store offered a sanctuary where black and white customers could share stories and shop in a common space. Within the sanctuary of the store, they discovered "store-bought," commercially distributed foods. These products included plug tobacco—Clark lists the colorful brand names: Johnny Reb, Southern Rose, Georgia Buck, Bull Tongue, Stud Horse, Captain Cash, Panther, Iron Clad, Bull Head, Blood Hound, Good and Tough, Bull Durham, and the celebrated Brown Mule. Familiar names for snuff included Tube Rose and Garrett. Images of banjos, opossums, and smiling black men decorated flour sacks to promote brands like Mama's Pride, Spread Eagle, White Lily, and Sunny Side.

Grace Elizabeth Hale notes that "country stores were the entry points into the region for the new northern ways of selling, the stage upon which many Southerners first encountered the new branded items with their colorful packaging, collectible trade cards, and eye-catching outdoor signs."

Southern writers were drawn to the country store as a setting for their stories. Elizabeth Spencer recalls how she and Eudora Welty stopped at a country store during a drive through the Mississippi Delta. As they entered the store, Eudora saw a sign on the store porch that read "No Loitering or Soliciting" and said to Elizabeth, "I think I'll loiter. Why don't you solicit?" Thomas Hines suggests that Faulkner viewed the country store as the place where rural people found a window on the larger world. In "Barn Burning" Faulkner describes the smell inside the store: "The store in which the Justice of the Peace's court was sitting smelled of cheese. The boy, crouched on his nail keg at the back of the crowded room, knew he smelled cheese, and more: from where he sat he could see the ranked shelves close-packed with the solid, squat, dynamic shapes of tin cans whose labels his stomach read." Even more evocative than smells were tastes associated with the country store. In *Light in August* Lena Grove orders a box of crackers and sardines. She eats them "slowly, steadily, sucking the rich sardine oil from her fingers with slow and complete relish."

John Egerton grew up eating Moon Pies in Kentucky and vividly remembers the store where he bought them: "I used to go in this little grocery store in Cadiz, Kentucky, where I grew up. It was called Albert Wallace's. Mr. Wallace was sort of a no-nonsense guy. He kept close watch on things. You could go in there and get a wedge of cheese, and crackers and bologna. He had fly paper hanging from little strings on the ceiling and an old oak floor. He had a drink box that you opened the top and slid a bottle down by its neck to the end and pulled it up. Double Colas and RCs and Dr. Pepper, as well as Coke."

Lee Smith associates Moon Pies with trips her family took in their car when she was a child: "We always took them on car trips because they were all wrapped up in their little wrappers. At a certain point, when everybody in the car would start getting really loud, we would get the Moon Pies."

The Moon Pie anchors the memories of Southerners in their history and culture. Today, like kudzu, the taste and image of the Moon Pie reach far beyond the region. Moon Pies are sold throughout the nation, as well as in overseas markets. Recent flavors include banana, chocolate, lemon, orange, strawberry, vanilla, and pecan.

Boxes of forty-eight pies are sold on the Internet for $29.56. Moon Pie websites list recipes that challenge the imagination. To make Moon Pie brownies, place chopped Moon Pies on the bottom of a dish, prepare and pour brownie mix on the top of the Moon Pies, and bake. There are other recipes for strawberry Moon Pie shortcake, raspberry Moon Pie, banana split Moon Pie, hot fudge Moon Pie, Southern Moon Pie, and deep-fried Moon Pie.

There are also Moon Pie festivals. Mobile, Alabama, claims that its Mardi Gras celebration, which began in 1703, is the oldest in the South. Each year the celebration begins with chants of "Moon Pie! Moon Pie!" Along with doubloons, candies, and beads, Moon Pies are thrown to excited crowds. Each year the University of Tennessee at Chattanooga hosts its Moon Pie Classic and its RC Cola quiz bowls, both of which draw teams from schools such as Carlton College, Indiana University, the University of Iowa, and Georgia Tech. And citizens in nearby Bell Buckle, Tennessee, host an annual RC and Moon Pie Festival. The festival features live entertainment, crafts, a 10k run, food, and the cutting of the world's largest Moon Pie.

Edward Baker, director of the North Carolina Institute for Public Health, at the University of North Carolina, grew up in Chattanooga and vividly remembers hearing the Moon Pie jingle each day on his local radio station. Baker recalled these lyrics, which he sang for me:

Moon Pies are delicious,
Tasty to eat.
They're only a nibble.
They cannot be beat.

Tony Diterlizzi's wonderful children's book *Jimmy Zangwow's Out of This World Moon Pie Adventure* takes the reader on an imaginary space trip. Jimmy Zangwow first visits the sleepy Moon, which gives him one thousand Moon Pies—a year's supply. Then he gathers milk from the Milky Way. Zangwow visits Mars and gives his milk and Moon Pies to the Martians. He finally returns home in time for dinner and has a Moon Pie with milk for dessert.

Cartoonist Sam C. Rawls and writer Ron Dickson have published *The Great American Moon Pie Handbook*. "Scrawls" grew up in Clarksdale, Mississippi, and is editorial cartoonist for the *Atlanta Journal-Constitution*. Dickson grew up in Shelby, North Carolina, works for Burroughs Corporation in Charlotte, and spends his leisure time on his sailboat, which proudly flies the official Moon Pie Flag.

Doug Marlette effectively used Moon Pies in his cartoon strip *Kudzu*. In one scene, inspired by fellow cartoonist R. Crumb, Marlette drew Moon Pies as they fell from the sky. Marlette's second novel also featured Moon Pies. He said of it: "My new novel is set in the civil rights period in Mississippi, and I have one of the main characters, who is down from Detroit, become addicted to Moon Pies during his stay. The Moon Pie sounds like a cliché, but actually

I do like the pies. I always feel a tug when I go through the Harris Teeter supermarket. I feel I really shouldn't be eating them. I don't like the health food version. I want the straight up pie. I like the ones with the Yellow Dye No. 2, the nanna flavor. It's outrageous, but there's something about the R.C. Cola and the Moon Pie, the Dr. Pepper and the peanuts. That is what we lived, and it was no big deal. It was just like the heat and the kudzu, just there."

The association of Moon Pies with the moon and the night sky assumes special importance in "Southern astrology." Southerners who are skeptical of traditional astrology can take comfort in a new set of "Southern signs" that include Okra, Chitlin, Boll Weevil, Moon Pie, Possum, Crawfish, Collards, Catfish, Grits, Boiled Peanuts, Butter Bean, and Armadillo. Those born between December 22 and January 20 fall under the sign of Okra and should take note: "Although you appear crude, you are actually very slick on the inside. Okras have tremendous influence. An older Okra can look back over his life and see the seeds of his influence everywhere. Stay away from Moon Pies." Those born between March 21 and April 20 are under the sign of Moon Pie: "You're the type that spends a lot of time on the front porch. It's a cinch to recognize the physical appearance of Moon Pies. Big and round are the key words here. You should marry anybody you can get remotely interested in the idea. It's not going to be easy. This might be the year to think about aerobics. Or maybe not."

An especially memorable musical tribute to the Moon Pie is Big Bill Lister's 1951 recording of Vic McAlpin's "R.C. Cola and Moon Pie." Born Weldon Lister, January 5, 1923, in Kennedy, Texas, an hour south of San Antonio, Lister is six feet seven inches tall and bills himself as "the world's tallest singing cowboy." He played rhythm guitar in the Hank Williams band and is best known for his recording of "There's a Tear in My Beer." The lyrics of "R.C. Cola and Moon Pie" have the ring of a Hank Williams piece:

> I may be just a country boy
> But Brother I get my thrill
> With an R.C. Cola and a Moon Pie
> Playing "Mabel on the Hill."

The Moon Pie has inspired a long list of musicians. Peter McKee, the only member of the Southern Foodways Alliance from the state of Washington, ended his presentation to the SFA's 2004 annual meeting by playing his banjo and singing his composition "Moon Pie." His musical group has been described as "Seattle's Slowest Rising Folk Group," and "Moon Pie" is a sequel to their 1994 song, "Do Certain Foods Really Need an FDA Nutritional Label?" which features lyrics like:

> Moon Pies don't need labels
> Despite the FDA
> 'Cause when you scarf a Moon Pie
> All reason fades away

Other songs inspired by Moon Pies include Andrew McKnight's "A Piece of Moon Pie," David Beebe's "Royal Crown and a Moon Pie," Tom Petty's "Moon Pie," and Kate Campbell's "Moon Pie Dreams." Caroline Henning sings,

> In the land of crazies, gentlemen and ladies
> I was born/I was born
> Long gone the fish fry
> Long gone the Moon Pie
> Long gone. Long gone.

Edwin Hubbard's *Moon Pie* appears on the Memphis Exotica Label. Hubbard has played with Isaac Hayes, Booker T, Steve Cropper, Duck Dunn, Chips Moman, Don Nix, Leon Russell, and Bill Black. A flautist, Hubbard describes his *Moon Pie* album as "a Southern treat, sweet and chewy and undeniably irresistible. It combines peppy flute music with down-home banjo pickin' backed with an assortment of instruments to create a sound called 'Afrobilly.'"

I conclude my Moon Pie journey with the voice of Chapel Hill's first lady of Southern cuisine, Mildred "Mama Dip" Council, as she reflects on the country store and the Moon Pie. Mama Dip bought her first Moon Pie at the country store in Bynum, North Carolina.

> The country store is important. We talk about it all the time, the older generation like me. Today you go to the freezer and take things out. But in the country store nothing was boxed up. The meat was hung in the loft of the store, the ham, and the shoulder and the strick o'lean.
>
> It smelled good because even the candy was laying out. The peppermint sticks weren't wrapped up. The hohound and the Mounds was three times as big as they are today. I remember we swapped eggs in the country for our goodies.
>
> Let me tell you about the country store. Everybody knowed everybody. We would ride to town on a wagon. People would sit

outside, and they could tell time by that shadow. Poppa could too. When dinner time came, he would say "Well the bell's gonner ring in a little bit." And that shadow would be real small, you know. Old people could tell the time of day with the shadow. People today don't know about it any more.

I love a Moon Pie. I'd eat one now if I had it.

Mountain Dogs

Fred Sauceman

Some are tonged out of crockpots. Some steam in glass-fronted metal boxes. One is scored, another splayed. Several are dunked deeply in oil. Others are charred brittle black on aging grills.

They're thrust out drive-through windows, hefted over deli counters, and plated on elbow-rutted bars.

In early anticipation of spring and the beginning of baseball season, we hit the hot dog trail in the winter of 2006 and discovered, in the mountain South, an amazing variety of interpretations and angles on wieners, buns, condiments, and cooking styles. And we met some folks who offered up solid frankfurter philosophy along the way.

The big-city dogs of Chicago, New York, and Philadelphia get most of the media attention, but the side streets and country backroads of southern Appalachia yield their own hot dog cuisine, a continuum from mustard-chili-onion loyalists to roasted red pepper revolutionaries.

We found hot dogs so neatly packed you can eat them while driving and others so chili-laden they collapsed into a beefy heap on contact.

We met mayonnaise adherents, chili minimalists, and red dog devotees. Our palette ranged from Styrofoam to aluminum foil to tissue to china.

We found irony along the way. Hot dogs are quickly made and quickly consumed, but many of the places where they're served in east Tennessee, southwest Virginia, and western North Carolina encourage leisurely loafing.

We found no hot dog sellers the least bit concerned about calories and cholesterol, and all we talked to spoke of quality, some going through dozens of dogs before deciding on the one that would be the centerpiece of their business, be it gasoline station or sit-down diner.

At Wallace's News in downtown Kingsport, Tennessee, selling hot dogs is almost a secretive enterprise. There's no menu and no sign saying they're available, but they pair perfectly with Marty Mullins's frozen Pepsis.

At the twenty locations of Pal's Sudden Service throughout northeast Tennessee and southwest Virginia, hot dog architecture is visible from a high-flying jet. The compact teal buildings are topped with twenty-two-foot fiberglass hot dogs made by a boat manufacturer. In 2001, Pal's became the first restaurant company ever to win the Malcolm Baldridge National Quality Award, and the regional restaurant chain celebrated half a century in business in 2006. Founder Frederick "Pal" Barger and CEO Thom Crosby estimate that during those fifty years, the nationally heralded corporation has sold 62.8 million hot dogs.

The Corner Dog House in Bristol, Virginia, has been using the same beanless chili recipe since 1963, spooned over stark red hot dogs. It's a walkup business only, in a quiet city neighborhood, with no drive-through.

Elizabethton, Tennessee's Sycamore Drive-In, a yellow-trimmed, white cinder block hut with three red, two-seated tables and one for four, has been an after-movie stopover for generations of Carter Countians. The Bonnie Kate Theater, just down Sycamore Street, is eighty years old this year. At the Sycamore, old bottles of Double Line, Dr. Enuf, Frostie, and Red Rock Cola, behind a trapezoidal encasement of glass, commemorate the region's love affair with soft drinks. Slightly salty, juicy hot dogs are dressed with chunks of sweet onion. Conversation ranges from the solemnity of the obituary page in the *Elizabethton Star* to diners' consensus that the late Don Knotts never was too funny as Ralph Furley on *Three's Company*.

Elizabethton's City Market features hot dogs fashioned by Johnson & Wales University culinary graduate Jennifer Hughes, and a duo of them goes for way under $2. The chili's thick and sharp, the onion's in shards, the dog's light pink, the bun's bready, and the mustard's fluorescent, in the style of a backyard picnic.

In Scott County, Virginia, I found a mayonnaise microclimate. Order a hot dog at Teddy's in Nickelsville, don't specify condiments, and it'll come with mayonnaise. Says owner Trish Kilgore, "I prefer mustard, but most people eat mayonnaise on their hot dogs around here."

Over in the county seat, at Gate City's Broadwater Drugs, you can eat a healing hot dog while waiting on a prescription. The seats still swivel at the old-time lunch counter, overseen by the steely but harmless leer of cook Jackie Tipton.

Down the hill a piece, the Campus Drive-In dresses hot dogs with antique chili, a blend of ground beef and spices simmered for hours. It's a holdover from founder Darrel Dougherty's Taylor Drive-In Theater days. Diners order it as a hot dog topping or in a bowl by itself. Gate City High School Blue Devil linemen mix it into their soup beans.

The chili recipe from Sammons Hot Dogs in Elizabethton, Tennessee, is buried in a vault at the Carter County Bank. It specifies double-ground beef, tomato sauce, a blend of spices, and, says owner Richard Sammons, "one unique ingredient you'd never find in another chili recipe."

Richard's father, Doran Sammons, knocked a hole in the wall at Cole and Sammons Market in 1950 and started selling hot dogs, 180,000 of them his first year alone. The business survives, having evolved into two red-and-yellow drive-around stands guarding opposite ends of Elizabethton. It takes about ten seconds to assemble a Sammons dog, a slightly smoky beef and pork blend. Condiments are packed well inside the bun to prevent dripping on customers' laps as they pull out onto Elk Avenue or Highway 19E.

Clara Robinson, owner of Mary's Hot Tamales in Knoxville, Tennessee, makes the chunkiest chili we found, a highly flavorful mélange of ground beef hunks, tomatoes, onions, and green peppers, doubling as a hot dog topping or the capstone touch to a "full house," a ladling of chili over handmade Mississippi Delta–style hot tamales.

It's like eating two sandwiches simultaneously at the Trail Blazer Market near Sulphur Springs, Tennessee. The chili sports dominant tones of Sloppy Joe. Half-moons of onion curls are arranged in chainlike interlock down the dog.

Malcolm's Meat Service in Bristol, Virginia, manufactures hot dog chili for the Blue Circle, on the Tennessee side of the city. Known for small, square hamburgers, the first Blue Circle opened in Knoxville in 1931, and Mike and June Marshall's place on Edgemont Avenue is the only one left.

Talk about location. Connie Swadley's Ballpark Corner Market and Deli sits right next door to Malcolm's, its supplier of wieners and chili, convenient when hot dog–crazed baseballers mob the place in the summertime. It's not uncommon for Connie to sell over four thousand hot dogs in a week that time of year. Across Randolph Street from the market are the Central Little League Field, the Virginia High School football stadium, and the two-thousand-seat DeVault Memorial Stadium, home to the Appalachian League's Bristol White Sox.

One of east Tennessee's most picturesque hot dog picnicking spots, in the Watauga community, surrounds Shirley Casey's T & S Country Kitchen. The building's about the size of a lawnmower shed. Shirley invites you to take a seat at one of the concrete picnic tables beside Brush Creek, near the spot where the first independent government in America was formed and next door to Tennessee's oldest business, St. John Milling Company, where Ron Dawson mills sweet feed for horses. Shirley's onions are bold, and she envelopes hot dogs with squares of yellow cheese.

T. C.'s Village Market in Blountville, Tennessee, is positioned to stuff travelers flying out of Tri-Cities Airport and students on their way to class at Northeast State Community College, both located right across Highway 75 from the store. Fishermen and -women bound for the banks of Boone Lake or the Holston River pack their coolers with T. C.'s hot dogs, assembled by an interior designer, Morgan Collins, daughter of owners Sam and Linda. Morgan symmetrically spaces three slices of pickled jalapeño peppers over the hot nacho cheese on the Super Dog. Her mother shreds homemade coleslaw every morning. Look for hot dogs up front and, for the tackle box, baby night crawlers in back, raised by the Mel-Bro Hatchery in Blountville.

The Fannon family abandoned their former building near the projects in Johnson City for a traveler's stretch stop off Interstate 26 in Unicoi County, Tennessee. Their steamed hot dogs fuel PTSA meetings, Methodist church suppers, and Unicoi Elementary schoolers. Etiquette does allow eating inside at the lottery table at the Unicoi Market and Deli, if you can squeeze in among the scratchers.

At the bottom of an Interstate 240 ramp in Asheville, North Carolina, John Vail ripped out a few extra gas pumps at his Exxon station and opened the 51 Grill on Merrimon Avenue. Staff there say the busiest time at this all-night eatery is between midnight and 4 a.m., after the city's bars let out. The alcohol-free 51 Grill serves Nathan's Famous Hot Dogs, like the ones sold at New York's Coney Island since 1916. The cumin-scented chili echoes Cincinnati. "It's not chili without cumin," says Stacey Harris, who makes it. At the 51 Grill, hot dogs are scooted over for side dishes, and not just fries. Applesauce, baked beans, and homemade macaroni and cheese, made from small pasta shells, are among the choices. The restaurant often boasts sanitation scores of 100.

"Burn it," diners demand at the Hill Top Drive-In on Highway 421 outside Boone, North Carolina. Owner Karen Wood's father, Harold Coffey, opened the business in 1958. Karen says of the crimson foot-long dogs, "People want them black. The more they blacken on the grill, the better they taste."

Hill Top hot dogs are split completely in two before they're grilled. The same procedure's followed at Boone Drug, in operation since 1919 downtown. There may be two reasons for the bifurcated wiener. More surface area is exposed to the grill, and if the condiments cause the frank to slide around on the bun, you're more likely to get a bite of meat every time since it's in two planks.

Boone Drug doesn't take itself too seriously. The menu reads, "In the early days we sold leeches for medicinal reasons. Now we have a group of them that gather here each morning and call themselves the Coffee Club." When a member of that club dies, the name is etched into a metal plate and affixed to the counter. Fountain manager Marilyn Farthing has worked at Boone

Drug almost twenty years. She says the hot dog chili's pretty basic, with lean ground beef, ketchup, and chili powder the ingredients you'd expect. The unexpected, moisturizing addition is tomato soup.

Bonnie Roop and Julie Arnold handcraft the coleslaw that tops dogs at Pierce's Grocery and Gas, a salvage store in Elizabethton, Tennessee. It's more carroty than other slaws, and half-and-half containers from the front counter account for the creaminess. Vinegar and a goodly dose of black pepper add finish.

The Shamrock in downtown Johnson City, Tennessee, has been selling pipe tobacco and hot dogs since the Great Depression. Across town, at the Red Pig Bar-B-Q and Deli, the cheese-blanketed all-beef-no-pork Hawg Dog comes with a glad handshake from the owner, Tom Carr, and a swig of sweet tea over crushed ice.

Keith Marsh, owner of the Dairy Cup in Mount Carmel, Tennessee, has been known to wrap his popular foot-long hot dogs in aluminum foil, pack them in dry ice, and ship them as far away as Maryland.

The Main Street Dog at Main Street Café and Catering in Jonesborough, Tennessee, is a bun-buster at a quarter pound. It's scored and grilled and served on a crispy grilled bun, with sweet relish or sauerkraut as toppings.

At Kingsport's strictly drive-through Purple Cow, a statuesque, surreal hot dog stands vertically out front, bunned and blanketed in the American flag, chained to a purple pole, sporting tennis shoes, and squirting himself with ketchup in preparation for his ultimate demise. The Cow's He-Man Garbage Dog comes deluged in mustard, chili, onions, nacho cheese, and jalapeños. It's served in a Styrofoam boat inside a tall brown bag, ideally flattened for use as a lap covering to protect the clothing from overflow.

At the Dawg House in Weber City, Virginia, piquant, spicy condiments enrobe the Fiesta Dog, described by my wife, Jill, as "a taco salad on a hot dog."

Skeeter's may be a blue-collar hot dog stand in Wytheville, Virginia, but owner Rick Patton and his staff tout the eighty-six-year-old restaurant's aristocratic lineage. First Lady Edith Bolling Wilson, second wife of President Woodrow Wilson, was born upstairs in 1872. Wytheville residents proudly call her the "Secret President," since she took over many routine duties and details of government when a stroke left her husband partially paralyzed in 1919. Rick says Skeeter's has sold over 8 million hot dogs, many of them dripping with a mild cheese sauce.

Back in Tennessee, a deep-fried hot dog corridor exists on Johnson City's Market Street. Neighborhood beer bars the Cottage and Terry's Apex dunk their dogs in hot oil for a brittle bite on the outside and a juicy interior.

Tom and Sharon Keller at T. K.'s Big Dogs Too! in Kingsport dress theirs Chicago-style, convincing mustard-chili-onion fans that tomatoes, cucumbers, sport peppers, dill pickles, and celery salt do indeed have a place between the buns.

And someone had to do it eventually. The menu at Cats and Dawgs in Asheville, North Carolina, balances farm-raised catfish filets with Vienna beef hot dogs. Not only are roasted red peppers among the hot dog toppings, when I asked for onions the cook responded, "Would you like white, yellow, or red, and would you like them sautéed?"

GB's Grill in downtown Corbin, Kentucky, sells its "world famous Dixie Chili" for $48 a gallon. In business since 1939, the red-hued diner is an eastern Kentucky sports museum. The walls chronicle the history of Corbin High School athletics, paying homage to luminaries like Bill "Big Eye" Hughes, who played football there in the late 1940s and early '50s. From a Kentucky Heroes poster near the cash register, the eyes of the late University of Kentucky basketball coach Adolph Rupp scan the room in search of double dribbles. On the opposite wall is the Redhound, Corbin High School's longtime mascot, a bipedal canine drawn by art teacher Mildred Gant in 1961.

The hot dogs we sampled were all different, but we found common ground among the people who prepare them: devotion to daily labor. Making a living by selling a food product often priced under a dollar and rarely over three dictates unending hours on the feet. Most of the businesses we visited have been around a long time. They've withstood cyclical fads and food vagaries, wild diets and economic downturns. Their owners and staff have made a respectable living for themselves and their families while creating friendly havens for their customers, who gather gratefully around the humble hot dog.

Scattered, Smothered, Covered, and Chunked
Fifty Years of the Waffle House

Candice Dyer

You, with the shaggy hair and the battered guitar case slung over your shoulder—you owe this lady something.

At 3 a.m., this Waffle House waitress (Flossie, Christelle, or some other salt-of-the-earth name) has fetched steaming heaps of starch to soak up the alcohol you just drank and replenish the carbs you burned in that sweaty encore. While pouring the coffee you need for the long drive ahead or the hoped-for assignation with that groupie, she has listened patiently to the catty, post-gig debriefing, when you complained about the bass player who, in turn, blamed the drummer, and you all groused about the chintzy club owner and the philistines in this small-town, small-time crowd who do not appreciate your musical genius.

She has winked, called you "hon," and buttered you up, in so many ways, after an exhausting show. The word *companion* derives from the Old French words for "with bread": someone with whom you share warmth and bread.

Talk about comfort food.

"You've been drinking and dancing and hoping for romancing but now you are in the all-night greasy spoon, clinging to the light, not wanting to go to the lonely house," scats Bert Neill, an Atlanta harmonica player. "If the waitress smiles and the guy at the other end of the counter is telling a rude joke, then for a moment you are in the kitchen of the world."

For musicians and others, these waffles provide a communion of sorts, the grease from the grill an anointing oil that lubes the gears of Southern nightlife. Waffle House is, by its very nature, a syrupy place, all bright yellow and full of cheery, unabashed sentiment. Who else cares enough to fire up the griddle at this unseemly hour? Where else could you swap one-liners with a waitress named "Sunshine"?

"We call her that because she's always in a bad mood and acts mean as a warthog," says Nathan Deen, a former cook describing an "iconic Waffle House waitress famous throughout a tri-county area" in coastal Georgia. Sunshine might act tough as cast iron, but a tender heart beats beneath that brown apron, he says.

"She doesn't want anybody to know how nice she really is. If you ask for a stupid, picky order like, 'half sweet tea, half unsweet,' she'll mutter under her breath, 'Choke, you bastard!' But she'll do anything for you—babysit your kids, take you in if you're homeless, take you in if your boyfriend's beating you."

Thus angels' bread is made the bread of man, philosophized St. Thomas Aquinas, and that sentiment is echoed by another theologian, the Rev. Billy C. Wirtz, the boogie-woogie musical satirist who has produced albums such as "Back-Slider's Tractor Pull."

"There's usually a waitress who has been there for at least fifteen years and seen it all," he says. "I knew a very seasoned lady who still wore hot-pants and drove a Camaro when she was in her sixties. When the bar rush came—the bands, the gay bar, the biker bar, the yuppie brats, the preacher who wants to save you, the whole shooting match at the same time—she could keep 'em all under control with her tough-but-kind personality."

So the Waffle House waitress surely functions as a high priestess in these nocturnal rites.

"We had a good-luck ritual after a really good gig, where we'd go to a certain Waffle House, and, if we considered the show worthy of the greats, we'd walk around the tree outside, reciting the set list," says Athens musician Adam Klein. "Then we'd go in and eat and talk with our favorite waitress, whose name was 'Dopey,' for some reason."

Dopey and Sunshine know their lines, and you, the road-weary performer, know yours. "Scattered, smothered, and covered, baby," with no cussing, in accordance with the chivalric code posted on the wall.

"There is definitely a symbiotic relationship between Waffle House and musicians, a whole culture and lifestyle unto itself," says Wirtz, who incorporates the restaurant's iconography into several pieces of his act. "Without the netherworld of Waffle House and the little hot-sheet, no-tell motels run by the Patels next door, rock 'n' rollers simply couldn't exist."

That argument holds a certain deductive logic, considering that rock 'n' roll and most other forms of American music originated in the South, as did Waffle House, which recently celebrated its fiftieth anniversary.

Joe Rogers Sr., a longtime grill cook, and Tom Forkner, a real estate "bidnessman," started with a modest, fourteen-stool diner in the Avondale Estates community of Atlanta. It had a simple mission: to "Take Care of the Poor Old Cash Customer" with cheap food and neighborly conversation.

Rogers drew inspiration from the most satisfying meal he ever ate: turnip greens, fatback, and cornbread served in the shack of an elderly African American couple when he was assigned, as a National Guardsman, to guard a Tennessee levee on a rainy winter day in 1937. In his restaurant, he aimed to re-create the heartfelt hospitality of these folks who invited him in from the cold.

"We wanted a restaurant for our friends to come in and eat and visit with us," Rogers explains on the Waffle House website. "We're not in the food business; we're in the people business."

And that means all people, all the time. Waffle House is one of those rare cultural icons that synthesizes Old South folksiness with a New South (read: racially integrated) ethos. In the early 1960s, when demonstrators against whites-only restaurants descended on the restaurant on Peachtree Street, Rogers cordially invited everybody to the counter, and, later, during the riots that roiled cities after the assassination of Martin Luther King Jr., Waffle House stayed open while most Atlanta businesses closed. Civil rights leaders took note.

As a result, both Usher and David Allen Coe can comfortably belly up to the formica. Waffle House sets the scene in videos for both the Blue Collar Comedy tour and the R&B group 112. Country singer Trace Adkins has warbled his downhome homilies on a promotional Waffle House tour, and during filming for "RU the Girl?" the divas of TLC usually held their snappy confabs in one of the booths.

"You're not a real Southerner if you don't go to Waffle House," T-Boz says. "We're keeping it real. Everyone can afford some eggs and some toast."

And even as the region succumbs to homogenized sprawl, Waffle House continues to "keep it real."

"It's one of the few elements of Southern life," Wirtz notes, "that has stayed true and not been ripped off and exploited by outsiders and then handed back to us in some generic, watered-down form, as is the case with country music, NASCAR, rasslin', and TV preaching."

The purist approach evidently works; the growing chain now boasts around fifteen hundred restaurants, serving 160 million customers a year in twenty-five states—mostly red states.

"Our Northern buddies just don't get Waffle House," says Chris Hicks, a guitar player with the Marshall Tucker Band. "But for us Southern boys, that glowing yellow sign is a comforting beacon. We live on the road, and when we see a Waffle House, we know we're at least within five hundred miles of home.

The appeal to musicians is obvious: inexpensive, belly-filling food served 'round the clock.

"Waffle House has been like an oasis in the desert for hungry musicians," says keyboard player Chuck Leavell, who has dined there with the Rolling Stones, the Allman Brothers, Eric Clapton, and others. "I can recall many times going there after a show and then getting back on a tour bus or back to my hotel room, all full of pecan waffles, eggs, and bacon, and then going to sleep."

Also, on a deeper level, the restaurants offer a touchstone of consistency in a knockabout, vagabond lifestyle.

"It's the one place that, no matter where you are, you know exactly what you're going to get," Hicks says.

At least with the food. The "people business" is another story.

With its unflinching, open-arms embrace of the "poor old cash customer," Waffle House offers a crash course in cultural diversity with every meal, the best seat for observing well-lubed people who are nonetheless at their least varnished.

Asked to name the kinds of people he has met at Waffle House in forty years of daily visits, during the day for coffee and at night after playing blues with some forty-odd (in some cases, very odd) bands, Ira T. "the Harmonica Man" White rattles off: old, young, Baptist, Catholic, educated, uneducated, black, white, thin, fat, bipolar, dope smokers, ex–dope smokers, jailbirds, alcoholics, ex-alcoholics, bikers, married, single, never married, married many times, Democrats, Republicans, Libertarians, veterans, nonveterans . . .

Naturally, song lyrics rise from snatches of overheard conversation. At one of the restaurants in Macon, folks still talk fondly about "Cowboy," an obstreperous regular who addressed everyone, repeatedly, with the signature greeting: "Get outta my pocket! You ain't mad, is you?" The late, great Cowboy made such an indelible impression on the musicians who drifted in from the bar next door that he has been immortalized in a song by the Roadhouse Blues Band titled, "You Ain't Mad, Is You?"

So along with the chocolate pie come memorable slices of life.

"One night in Statesboro, every single person in the place jumped behind the counter and hid," recalls Athens roots rocker Dodd Ferrelle, "because there was a guy in his underwear waving around a shotgun in the parking lot."

A real-life grease fire in Mississippi was the basis for Wirtz's classic ballad "The Waffle House Fire," and a lost weekend in South Carolina yielded a ditty titled "Honky Tonk Hermaphrodite."

"Several couples walked in, wearing tuxedos and prom dresses," Wirtz says. "As I looked closer, I realized the people in the dresses were men. In the early '80s in Greenville, that sort of thing could raise an eyebrow and tighten a buttcheek here and there, but there they were at the Waffle House, no problems."

Like other aspects of Southern social life, the mood of Waffle House alternates between Saturday-night hell-raising and Sunday-morning sanctity.

"If you're in an unfamiliar town on a weekend night, check the local liquor laws and get out of there half an hour before the 'idiot rush' of the bars," he says. "And don't go there between 11 a.m. and 2 p.m. on a Sunday because you get the slow-moving church crowd. I've had many a good meal spoiled by not knowing just when to leave."

Deen says the Waffle House employees regard working the rush after "last call" as a hard-earned "badge of honor." "It's like the Marines who serve a four-year tour of duty and hate it at the time but brag about it later," he says. "If you can work a double-shift on New Year's Eve when the bars let out, with a cook out sick and only two waitresses, you've accomplished something. You dread dealing with the drunks, but they usually leave good tips."

Unlike the "crotchety bastard coffee drinkers who only leave a quarter because that was a good tip back in their day," Deen says, referring to the weekday-afternoon crowd of retirees brimming with theories and advice. "We call one group the 'Einstein Club,'" White says, of his rival coffee klatch. "Don't matter if it's going to the moon or heart surgery, those sumbitches have been there, done that, and have all the answers to all the world's problems. But they really don't know squat."

Deen, twenty-eight, worked as a Waffle House cook for about a decade, he says, until his rehab counselor advised him to seek other employment. Based in Darien, Georgia, he has cultivated a following in Georgia coffeehouses as the "Waffle House Poet" with his spoken-word performances about life at the grill of what he grandly calls the "Fluorescent Palace."

"Most people seem to just disregard it as a place where old men go to drink coffee during the day and drunks go to sober up at night, but it's so much more than that," says Deen, who has filled a tall stack of coffee-stained notebooks with his reflections. "The Waffle House has been my Muse."

His resulting work is, like the bar rush on a full-moon Saturday night, blazingly candid, poignant, and funny.

"When you show up at 3 a.m. so drunk you can't even order your patty melt correctly and you look over and see a broken soul in a paper hat being screamed orders at by waitresses; I'm that guy," Deen writes. "Did you ever once stop and feel sorry for me? You shouldn't have. I was more messed up than you were."

He says he took up the spatula in emulation of "Buddy," the "baddest Waffle House cook around," whose prowess with the waitresses and access to limitless food signified the "coolest job around."

"I wanted to be just like him," Deen says. "He told me, 'Flipping eggs is just like jerkin' off—all in the wrist.' And so began my Waffle House career.

Every king has his castle, and I still consider Waffle House my castle. They're good folks who work there, a family. They'll pass the hat for you when you get arrested or keep you from having to live under a bridge."

White agrees: "If you are in trouble, these folks at Waffle House are the ones you want to see. There really isn't any sort of class-envy. When we walk through that door, every one of us is the same. It's very strange and strangely comforting."

Deen, who works as a telemarketer now, says he misses the feel of the spatula, and the cranky ministrations of the ironically named "Sunshine." "In a way I am the quintessential Waffle House employee," he says. "I'm a fractured human being, a bastard child of the pine-tree kingdom with no trust fund and no roots to grow from. I'm making this life up as I go along. That's what most Waffle House people do."

That is what most of us do, actually: make it up as we go along. Waffle House just nourishes us—and our music—while we do.

Let Us Now Praise Fabulous Cooks

John T. Edge

In January 1986, the *New Yorker* rejected an advertisement from the Jargon Society, a North Carolina literary press, for *White Trash Cooking* by Ernest Matthew Mickler. Camera-ready art and a check for $900 were returned. "We thought the title might offend our readers," a spokesperson for the magazine said.

"That just goes to show you how much the *New Yorker* knows about anything involving gravy," said Georgia-bred Roy Blount Jr., an early proponent of the book and a putative kinsman of Florida-born Mickler. Blount did not stand alone; admirers of the work were many. In *Vogue*, Barbara Kafka wrote that Mickler "sees clearly, without condescension." Bryan Miller of the *New York Times* dubbed Mickler the "Escoffier of icebox cake and bucket dumplings," and proclaimed *White Trash Cooking* "perhaps the most intriguing book of the 1986 spring cookbook season." Colman Andrews, now the editor in chief of *Saveur*, then the food editor of *Metropolitan Home*, called *White Trash Cooking* "the best American cookbook of the century, by far."

Upon receipt of a galley, a correspondent from Monroeville, Alabama, wrote, "I have never seen a sociological document of such beauty—the photographs alone are shattering. I shall treasure it always. . . . Now that it's harder than ever to identify the genuine article on sight—with two generations of prosperity white trash looks like gentry—we've long needed something other than the ballot box to remind us of their presence: *White Trash Cooking* is a beautiful testament to a stubborn people of proud and poignant heritage." (Harper Lee knew a good thing when she saw it.)

White Trash Cooking was among the most unlikely best-sellers to ever climb the charts. For those who did not dog-ear a copy, mixing Goldie's Yo-Yo Puddin' or Mona Lisa Sapp's Macaroni Salad, baking Resurrection Cake, Grand Canyon Cake, and Vickie's Stickies, for those who have never had the pleasure of pondering recipes for Canned Corn Beef Sandwiches, Potato Chip Sandwiches, and Girl Scout One-Eyed Egg—and for those who once knew but have since forgotten their glories—a primer is appropriate.

White Trash Cooking was published with a spiral binding, in the manner of the South's beloved community cookbooks. The background for the cover image of a fleshy-armed woman in a flower-print tank top was a patchwork of Tabasco sauce, Ritz crackers, and Velveeta cheese bricolaged with those country icons Uncle Ben, Aunt Jemima, and Martha White, all of which was overlaid on a photostat of mulched turnip tops and precisely rectangular turnip roots—the sort of vegetable matter that does not come fresh from the farm but straight from the can.

On the inside cover, Jonathan Williams of the Jargon Society declared, "If you were trying to explain what these recipes and snapshots were all about to some grand maître like Paul Bocuse, you'd say: 'Listen here, buddy, this be's the victuals of white, Southern rural peasants . . . Hit'll eat!'" Williams suggested that the reader imagine Bocuse and his ilk "swooning over such delicacies as 'Big Reba's Rainbow Icebox Cake,' 'Tutti's Fruited Porkettes,' and the 'Cold Collard Sandwich,' as the Durkee's dressing drips over their cravats."

But Williams also hinted at a deeper meaning, one that eluded many a wink-and-nod reader. After complimenting Mickler's "snapbean prose style," Williams, a countercultural poet and publisher who called himself an "aristo-dixie-queer" and called Mickler the "Carmen Miranda of Moccasin Creek," argued that, in congruence with the collected recipes, the forty-six photographs at the center of the book "fill out a picture of Southern living suggested by the photographer William Christenberry."

Regard the photographs—and the text—of *White Trash Cooking* closely and likely you will discover that the citation was apt. Christenberry, among our region's most talented and forthright photographers, was born near Hale County, Alabama, the same Black Belt county that writer James Agee and photographer Walker Evans chronicled in their Depression-era masterpiece, *Let Us Now Praise Famous Men*. Early in his career, Christenberry claimed the work of Agee and Evans as his lodestar. And after a week of alternately thumbing *White Trash Cooking* and *Let Us Now Praise Famous Men*, I can't help but conclude that Mickler read the words of Agee or saw the photographs of Evans. At the very least, Mickler, like Christenberry, was influenced by their unflinching and sympathetic style of documentation.

The Agee-Evans-Mickler triangle may not be provable, but I do know, thanks to an oral history collected late in life, that Mickler read Zora Neale

Hurston. "Child, that just blew me away," Mickler said of his first encounter with the writings of the Florida-born and Barnard-trained anthropologist, best known for her novel *Their Eyes Were Watching God*. "[S]he walked on the shell ground I walked on. Played out in the same woods, saw the same rivers, and that's what made her."

Hurston documented the lives of working-class blacks. Mickler, like Agee and Evans, focused his lens—and cocked his ear—in an attempt to capture the pathos of everyday whites. Agee and Evans brought to life people unheralded. So did Mickler. Agee wanted readers to apprehend that "these I will write of are human beings, living in this world . . . and that they were dwelt among, investigated, spied on, revered, and loved." *Let Us Now Praise Famous Men* affirmed humanity: "If I could do it, I'd do no writing at all here," said Agee of the effort. "It would be photographs; the rest would be fragments of cloth, bits of cotton, lumps of earth, records of speech, pieces of wood and iron, phials of odors, plates of food."

Mickler embraced the written tradition. And he aimed for nobility, invoking Welty and Faulkner, O'Connor and McCullers: "They all tell us, in their own White Trash ways, that our good times are the best, our bad times are the worst, our tragedies the most extraordinary, our characters the strongest and the weakest, and our humblest meals the most delicious. There ain't much in between."

But Mickler, like Agee, also relished the gut-punch of photography. A reviewer for *American Photographer* noted that Mickler's pictures "evoke a palpable social strain, and are filled with the sympathy and goodwill of a photographer who sees the joy in what might best be called the 'supper class.' [T]here is more than a hint of pathos in the way Mickler has organized his pictures. Close-ups of frying hush puppies and plates gobbed over with grits, beans, creamed corn, and biscuits are interspersed with melancholy interiors of white-trash homes. . . . Subtly, Mickler reminds us that it takes a dirt-poor people to produce a diet as rich and raunchy as *White Trash Cooking*."

Like *Let Us Now Praise Famous Men*, which was rejected by its commissioning agent, *Fortune* magazine, *White Trash Cooking* wasn't warmly received by publishers. The name was the matter. For want of a title that would not offend, a half-dozen New York houses turned down the cookbook. But the Jargon Society, in the person of Jonathan Williams, saw merit where others saw a goof at best, a libel at worst.

A poet and contrarian, Williams was a veteran student of North Carolina's Black Mountain College, an early and important locus of free thought and Southern dissent, where artists in residence at various times included Ben Shahn, Robert Motherwell, Robert Rauschenberg, and Cy Twombly. On the

Black Mountain College campus, Buckminster Fuller built his first geodesic dome, John Cage staged the first multimedia happening in the United States, and the *Black Mountain Review* published the likes of Allen Ginsberg.

When Black Mountain College closed in 1957, Jonathan Williams threw himself wholesale into the work of the Jargon Society, declaring his mission to "keep afloat the Ark of Culture in these dark and tacky times!" Often dismissive of the bourgeoisie, Williams savored the vernacular speech and traditions of his Appalachian neighbors. In Ernest Matthew Mickler, Williams found a swampy analogue to those mountain folk, touting Mickler as a poet laureate of the underclass, one of the coterie whom Jargon celebrated as "strays and mavericks . . . those afflicted with both vision and craft."

Mickler, baby-faced with the unstudied good looks of a country boy come to town, was born in 1940, in Palm Valley, Florida, near St. Augustine. His father was a shrimper. His mother worked as a cook and a filling-station attendant. Mickler was fond of telling interviewers that his family lived without electricity until he was seventeen or eighteen, in "the middle of the swamp" at "an old fish camp." He described the buildings as "crude-cut cypress," the family privy as "out-of-doors."

Mickler's father died when the boy was six. Mickler called him a "mean old son of a bitch." He once called his mother, Edna Rae, "the lowdowndest White Trash that ever walked the face of the earth," but aimed to flatter. "Mama was a great fisherman," Mickler said, "redfish, bass, trout, drum on the hook and line. Mullet in the net. And she shrimped too. Caught tubs of fish."

Mickler took great pride in place, although he was not wholly provincial. When he was a teenager, Mickler, along with Petie Pickette—granddaughter of the woman he called Mama Two, the woman who gave the world Tutti's Fruited Porkettes—scored a regional country-and-western hit with the single "Our Love." The duo toured the South and, depending upon the story told, either opened for, sang backup for, or merely conversed in a hotel lobby with Patsy Cline and Roy Orbison. "We were not big time," Mickler said later. "We elbowed with them."

In his mid-twenties, Mickler went to college, earning a bachelor's degree at Jacksonville University. At the suggestion of his primary professor, Memphis Wood, he applied for and won admission to the master of fine arts program at Mills College in Oakland, California. While in Oakland, Mickler likely concocted the idea for *White Trash Cooking*.

Apparently, Mickler and his friends first envisioned a campy television show, a kind of drag-queen riff on the Galloping Gourmet. The book came into focus later, as Mickler traveled the gay vagabond circuit from the Bay Area to New Orleans and on to Key West. He shopped the project for a couple of years, soliciting introductions to editors and publishers. To no avail. And then, while working as a caterer in Key West, Mickler received a call from Jonathan Williams, who, on behalf of the Jargon Society, offered a modest contract, a poet's-eye edit, and, no matter the ruckus, a pledge to retain the original title.

Williams understood the power of the title. He knew that printing the epithet was an act of transcendence, a marker of movement beyond the constraints of stereotype. Mickler proclaimed "White Trash" to be a badge of honor. Black Southerners responded positively to the book, recognizing the ascendance of white trash as concomitant with the liberation of their people.

Mickler delineated lowercase white trash and uppercase White Trash, arguing that "manners and pride separate the two. Common white trash has very little in the way of pride, and no manners to speak of, and hardly any respect for anybody or anything." White Trash, however, "never failed to say 'yes ma'm,' and 'no sir,' never sat on a made-up bed (or put your hat on it), never opened someone else's icebox, never left food on your plate, never left the table without permission, and never forgot to say 'thank you' for the teeniest favor. That's the way the ones before us were raised and that's the way they raised us in the South."

In one of the preambles to *Let Us Now Praise Famous Men*, Agee fretted about the "emasculation of acceptance," acknowledging that when an audience brings a work to its bosom, it smothers the potential to shock, to change perceptions, to catalyze action. And so it was with *White Trash Cooking*.

Within six months of publication, Jargon, overwhelmed by the response, sold the rights to Ten Speed Press of Berkeley, California, an upstart that earned a reputation for savvy marketing with *What Color Is Your Parachute?* Through the summer and fall of 1986, the book sold strongly, and by January 1987 *White Trash Cooking* was number eight on the *Publishers Weekly* roster of paperback best-sellers. At a time when health-conscious cooking was all the rage—*Spa Food*, *The New American Diet*, and *The Four Seasons Spa Cuisine* were three of the books that made their debut alongside *White Trash Cooking*—Mickler's book was a thumb-of-the-nose at the calorie-obsessed.

Mickler became a media celebrity, cooking chicken feet and rice on *Late Night with David Letterman* and starting an on-stage trash-can fire in the process. He became an arbiter of pop culture. When Tammy Faye Bakker, wife of the fallen PTL founder Jim Bakker, offered her Sloppy Joe recipe to the PTL's 900-line callers, Mickler defended Tammy Faye's inclusion of canned chicken gumbo soup and her instructions that a cook will "know if you have enough ketchup when it gets to the right degree of redness." He told a reporter, "I bet it's delicious. But I like my Sloppy Joes on cornbread, which is real lowdown."

Soon, more than 200,000 copies of the book were in print. But trouble followed money. In December 1986, in the wake of a *People* magazine article that mentioned a $45,000 royalty, an attorney representing the Ledbetter family of Alexander City, Alabama, threatened suit and received compensation for Mickler's unauthorized use of their daughter's photograph on the book cover.

The Ledbetters joined an unlikely cadre of people who, taking note of the book's success, threatened suits against Mickler. The most curious complainant was the Junior League of Charleston, publishers of *Charleston Receipts*, the ultimate white-glove Southern cookbook. The good ladies of Charleston claimed that twenty-three recipes in *White Trash Cooking*, including roast possum and broiled squirrel, were lifted almost verbatim.

Mickler went to work on his second book, *Sinkin Spells, Hot Flashes, Fits and Cravins* (now available as *White Trash Cooking II*). The back cover shows Mickler in his prime, tending a cast-iron skillet roiling with grease. In the background, at the sink, is a man in briefs and a white tank top—his partner Gary Jolley. With *White Trash Cooking* Mickler outed the South's White Trash. With book two, he outed himself.

"I casseroled them to death," Mickler said of *Sinkin Spells*, the book he had written and collected in fits and starts, much of it while on book tour for *White Trash Cooking*. No matter what Mickler might suggest, *Sinkin Spells* was a more mature effort, one that used the recipes and the folio layout, but shifted the focus to food ceremonies, like the dinner after a cemetery cleaning, the casserole luncheon of a quilting circle, even the wake of Mickler's own mother.

The story of the wake was Mickler's best piece of writing, in which a woman named Chestine flails at her neighbor, grabbing her dress "like a bulldog," and Naireen Sikes, known for wearing "the tightis clothes you ever witnessed," makes the "best, damn perlow" in "these scrubs." Meanwhile, respect for Mickler's mother is conveyed by deviled eggs, served in such quantity that "everybody's hens had ta been a layin double."

"One Side of a Conversation between Gracie Dwiggers and Rosetta Bunch about Edna Rae's Wake and Funeral, over the Phone" was one of Mickler's last efforts. *Sinkin Spells, Hot Flashes, Fits and Cravins* was published on Monday, November 14, 1988. Mickler died of AIDS the very next day.

Downhome Food

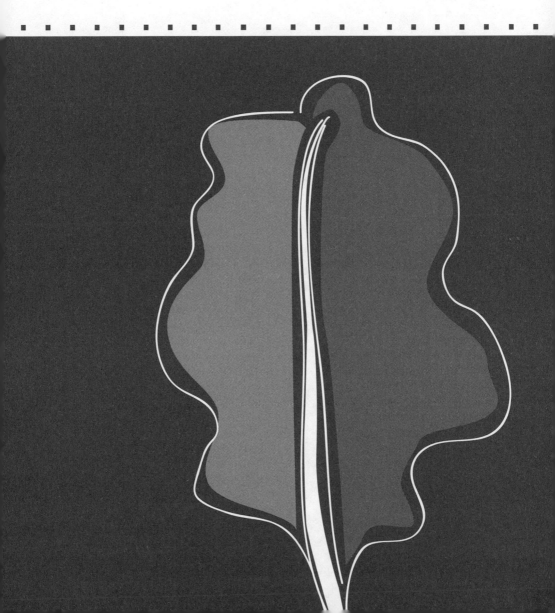

Molly Mooching on Bradley Mountain

Mary Hufford

Columbine: Pierrot, I'm growing tired of caviar and peacock's
liver. Isn't there something else that people eat? Some humble
vegetable that grows in the ground?
Pierrot: Well, there are mushrooms.
Columbine: Mushrooms! I had forgotten!
    From Aria da Capo, *by Edna St. Vincent Millay*

You could just go on and on about the molly moochers. There
are so many ways to fix them.
    Laffon Pettry, Drew's Creek, West Virginia

At sixteen, assigned to the role of Columbine in a high school play, I had no
idea what I was talking about when I said I had forgotten about mushrooms.
For me, there was nothing to forget. Button mushrooms were filler material for salads and Campbell's soups. Even though I attended high school
in Pennsylvania's Allegheny foothills, I had never hunted mushrooms, not
even morels, the most unmistakable of the edible wild fungi. Decades would
pass before, in the 1990s, I encountered the premier conditions for rearing
ardent mycophagists (mushroom eaters): the forest of the southern West
Virginia coalfields, where rich deposits of humus support the world's richest temperate-zone hardwood system. There are more than forty dominant
canopy species, forty woody understory species, and more than twelve hundred herbaceous species in this forest system, which reaches from northern
Alabama into Ohio and Pennsylvania. Over many generations, mountain

communities have developed a richly variegated seasonal round, from digging ramps (wild leeks) and gathering wild greens in the spring, to gardening and berry picking throughout the summer, digging ginseng, goldenseal, and other medicinal and edible roots, harvesting fall fruits and nuts, and hunting and fishing through most seasons. A high point in this annual round is the springtime hunt for morels, known throughout southern West Virginia as "molly moochers." Hunting molly moochers, or "molly mooching," people travel throughout the hills, checking their secret places just after the first warm spring rains.

At the head of Drew's Creek, on a late April evening in 1998, I was processing ramps with members of the Delbert Freewill Baptist Church. Ramps, wild cousins of the leek, are the first of the wild edibles to appear in the spring. These ramps would be consumed the next day at the Pine Knob Ramp Supper, an annual fund-raiser that supports the community center known throughout the valley as "the Ramp House." As we chopped off the rootlets and peeled away the slippery outer membrane (jokingly referred to as the "slimer") for the next day's feast, we were already caught up in the time of molly moochers.

"I found one today," said Jenny Bonds. "A little tiny one."

Laffon Pettry reported that a neighbor of theirs had found fifty-six of them already.

"Where'd he find them at?" Jenny wanted to know.

"Behind our house used to be an old apple orchard," Laffon answered. "He found thirty-seven yesterday."

"Gladys was finding them out there," volunteered Delores Workman.

"Gladys," Laffon chuckled, thinking of her niece's passion for morels. "The Queen of the Molly Moochers!"

Within days of this conversation, molly moochers would be simmering in skillets throughout the hills and hollows surrounding the headwaters of the Big Coal River. Calling at the homes of friends on Drew's Creek and in Sundial and Stickney, I had multiple invitations to eat molly moochers in the space of an afternoon. Jenny Bonds, who had molly moochers soaking in salt water, urged me to come back. Just up the hollow, Judy and Wayne Griffy were eating theirs already, rolled in flour and fried in butter. "Have you ever had molly moochers?" Judy asked. "Try one!" I popped one into my mouth, not quite prepared for the sensations that followed. There was the familiar texture of the butter-flavored coating, the wrapping for delicacies I knew well, such as zucchini, squash blossoms, and oysters, and the satisfying release of juices as I began to chew. But the flavor spreading over my palate was not the flavor of any of those. It was a series of hints, of the tenderest, choicest cut of beef, marinated to perfection in hazelnut oil or liqueur. Intensely but ethereally earthy, it gathered the juices into a taste like no other, leaving me startled and eager for more. In Sundial, Randy and Debbie Sprouse offered me molly moochers that had been dipped in beer batter and sautéed in butter. I tried again to identify the salient flavor, nutty, light, savory, but ultimately elusive. An hour later, in Stickney, I was facing another plateful in the home of Dave and Glenna Bailey. "Here, hog this!" Dave invited me. I obliged.

I began asking about molly moochers, where and when to get them, what to do with them. I asked everyone I talked to over the next few weeks.

"Some people call them 'merkles,'" Mae Bongalis told me. "They look like a corncob."

"Some people call them 'sponges,'" said Elsie Rich, a descendant of Floyd Williams, an English pioneer. She had married an Italian immigrant, who referred to morels as "spugna," a term shared with the classical Roman gourmand Apicius.

"How did they get the name 'molly moochers'?" I often asked.

"Old timey people called them that," explained Mary Allen, an older woman herself, who grew up on Peachtree Creek.

"Maybe that's from the Irish," suggested a man who lived over on New River.

In every public establishment I heard talk about where they grow and how hard they are to find, unless you know the local history and ecology. "Buddy, I'll tell you," said Kay Miller, one evening in the Sundial Tavern. "If you come home with some mushrooms, man, you have been on a hunt."

"I love them," agreed Randy Sprouse. "Deep fry them in beer batter."

"They say there's a real good place up in Peachtree," said Kay Miller.

"Up on Molly Daniel's place," offered Randy, referring to a stand of old growth in Jarrold's Valley, at the confluence of the Marsh and Clear forks.

"But I've never hunted up there," said Kay. "I've only been up in Dry Creek and Rock Creek."

"Is there more than one kind of molly moocher?" I asked.

"Oh yeah," replied Kay. "It depends on what kind of tree you find them under. If you find them under apple trees, they're white. If you find them under sycamore trees they're yellow."

"Some of them are cone-shaped, some of them are round," Randy added.

"If you find them on the top of the mountain," continued Kay, "they're brown, or black. They're not as good as the ones you find down low."

A global passion for morel mushrooms, which seeps into the scientific names for species *esculenta* and *deliciosa*, also informs the variety of common names for morels. These names are brimming with images and clues for locating an object of desire: sponge, honeycomb, pinecone, snakehead, haystack, corncob, brains, tulip morels, hickory chickens, orchard mushrooms. The Cherokee, who rolled them in cornmeal and fried them, knew them as *Ahawi sayoniyusti*, meaning "like a deer antler." Etymology reveals a European search image within the name for the genus itself. Early German terms included morus, alluding to the morel's likeness to a mulberry (*Morus rubra*). In *The Romance of the Fungus World*, Rolfe notes that the word *morchella* first appeared in the scientific literature in 1719. European names for the morel are quite similar: *morchella* (Bulgarian), *morkel* (Danish), *morille* (French), and *morchel* (German). The old High German *morha*, which meant "carrot" or "parsnip," was diminutized to *morhila* in reference to the mushroom, from which *morchel* derives. The diminutive conveys the affection with which the morel was regarded in Europe.

The term "molly moocher" appears to be unique to central Appalachia. Perhaps "molly," the Irish nickname for Mary, is a play on the French *morilla*, which might have sounded like "Maria" to the ears of the Irish who came to the region in the mid-nineteenth century to work on the railroad. Another possibility is suggested by the Latin name for "apples," *malus*. Morels fruiting around apple orchards could be thought of as *malus morchella*, a term that could be playfully and meaningfully shortened to "molly moochers." But that is, of course, sheer speculation. (To the question of what it could mean to "mooch" mollies, we will return shortly.)

Morels are also referred to as "dryland fish," as pleasing to the gourmet palate as choice seafood. "Aren't they the best things you've ever eaten in your life?" exclaimed a young woman from Rock Creek. "You fry them up like oysters. I've eaten them until I was sick." The distinctive look of the fleshy fungus is accounted for in a Silesian tale of how the devil, once in a rage, tore an old woman to shreds and scattered her parts all over the forest. Wherever a part landed, a mushroom grew, as wrinkled as the skin of the wizened dame herself.

The Silesian tale also bears on the etiology of the craving for morels, which, like tomatoes, Parmesan cheese, meats, fish, and other mushrooms, stimulate what was officially recognized in the 1980s as a fifth taste: umami. In 1908 Kikunai Ikeda of Tokyo Imperial University, investigating konbu (Japanese kelp), coined the term to describe the taste of the deliciousness trigger, glutamate. Our first encounter with umami is in breast milk, and it signals to us that a particular food contains vital nutrients. Morels, which contain more protein than most vegetables, along with vitamins A, B, D, and K, possess a number of well-known umami-like taste contributors, as well as a unique glycoside, S-morelid. Thus, morels may look like many things, but they taste only like themselves. The flavor of morels is so difficult to describe because it is the flavor of morels. The only way to communicate the flavor is by sharing the mushrooms.

The morel has steadfastly resisted domestication, although aficionados have found a few ways to encourage them. (Peasants in eighteenth-century Germany, for example, set fire to the woods each year to stimulate morel production, until the government banned the practice.) Mycologist Tom Volk argues that the reason morels are so difficult to cultivate is that the main part of the fungus is a microscopic underground structure called a mycelium, which feeds on dead and dying organisms or forms symbiotic relationships with trees. Forest soils are teeming with mycelia, which are the most massive living component of soils. Each network may eventually weigh several tons, forming, if one is willing to count such networks as individuals, the largest organisms on earth: "Larger than baleen whales or sequoia trees," writes David White.

Morels form associations with apples, elms, and pine trees, and they can also digest dead matter, converting it into the rich humus on which hardwood forests depend. As long as there is a source of nutrition, the morel mycelium seems able to grow indefinitely underground through cloning; in the wild, it appears to fruit mostly in response to habitat disruption—a forest fire or the death of a plant partner. This is why morels are so often found on burned ground and around old orchards and dying elms.

In this part of West Virginia, through the first half of the twentieth century, farmers grew their "heavy vegetables" (corn, beans, and winter squash) on rich "benches" of soil high in the mountains. When these "newgrounds" wore out after a number of years, farmers planted apple orchards. Apple trees were once ubiquitous in the mountains. "I've seen a thousand bushels of apples come out of that hollow in one season," related Dennis Dickens, an octogenarian living on William's Branch of Peachtree Creek in the 1990s. The orchards that matured with the woods were pruned and harvested for decades by people hunting and gathering in those areas. As the orchards have aged and declined, they have become premier spots for molly mooching. "Once the apple trees lose their spurs," cautioned Kay Miller, "the molly moochers stop coming."

Whether farmers planted orchards with morels in mind or not, morels are one reason people remember where the old orchards are. I went molly mooching on Bradley Mountain one spring afternoon with Dave Bailey, his son Terry, and their friend Woody Boggs. We met at the mouth of Hazy Creek, near a tiny settlement that was known as Launa before the Raleigh-Wyoming Coal Company renamed it Edwight. Descendants of people who settled Launa still live there. Dave and Terry climbed into the back of Woody's pickup truck, while I rode along in the cab, with the tape recorder running. It was the morning after a warm spring rain. "It has to be a warm rain," Dave Bailey had said. "It can't be the cold May rains. Those are different." It had to be the kind of rain, as Woody put it, where you could hear the molly moochers pop out of the ground. "You can hear them pop up in a thunderstorm," he insisted. So off we drove, in pursuit of the cacophonous toadstools.

Bradley Mountain, in the late twentieth century, was both devastated and bursting with life. People had moved away decades ago, but returned year after year to harvest Lige Bradley's "Wolf River" apples and prune the trees. The scars of logging roads and strip mines visible on the mountain slopes were mitigated by the color slowly bursting into view around them: the green buds of "soft maples," the orange-russet blooms of hard maples, the white blossoms of dogwoods, and the fuschias of redbuds. Along the road here and there a forsythia (known locally as "shower of gold") or a quince (known as "fire on the mountain") marked the sites of former homes. "Before we go any farther, I want to tell you something," Woody Boggs announced. Waving at the mountain to our left, he continued, "All the trees on this side of the mountain are made of wood." He paused for effect. "And the trees on the other side are too."

Turning left into the Irene Hollow, we began a steep ascent, lurching and creaking along the rutted, unpaved route to the top of Bradley Mountain. "You should have seen this road before they fixed it!" Woody commented, seriously. He downshifted again and we bounced our way around and through a terrain of overwhelming contrast, in view of scalloped and serrated ridgelines, sheer drops into deep crevasses, and the softer cleavages of hills and hollows in an earlier stage of spring. Our first stop was at the charred remains of a campfire, beside a bowl-shaped cove.

Molly moochers are hard to recognize. Was that dark spot across the hollow a husk of a nut or one of the black morels? Was the bulge beneath the nearby leaves a yellow morel or a mayapple? In the time it took my companions to fill their sacks, I found three molly moochers. When we placed our open bags on the ground to assess the day's take, I showed Dave my meager findings. His eyes twinkled. "You know what I'm going to do? Give me the address of where you work, and I'm going to send these to somebody there, with a note that says, 'Look what Mary found.'" At my look of chagrin, he threw his head back and filled the air around us with the generous, contagious guffaw that is his trademark.

Local people's comments reveal that the relation between forest and community transcends the individual, and reaches into the future. "We were taught never to cut down the nut trees," Virgil Jarrell, of Sylvester, commented, "because they're good for the animals." Another man told of a co-worker who refused to cut down hickories. "The boss had to go along behind him and cut down the hickories." As it happens, nut trees are associated with morels. Older residents counsel against destroying den trees and bee trees, which happen also to provide the dead matter on which mycelia feed. Cutting such trees is a grave error—what one sawmill operator called "robbing the land."

Let us return then to the notion of mooching. Mooching suggests a free ride at someone else's expense. But what exactly is being mooched and who is doing the mooching? In one sense the fungi are moochers, availing themselves of carbohydrates produced by trees that are the property of absentee owners. Are those who hunt for molly moochers also mooching? If they are, it is not the property of the landlords, for molly moochers are not merchantable timber, nor are they minerals.

Neither animal nor vegetable nor mineral, molly moochers are anomalous. They call to mind the tricksters of world mythologies, whose antics give rise to landforms, cultures, and constellations. They are like the empty bowl that Lewis Hyde says is the ticket to entering the economy of gift exchange. "A gift," he wrote, "is a thing we do not get by our own efforts. We cannot buy it; we cannot acquire it through an act of will. It is bestowed upon us."

Molly moochers are bestowed in the moment of recognition, a moment that issues an imperative to molly mooch, no matter when the recognition strikes. "It's hard to let them get big," confessed Laffon Pettry, "because you're afraid someone else will beat you to them." The time of molly mooching trumps ordinary time. One woman recalled coming upon molly moochers while retrieving a golf ball that had gone across the creek when she was practicing. She dropped her club, forgot about the ball, and "brought back a shirt-full of molly moochers."

Dave Bailey recounted a similar feat of recognition: "Coming up the road in the car last spring, down at the Dairy Queen, me and my son. He was driving. I was setting there just looking out the window. And on the bank, I seen a molly moocher. In the car, going! I said, 'I seen a molly moocher.' 'No you didn't!'—I said, 'Turn the car around.'—'You didn't!'—I said, 'Turn around!' He turned around, went back. And there it was! That thing was that tall, that big around."

"You should have seen it," verified Glenna. "It was huge!"

"And I went back down there," resumed Dave, "and got a sackful. Boy, they were great!"

The following spring, Dave met me at his door with another trophy: a "boss" molly moocher from Hazy Creek. Measuring about eleven inches, it was the biggest I've ever seen. Later when it came up in conversation, I couldn't help myself. "How many pounds of meal did it take to coat that molly moocher? Fifteen?"

He paused and grinned. "No, twenty-five. It took twenty-five pounds of meal to coat it. We had to use a pickup truck to winch it out of the ground! It took two men to get it onto the picnic table, and the top hung over one end. We had to slice it with a chainsaw! It fed the whole community!"

Molly moochers are the effect, not the purpose, of living well. Community life is the habitat for molly moochers, which molly moochers help to renew. "We give them to our friends," said Laffon Pettry. "We've got lots that can't get out. . . . Gladys found fifty-one on Friday, and she sent them to her friends that were sick and couldn't get out and get any. I didn't find but twenty-five, but I gave mine to my friends too. We both feel that if we give them to our friends and things, that we'll find more. It's just our belief. If we give away what we find today, next time we'll find more."

Molly moochers, humble esculents, spring into view when their nutrients have run out, and become gifts to be kept in motion lest they be wasted.

Laffon Pettry's Recipe for Molly Moochers

"Make up a batter like you're fixing for chicken, dip the molly moochers in that, then roll them in cornmeal and deep fry them."

Her Ways to Preserve Molly Moochers

1. "You can fry them like you would to eat them. Put them on a paper towel and drain them. Then put them in a plastic bag and freeze them."
2. "You can fry them, place them in glass jars, and give them a fifteen-minute water bath. That seals your lid, you know. But be sure that you salt them to preserve them. But you don't have to salt them if you freeze them."
3. "Dry them: String them like beans and hang them."
4. Or make a wreath: "You gather them. You don't put water on them. You take a paper towel and you wipe all the dirt you can get off of them, just let them lay anywhere, on your sink or kitchen, anywhere, to dry them. They will petrify—they'll get real, real hard. Then you take a styrofoam, and you stick the molly moocher stems in the styrofoam, place them in a wreath. You can also use nuts and different things with them."

Deep Roots

Wendell Brock

It's an ovenlike ninety-eight degrees on a September day deep in southwestern Georgia, and my brother Wade and I are in his pickup truck, hurtling across what seems like an endless flat desert of peanut fields. This is the height of the goober-gathering season, and Wade—who works for a large peanut-growing operation—is monitoring a phalanx of combines as they do their dirty business: picking Georgia Green runners off stems sprawled in the dirt while belching so much dust that we have to keep the windows rolled up.

With thousands of dollars' worth of runners plowed up and ready for harvest, Wade's moods shift as fast as the weather. He watches as an old family friend, Davis Wacaser, operates a John Deere tractor that's pulling one of the combines. Once the basket atop the picker is full, Wacaser dumps the load into a red wagon, and worker Roy Ortiz shuffles the mounds into smooth piles. Soon the wagons will be attached to warehouse-sized dryers, which blast the peanuts with hot air until they are dry enough to store safely. (The worst job I ever had was in the summer of '79, at Climax Milling Company, or "the mill," as we called it, a peanut purchaser and feed-and-seed outfit in the tiny nearby town of Climax, where my task was to dig down into the sweltering peanut trailers for samples to test for moisture. Imagine a hair dryer from hell blowing peanut dust into your face, and you get the idea.)

Peanuts, groundnuts, goober peas, ground peas . . . Wade and I grew up in this nutty, non-nut culture. (Peanuts aren't nuts and don't grow on trees; they're legumes, edible seeds enclosed within pods, like beans, peas, and lentils.) Our father, Charlie Wade Brock Sr., farmed peanuts, and our mother, Virginia, worked for years as a bookkeeper at the mill. Thus the cyclical rituals of this crop are encoded in my family like the habits of migratory birds. But I fled the dust and heat more than twenty years ago, leaving Wade to take over the family vocation. He now lives on the land that's been tilled by our ancestors since the early 1800s, smack-dab in the middle of one of the most prolific peanut-growing regions in the United States. Georgia is the nation's number-one state for peanuts, and Decatur and Mitchell counties—where Wade also tends more than twelve hundred acres of goobers for Bishwell Farms—are located in one of the richest peanut regions in the state, which has an annual yield of almost 2 million pounds, about 44 percent of all the peanuts grown in the United States.

Although China and India lead the world's peanut production, they use the nuts mostly for oil. America, on the other hand, has had an appetite for the humble, protein-rich legume itself since colonial times. One of the first references to peanuts in an American cookbook appears in Sarah Rutledge's *The Carolina Housewife*, published in 1847, which offered recipes for "Ground-nut Cheese Cake," "Ground-nut Cake," and "Ground-nut Soup" (which survives in Virginia today as peanut soup). The legume's appeal really exploded in the early 1900s, when peanut butter was introduced at the World's Fair in St. Louis in 1904. Americans now eat more than 700 million pounds of the smooth or chunky lunch-box staple each year.

Aside from its place in America's pantry and at ballparks, the goober pea is embedded in the history of the republic. The so-called father of the peanut, George Washington Carver, began his peanut research in 1903 at Tuskegee Institute, in Alabama, and subsequently developed more than three hundred products using peanuts, including flour and an oleaginous base for cosmetics. Around the same time, an Italian immigrant by the name of Amedeo Obici perfected a system for blanching (removing the reddish skin from the kernel) whole roasted peanuts. In 1906 he and his partner, Mario Peruzzi, founded Planters, the first company in the country to successfully market roasted and packaged shelled peanuts, and in 1916 they introduced the dapper, top-hat-and-monocle-wearing mascot Mr. Peanut.

Peanuts may be one of the most iconic of American foodstuffs—they've even played a role in our politics, as when Jimmy Carter drew on his salt-of-the-earth, peanut-farming credentials to become president of the United States—but we can't claim the versatile goober pea as our own. The peanut (*Arachis hypogea*) is indigenous to South America, where Peruvian tribes placed peanuts in their graves as early as 750 BC. Two thousand years later, beginning with Columbus's arrival in the Americas, New World explorers transported peanuts to Europe—as they did tomatoes, chiles, potatoes, and the cacao bean. The Portuguese later disseminated them to Africa (via the slave trade) and Asia. Eventually, the well-traveled peanut made its way to North American shores with slaves from West Africa. The name *goober* probably comes from *nguba*, Congolese for "peanut"; and early American colonists called both the peanut and the similar (but now rare) Bambara groundnut (*Vigna subterranea*) some variation of the word *pindar*, from the Angolan *mpinda*. Thomas Jefferson, in his *Garden Book*, wrote of planting "peendars," and I grew up hearing my father (who passed away in 1973 at the age of fifty-four) speak of "pinders," a moniker he no doubt picked up from African American farmhands.

Peanut seeds go into the ground in the spring, after the last frost, and by the summer grow into lush vines with jade green foliage resembling watercress and yellow flowers the size and shape of violets. Once pollinated, the buds miraculously push themselves down into the soil, where they mature into seedpods that are harvested in the fall. The first time you snatch a bunch of these dirt dwellers from their sandy beds and crack into their light tan shells, you may be surprised to see that they are wrapped in a light pink skin—not brittle red husks—and that the kernels taste green, raw, and milky. The major varieties include runner, Spanish, Valencia, and Virginia.

In the five hundred years since they were taken from the Americas by the conquistadores, goobers have been incorporated into the cuisines of Africa and Asia, and they are still savored all over Mexico and Central and South America. In Mexico, they are roasted with chile powder or pureed with chiles to make a salsa for chicken. In Brazil, peanuts turn up in all manner of candies; they are also sometimes crushed and mixed into cachaça-based cocktails called batidas, and they are a primary ingredient in *vatapá*, a thick sauce made from dried shrimp, coconut milk, and spices that's stuffed into *acarajé*, a deep-fried black-eyed pea fritter sold on the streets in the state of Bahia. Like their American counterparts, the Chinese also snack on roasted and boiled peanuts. They grind them up for use in soups, too; and to Sichuan dishes, like kung pao chicken, peanuts are added for crunch. Peanut sauces virtually douse the cuisines of Southeast Asia. Indonesians use peanuts in their gado-gado salad dressing, and the Vietnamese put them into the dipping sauce for *goi cúôn* (summer rolls); and, of course, there's Thailand's wonderfully sludgy saté dip, a puree of coconut milk, peanuts, and curry paste. The Thais also sprinkle the nuts on the classic noodle dish pad thai and mix them into green papaya salad and masaman curry. When I was in Bangkok, my friend Poj packed me off for Chiang Mai, in northwestern Thailand, and insisted that I try the city's garlic-and-chile-studded sausage. To my surprise, the pork links arrived with a dish of *nam prik ong* (a tomato-chile paste mixed with ground pork), cabbage, cilantro, and—ta-dah!—fried salted peanuts.

Peanuts are so omnipresent in Africa that they are often mistaken for a native of that continent. Nearly every nation has a peanut stew or soup: in Senegal it's *mafé*, a lamb, chicken, or beef concoction made with peanut butter; in Ghana, ground peanuts are added to a simmering pot of chicken, tomatoes, onions, and stock.

In the American South, most of the peanut people I know are purists, and their tastes for goobers are personal and specific. "When I was growing up, the only way you ate a peanut was at a ballpark, or you just ate them in the shell, or people put them in their Co'-Colas," says Virginia peanut farmer Dee Dee Darden, pronouncing "Coca-Cola" the time-honored Southern way and causing my own memories to fizz up like peanuts in a bottle of pop. "But I would not think of boiling a peanut," continues Darden, who raises peanuts with her husband, Tommy, on their farm near Smithfield, Virginia. "I don't know why you would want to mess up a good peanut to boil it."

Au contraire, says my brother Wade, who likes 'em wet. "I'd like to boil some of those big Virginias," he says as we hover around a steaming pot of runners in his backyard. Cooked in the shell in briny water, boiled peanuts come the closest to honoring the nut's tender, leguminous quality. Perfect little snack peas in a pod, Wade's dainty, sweet morsels taste nothing like the overcooked and oversalted boiled "P-nuts" I've been buying at roadside stands for many years now, in a desperate attempt to re-create the tastes of my past—for it seems that once you experience the genuine article, you can't get the taste out of your system.

"I remember when I went away to college," recalls Darden, who grew up in Suffolk, Virginia, once known as "the Peanut Capital of the World," "and when I came back home and we got closer to the peanut area I told everyone in the car, I said, 'Put your windows down. Y'all smell?' I said, 'That's peanuts. Now we are getting close to home.'" As Wade and I crisscross the hazy-hot fields, I know exactly what she means. Peanuts toasting in the sun: it's one of the memories I've come back for.

Peanut Butter Swirl Ice Cream
Makes about 1 quart.

1 cup milk
¾ cup sugar
3 large eggs
1 cup smooth natural peanut
   butter

1½ cups heavy cream
2 teaspoons vanilla extract
1 cup salted roasted shelled
   peanuts, chopped

Heat the milk in a small saucepan over medium heat until just hot. Meanwhile, beat the sugar and eggs together in a medium-sized bowl until thick and pale yellow.

Gradually whisk the hot milk into the egg mixture in the bowl, then pour the milk-egg mixture into the saucepan. Return the saucepan to medium-low heat and cook the custard, stirring constantly with a wooden spoon, until it is thick enough to coat the back of the spoon, about 5 minutes. Remove from the heat and stir in half of the peanut butter. Strain the custard into a large bowl, let cool briefly, stirring often, then stir in the cream and vanilla. Cover and refrigerate until cold, 6 to 8 hours.

Process the mixture in an ice cream maker according to the manufacturer's directions, adding half of the nuts to the ice cream 30 seconds before it has finished churning. Transfer to a bowl, quickly swirl in the remaining peanut butter, cover, and freeze until hard. Serve ice cream sprinkled with the remaining nuts.

You can gild the lily by topping this ultra-peanut ice cream with chocolate sauce or hot fudge.

Based on a recipe in Bruce Weinstein's The Ice Cream Book *(William Morrow and Company, 1999).*

Tough Enough
The Muscadine Grape

Simone Wilson

Researchers at the USDA Agricultural Service and Mississippi State University have recently discovered that France's red wine and the South's muscadine grape share a common ingredient. It's called resveratrol, which acts as a natural "heart guard." Red wine shows high concentrations of resveratrol, but muscadines have an even higher concentration, especially in their skins.

Resveratrol consumption in France has been linked to its countrymen's intake of red wine, which in turn creates what is now commonly known as the "French paradox." The paradox is that in France few people die of coronary heart disease, even though they indulge in a relatively high-fat diet.

The good news for us? We might just be one step away from a "Southern paradox." Two ounces of unfiltered muscadine juice have twice as much resveratrol as two ounces of red wine.

While older people from rural parts of the South might remember their mom's muscadine jam, the sweet and musky flavor of muscadine wine, or the bitterness of a fresh muscadine's skin, today they'd be lucky to find a grocery store that sells muscadines. We found them at the farmers' market at the Memphis Agricenter.

Muscadines are wild grapes first discovered in 1524 by the explorer Giovanni de Verrazzano in North Carolina's Cape Fear River Valley. They were most likely named after the French muscat grape, which is similar in its sweet flavor and musky scent. The grape Verrazzano found, unlike the common dark-purple grape, is a greenish bronze and is also known as a scuppernong, after a small town in North Carolina where it was first grown. Because it thrives in a warm and humid climate, the muscadine is largely grown in the South, with most of the grapes being used to make wine and juice.

Many different varieties of muscadines have been cultivated since Verrazzano's discovery, but the fruit is still that firm, tough-skinned, seed-studded, marble-size grape that for many is only edible if processed in a certain way. A fresh muscadine has a more pronounced flavor than a garden-variety red seedless grape found at the grocery store. It's in season from mid-September until late-October and is hand-harvested, since not all muscadines on one vine ripen at the same time.

The secret to enjoying the muscadine is in your approach. One way is to simply pop it in your mouth and chew. But if you don't care for the grape's tough skin and bitter seeds, you can try squeezing and spitting. First, you squeeze the grape's pulp into your mouth. Then you separate the pulp and seeds with your tongue, spitting out the seeds or swallowing them whole.

If that's not for you, there are a number of other ways to remove the skin and to strain the seeds for jam or jellies. Muscadines also make delicious fall pies and cobblers (using pulp and skin, no seeds). And there is always wine, juice, and research.

At the USDA Southern Horticultural Laboratory in Poplarville, Mississippi, geneticist Steve Stringer is working hard to cultivate a more consumer-friendly muscadine—maybe even one that is seedless. "Our goal is to come up with cultivars that have softer skin, melting flesh, and less bitterness but still have that characteristic muscadine flavor," Stringer says.

But a more appealing muscadine might mean a less disease-resistant plant and possibly lower resveratrol levels—the very quality that makes the skin so tough and the grape so good for your heart. It is the paradox within the "Southern paradox."

Making a Mess of Poke

Dan Huntley

In late spring in York, South Carolina, when Frances Meeks's body tells her it needs poke sallet, she does not lollygag. She grabs a paper bag and heads to the woods to pick poke. Or, in the parlance of pokedom, "a mess of poke."

"I can't explain the feeling, but I gots to have it. There's something in those greens that does my body good," said Meeks, a seventy-four-year-old retired textile worker and mother of nine and "twenty-seven grands and great-grands." "People say it's a spring tonic, that it purifies your blood. I don't know about all that. I just know I feel better after I eat it and spring ain't officially here until I've had my first poke."

OK, here's the perfunctory paragraph of encyclopedic factoids: Poke, or pokeberry (*Phytolacca americana*), is a perennial plant that grows up to eight feet tall and is found throughout the United States. The proper term is *poke sallet* (old English for "salad"). The hearty plant thrives along the edges of fields, woodlands, and highway rights-of-way in recently disturbed soil. Poke sallet is rarely sold in groceries, partly because it's difficult to grow commercially; also, it abounds in the wild and can be harvested freely. Picking season in the Carolinas is spring through early summer. The leaves of young plants, two to three feet tall, can be gathered and boiled (changing the water several times to get rid of the bitter taste) for eating. The roots, stems, and purple berries of mature poke plants are poisonous. Though experts disagree on just how poisonous, it's agreed you shouldn't eat poke leaves raw and that you shouldn't ever eat roots or berries. (In any doubt? Use Swiss chard.)

But here is the most important paragraph for foodies: Cooked poke tastes better than it looks. Close your eyes. Minced and topped with Parmesan slivers and a dollop of crème fraîche, it could be a cloud of creamed polenta. Puree it with olive oil, fresh basil, roasted garlic, and pine nuts, it could be pesto's country cousin.

Most poke sallet recipes start with its being thoroughly washed and then boiled. It's usually then sautéed with bacon grease or salt pork. Some recipes call for sautéing green onions in the grease before adding the poke. Often it's prepared like a wilted spinach salad, with garnishes of sliced boiled eggs and crumbled bacon, maybe a little vinegar.

If you can't find poke in your yard or by the roadside, check farmers' markets. The coolest thing about poke is that it's immortalized in song: "Polk Salad Annie." Aside from not being able to spell, rockabilly raconteur Tony Joe White penned perhaps the most funked-out and inscrutable lyrics in all rock music when he wrote this ode to poke in the late 1960s:

Every day 'for suppertime
She'd go down by the truck patch
And pick her a mess o' polk salad
And carry it home in a tote sack
Polk Salad Annie. Gator's got your granny
Everybody said it was a shame
'Cause her momma was aworkin' on the chain gang
(a wretched, spiteful, straight-razor totin' woman)
Lord have mercy. Pick a mess of it.

Food writer John T. Edge says poke sallet—along with fried chicken, pork barbecue, and chitlins—is among the most "fetishized of Southern foods." "Southerners, particularly ones who have moved away, probably spend more time talking about poke sallet than they ever did putting it in their mouth," jokes Edge. "With much of the rural South in retreat, people seek out poke. It's as much ingrained in whites as it is in blacks. It's slightly veiled as poor folks' food, but it's really a marker of frugality. People are proud of their poke roots."

Dori Sanders was raised on poke in rural York County, South Carolina. "It's a spring ritual, a rebirth," said Sanders, a peach-farming novelist whose culinary skills have been featured in *Gourmet*. "Don't get me started on poke and creasy greens [similar to collards]. I could go all day. Pan fry it with some streak-o-lean and some skillet cornbread. Oh my Lord, take me home." The author of *Dori Sanders' Country Cooking* says that folks raised in the rural Carolinas have a natural affinity for this noble weed—poor people could afford it and they needed the nutrition. She's so fond of the vegetable, she makes a poke quiche.

"You can't fill your belly with anything that costs less money than a pot of free poke," she says with a chuckle. "A lot of us were raised poor on the farm. We ate poke out of necessity back then. We can afford store-bought greens now, but we still come back for another plate of poke. Why? Because it connects us with our past."

Marianne Turow says that, nutritionally, poke packs a powerful package of iron, beta-carotenes, antioxidants, and vitamin A, but she says there is no scientific evidence to support the claim that some people are physiologically "compelled" to eat certain foods—that their bodies "tell them" to eat poke in the springtime. "As best we can tell, it's folklore," said Turow, an associate professor of nutrition at the Culinary Institute of America in Hyde Park, New York. "When I was pregnant I craved a bag of potato chips. What was my body telling me? That I needed more sodium?"

Turow's theory is that people who grew up eating poke sallet learned to associate it with spring's arrival and with living in a pastoral setting. "And as they've grown older, they want to return to that time and place," Turow says. "What poke really is, is good roughage to cleanse the digestive system. What people have added to this plain leafy vegetable is romance."

Poke Pie (Quiche)
Serves 6 to 8.

2½ pounds poke
2 tablespoons olive oil
3 cloves garlic, minced or grated
½ teaspoon minced fresh basil
½ teaspoon minced fresh sage
½ cup all-purpose flour

½ cup cornmeal
½ teaspoon salt
3 large eggs, lightly beaten
¼ cup freshly grated Parmesan
   cheese

Pull the leaves from the poke plant, discard the stems, and rinse the leaves well. Bring a large kettle of water to a boil. Add the poke leaves and boil for 3 to 4 minutes. Drain in a colander and discard the water. ("You may repeat the process with new water if you like; I don't," says Sanders.) Chop the poke roughly and set aside.

Preheat the oven to 400 degrees. In a large cast-iron skillet, heat the oil over medium heat until the oil begins to jump a bit. Add the garlic, basil, and sage and sauté, stirring occasionally, for 2 minutes. Add the blanched poke leaves, stir to combine, and remove from the heat. Set aside.

In a small bowl, blend the flour, cornmeal, and salt and sprinkle the mixture over the poke in the skillet. Pour the eggs over the top and mix well. Sprinkle with the cheese.

Cover the skillet and bake for 50 minutes. Uncover and bake for 10 to 15 minutes longer, until nicely browned. Remove from the oven, cut into slices, and serve.

Adapted from Dori Sanders' Country Cooking: Recipes and Stories from the Family Farm Stand *(Algonquin Books).*

Frank Pressley's Poke and Eggs

1 large bag of poke (a mess)
Handful of dock sorrel
   (if available)
Salt and pepper to taste
6 slices bacon

A few drops of vinegar
4 large eggs, hard-boiled and
   chopped
Sprinkle of sugar (optional)

This is in the words of Pressley, a longtime poke aficionado from Appalachia, quoted in *Smokehouse Ham, Spoon Bread & Scuppernong Wine: The Folklore and Art of Southern Appalachian Cooking*, by Joseph E. Dabney (Cumberland House):

I break off just the tender leaves on top and the buds [of the living plant]. I leave it where it'll sucker out and make more. I take the tender shoots to the house, chop it up and put it in the pot, cover it with water, and parboil it five minutes. If dock is available, I put in a handful to cook with the poke. I pour that water off and parboil it again for five minutes with salt and pepper, and drain it off for a second time. Then I fry the bacon good and crisp and put the poke in the skillet and crumble the bacon up on it. I heat it good and fry it till it's sort of tender, put a lid on it and smother it a bit and then put a few drops of vinegar on it and sprinkle the chopped eggs on top. Sometimes I sprinkle a little sugar on it. Usually though, I like it pretty natural.

Plain Ol' Poke Sallet
Serves 4.

1 pound poke
1 slab "white bacon" (salt pork), ¼
   inch thick; or 2 slices breakfast
   bacon; or 2 tablespoons butter

2 green onions, chopped
Salt

Rinse the poke very well to rid it of dirt, grass, or twigs. Be sure to cut off any roots on the bottom; they are poisonous. Place the leaves in a large pot and cover with water. Bring to a boil over medium-high heat and boil for 3 minutes. (You may need to use a wooden spoon to push the greens down into the water while boiling.) Drain. Repeat the process. Set the greens aside.

Fry the bacon to render the drippings—or melt the butter—in a skillet. Remove the meat from the skillet, leaving about 2 tablespoons of the drippings; if you are using breakfast bacon, reserve the meat. Sauté the green onions in the drippings over medium heat. While the onions are cooking, cut the greens into strips about ½ inch wide. Add them to the skillet and stir to mix and coat them with drippings. Cook for 6 to 10 minutes, until the greens are tender and seasoned but not mushy. Add salt to taste. Serve immediately, crumbling the reserved breakfast bacon over the top if you wish.

(Another way of finishing cooked poke is to whisk 3 or 4 fresh eggs and pour them over the sautéed poke, then continue cooking, stirring once or twice, until the eggs are set.)

Adapted from Butter Beans to Blackberries: Recipes from the Southern Garden, *by Ronni Lundy (North Point Press).*

Green Party

Julia Reed

When I got married, my friend Elaine Shannon sent me a stack of wonderful old Southern cookbooks, which prompted a lively e-mail correspondence about the food we each grew up eating. In one of her dispatches Elaine, who is from Georgia, reported that her grandmother had two biases about food: roast beef had to be cooked until it fell apart, and she couldn't abide collard greens. To her, Elaine wrote, "collards were worse than useless, and any house where they had been cooked had to be burned to the ground. She was a turnip-greens woman."

I didn't know it at the time, but my own mother, until recently, was one too. (She grew up in Nashville, a place described in *Nashville: Personality of a City* as "the turnip-greens and hog-jowl center of the universe." Alfred Leland Crabb writes, "These two were used in fitting combination . . . by 1810, and the townspeople's appetite for them has not waned.") I discovered her allegiance this year when I was appointed cook for Thanksgiving and called her from the produce aisle to ask how many people were coming so I'd be sure to get enough collards.

"Collards?" she roared with such disgust I almost dropped my cellphone. "They are tough and, well, just awful." I responded that I had recently eaten some of my friend Robert Carter's braised collards at the superlative Peninsula Grill in Charleston, South Carolina, and that they were some of the most delicious things I had ever tasted. She was unimpressed and told me that I had best bring home some turnip and mustard greens, too.

I had no idea there were such passionate greens factions. I guess since the South lost the war, its residents have to find things to argue about among themselves. I managed to negotiate a peace in my own family by quietly going on and making Carter's collards anyway, and now everybody's a convert.

I'm not so sure I could have convinced Elaine's grandmother, but at least she wouldn't have had to burn down the house.

In her day the only way people cooked greens was to boil them with a ham hock or a piece of slab bacon for hours until the house smelled so sour that it was indeed almost uninhabitable. Since collards are thicker than mustards or turnips, they cooked the longest, and the stench was the worst. But in Carter's recipe, they aren't boiled to death, but braised for just fifteen minutes or so in degreased ham stock. Not only is there no stench, but you get the great pork flavor that is such a complement to greens, without the fat.

In *The Gift of Southern Cooking* Scott Peacock writes that he grew up in Alabama, where they were "segregationists," favoring turnip greens over all others, while his co-author, Edna Lewis, who hails from Virginia, took the more democratic approach of mixing lots of greens up in one pot. Their recipe follows her tradition, cooking such "Southern" greens as mustard and turnip with more widely grown varieties like watercress, escarole, kale, and chard. They boil theirs, but, like Carter, they do it in degreased pork stock and only for fifteen to twenty minutes.

Inspired by her Jeffersonian attitude, I made that recipe the day after Thanksgiving, and I don't think I've ever seen my father so happy. Any time he gets to eat greens—of any kind—two days in a row, he considers himself extremely lucky, and he is not alone. In 1984, at the annual Collard Festival in Ayden, North Carolina, a man named C. Mort Horst set a world record by eating seven and a half pounds of collard greens in thirty minutes. (However, it was reported that he kept them down just long enough to claim his prize.) A year later, a woman named Colleen Bunting contributed to an anthology devoted to collards called *Leaves of Greens: The Collard Poems*. In one of the poems she addresses Elaine's grandmother's prejudice: "Some say collards don't smell so nice, / But eat them once, and you'll eat them twice."

An earlier poet named Cotton Noe wrote in 1912, "I have never tasted meat / Nor cabbage, corn nor beans / Nor fluid food one half as sweet / As that first mess of greens." The great Tony Joe White had a hit song in the late '60s called "Polk Salad Annie." Poke sallet is a wild green and hard to come by these days, but the song remains a personal favorite because of its chorus, which includes the immortal phrase " 'cause her momma was aworkin' on the chain gang."

All of these writers would have been referring to greens cooked the old-fashioned way and served with the classic accompaniments of pepper and cornbread, which is useful for dipping into the much-prized pot likker. Pot likker has plenty of nutrients; some people have been known to eat bowls of it by itself as a sort of soup. It also came in handy for Senator Huey P. Long as filibuster material. In *The Natural Superiority of Southern Politicians* David Leon Chandler quotes from some of Long's more memorable rants devoted to blocking various pieces of legislation from the Roosevelt White House. At one point the senator, who hailed, of course, from Louisiana, dictated the recipe for pot likker into the *Congressional Record*: "First let me tell the senators what pot liquor is. Pot liquor is the residue that remains from the commingling, heating and evaporation . . . anyway it is in the bottom of the pot." He went on to hold up a wastebasket to demonstrate how to properly put turnip greens into a pot, and followed up with instructions on how to make a Sazerac cocktail and oysters Rockefeller.

Pot likker is full of nutrients because the greens themselves are. Collards and their close relatives mustard greens and kale are excellent sources of calcium, iron, and vitamins A and C. (Mustards are also rich in thiamine and riboflavin.) Chard, a member of the beet family, has many of the same nutrients as its cruciferous cousins, plus lots of phosphorus. It also has a less pronounced flavor, so it's good to mix it with other, more peppery greens like mustards or watercress, and the French like to use it in gratins with eggs and milk and sometimes Gruyère or Parmesan. (See Daniel Boulud's wonderful gratin of chard with finely chopped mushrooms and his Swiss chard strudel in *Cooking with Daniel Boulud*.)

Greens also have almost no calories, so without the addition of the pork they are the perfect diet food. My best friend Jessica Brent has come up with a healthy way to prepare them that is so good it satisfies even die-hard traditionalists like my father. She puts three or four bunches of cleaned and stemmed mustard greens in a big pot with a half cup of olive oil and two cups of dry white wine (and salt to taste) and steams them until they are tender, about twenty minutes. The vegetarian chef Deborah Madison braises collards or turnip greens in brown butter and does a wonderful recipe of twelve cups of mixed greens sautéed in olive oil with garlic, a cup of chopped parsley, a cup of chopped cilantro, and two teaspoons each of paprika and ground cumin.

Some people, though, really miss their pork. In Afghanistan I met an American aid worker who grew kale in her garden there, and all she could talk about was how much better it would be if she could only get her hands on some bacon. For folks like her, I offer two recipes: Robert Carter's collards with country ham, and one for mustards braised with bacon from Donald Link at New Orleans's very fine Herbsaint. Kale could be used successfully in both.

Robert Carter's Braised Collard Greens
Serves 6.

1 pound collard greens, cleaned and stemmed	¼ cup (about ¾ ounce) thin strips of country ham
2 tablespoons olive oil	2 tablespoons minced shallot

⅓ cup aged sherry vinegar, or
more to taste
⅓ cup tupelo honey, or more to
taste
½ cup Smoked Pork Stock (recipe
follows)

Salt and freshly ground black
pepper to taste
¼ cup butter

Cut the greens into chiffonade about ½ inch wide and blanch in salted boiling water for 10 seconds. Drain, refresh in ice water, and squeeze dry.

Heat the oil in a large sauté pan over medium heat. Sauté the ham and shallot. Deglaze the pan with the vinegar and stir in the honey. Add the stock and bring to a simmer.

Add the greens and cook at a healthy simmer until tender, 10 to 15 minutes. Remove the greens to a bowl using a slotted spoon. Heat the cooking liquid and boil until it is reduced to about ¼ cup. Taste and adjust seasonings. (You may want to add a little more honey or vinegar.) Add the butter, stirring constantly until it melts. Return the greens to the pan and toss to coat.

Smoked Pork Stock
Makes about 9 cups.

2 pounds ham hocks; or 1 (2-pound) piece of Smithfield ham or other
cured country ham

Rinse the ham hocks or ham and put them in a large stockpot. Add 1 gallon water. Cook, covered, at a full simmer for at least 2 hours, or until the stock develops a strong flavor. Strain and discard the meat. (Or use the meat to make ham salad or to flavor soups or beans.)

Cool the stock completely and skim off all the fat. (Ham hocks will produce more fat.) The stock may be refrigerated for up to 1 week or frozen for 6 months.

Bacon-Braised Mustard Greens
Serves 4 to 6.

2 or 3 bunches of mustard greens
(about 3¾ pounds total; 16
cups trimmed)

8 ounces thickly sliced lean slab
bacon, diced
1 large onion, diced (2 cups)

1 teaspoon chopped garlic

1 teaspoon hot red pepper flakes

3 tablespoons sugar

½ cup apple cider vinegar

½ cup chicken stock

Salt and freshly ground black
    pepper to taste

Rinse the greens well. Cut out the stems and thick veins; tear the leaves into 4- or 5-inch pieces.

Cook the bacon in a large sauté pan until the fat starts to render and the bacon begins to brown. Add the onion, garlic, and red pepper flakes and sauté until the onion is soft, about 7 minutes. Add the sugar, vinegar, and stock. Heat to boiling, add the greens, and cook slowly, stirring often as the greens begin to release their own liquid. Reduce the heat and simmer the greens until tender, 10 to 20 minutes, stirring occasionally. Season with salt and pepper.

Adapted from Donald Link, Herbsaint Restaurant.

Something Special

Carroll Leggett

Cornmeal dumplings.

I was doggone near grown before I knew they were something special.

It was during my summer at East Carolina University. I signed up for an early-American lit course taught by an inspired teacher named Miss White—a frail, gentle lady who gave top grades for a minimum amount of work. I am sure "Miss White" had more of a name than that, but, honestly, I don't remember what it was.

So she will be just "Miss White," who wore dresses with lots of material—rayon, maybe—that hung to her ankles, and sensible shoes, and had long, bony arms that she flung about excitedly as she spoke. That summer she came by a set of store-bought teeth. Getting those dentures must have been a major investment for a teacher in a state institution that had not yet come into its own, and then she had to come to terms with them before a class of schoolmarms, who had to pass her course for recertification, a wide receiver from the football team who desperately needed an A in something, and me. For the first several days, I kept my hands semicupped and ready to shag them if, by chance, they happened to fly out and over my way. Better in my direction, though, than toward Number 23, who didn't catch a single pass the fall of '61.

That summer in Miss White's classroom, I sat on the front pew in fire-breathing Jonathan Edwards's seventeenth-century New England church, heard him preach "Sinners in the Hands of an Angry God," and learned what Hell is all about. And in her class one hot, muggy ECU morning (in Greenville, like London, it seemed to rain every day), I discovered that food I had considered quite ordinary—cornmeal dumplings—was really something extraordinary.

Miss White had visited farther Down East the weekend before—somewhere near Wilmington, I believe—and, as she explained it, had had a remarkable culinary experience. She opened the class by telling us of her mystical experience—she had eaten her fill of cornmeal dumplings, a dish that she thought was extinct. Fighting to keep her teeth firmly anchored in her excitement, she described each bite with such relish that you would have thought she had eaten the fabled orange soufflé at Washington's now extinct Lion d'Or.

The schoolmarms were duly reverential but didn't have the slightest idea what a cornmeal dumpling was. For Number 23, it didn't matter. He had kicked off his Weejuns and was dozing—visions of cheerleaders and pom poms dancing in his head, I suppose.

As for me, I had bolted upright and was saying to myself, "Great God a'mighty, cornmeal dumplings like my mother makes? This woman must be nuts."

As they say Down East, "Miss White weren't from here," but, glory, did she ever have a deep appreciation of a uniquely eastern–North Carolina food, the common cornmeal dumpling. Her description of the dinner was rapturous; her enthusiasm was infectious; and I left Miss White's class determined that someday I would tell the world about cornmeal dumplings myself, excite my listeners as she did me, and secure for the dumplings their rightful place in Southern culinary history. In doing so, I would ensure that the art of cooking cornmeal dumplings would not perish from eastern North Carolina, the South, the earth, and the universe.

Now is my chance.

So what the Hell is a "cornmeal dumpling"?

My theory, and mind you I am no scholar, is that cornmeal dumplings evolved out of necessity and an abundance of corn in agrarian, eastern North Carolina—the only place I have found them.

When farming in eastern North Carolina still was labor-intensive, you had to feed all the family and the hired help—"field hands," as they often were called. Folks who primed tobacco, plowed corn, stacked peanuts, and picked cotton could work up a voracious appetite. The phrase "eat like a field hand" had real meaning. When labor got tight, all things being equal, hands would choose the employer they thought would feed them best at dinner (noon). It was a challenge to cooks, many of whom labored over hot woodstoves well into the 1940s and even '50s.

My daddy made a living by doing a little farming and running a service station beside Highway 17 between Windsor and Williamston. Our house was just behind and to the side of it on a slight knoll, and it was Daddy's practice at noon, since there were no restaurants within miles, to invite salesmen or visitors to "have dinner" with him. Generally, my mother was not amused by his generous and hospitable spirit, but early on reconciled herself to the fact that peddlers, deliverymen, and assorted strangers might have their feet under her table.

"T.C. thought I was supposed to feed everybody who walked through the yard," Mother recalled in her old age. So she and Ada, the cook, couldn't think in portions. They had to think in pots-full.

Besides running a store and pumping Sinclair gasoline, Daddy also brokered cucumbers for a pickle company, picked peanuts for other farmers, and ran a grist mill on Saturdays, usually taking his pay in shares of the ground meal. I am told by my friend Judge Peter Hairston, who is now past ninety, that the miller usually kept 5 percent. Therefore, we always had plenty of fresh cornmeal. And we always had "hands" about the place—doing one thing or the other and indulging me—who had to be fed.

One—a slight, animated character named Bill Gillam—wandered in and out of our lives, showing up, working awhile, then disappearing for long periods of time. Daddy always gave him work, and he loved Mother's cooking. She said she always could tell when Bill was about to leave again, because he would hoard biscuits, stuffing them in his old coat pocket when he thought she wasn't looking. Guess they were his version of hardtack.

"T.C., you'd better be looking for help, because Bill will be gone soon." She was usually right.

Field work, especially plowing, was hot, dirty business, but Bill Gillam had his own way of coping with the Bertie County heat. Locals were used to Bill's antics, but strangers driving by often were startled to see Bill across the field, walking briskly behind "Little Mule" and plowing while wearing one of Mother's old, discarded print dresses.

The easiest way to feed Bill Gillam and the rest of the hands at dinner and send them back to the field with full bellies was to "boil the pot." Ada, who cooked and tended to me on the side, put a huge pot of water on the stove and dropped in pieces of seasoning meat—usually fatback or side meat. (Never shoulder or ham—that would be eating "too high on the hog.") After the meat boiled awhile and she could see a skim of grease on the top, she added collards, cabbage, or some other kind of greens. Later she put in potatoes and, last, the cornmeal dumplings, because they lay on top of everything in the pot, partially submerged in the pot likker, and half boiled and half steamed until done.

Dinner came out of that one pot. Each person got a piece of the seasoning meat, some greens, potatoes, and cornmeal dumplings. The servings were generous, and there was plenty more where that came from.

Making cornmeal dumplings sounds easy, but there is art to it. They are nothing more than plain (not self-rising) cornmeal, warm water (using the pot likker makes them tastier), salt, and a bit of flour to help "bind" the cornmeal if it is coarse-ground.

Ada would mix the ingredients and then pinch off enough to make a ball a little larger than a golf ball by rolling it around in the palm of her hand. The trick is to make it soft, but yet firm enough to hold together when you put it in the pot. Holding the dumpling in her palm, she would flatten it with her fingers until it was about two or three inches across and a half inch thick and lay it gently on top of the vegetables in the pot. When she had made enough dumplings to cover the boiling vegetables, she would put the lid on and let the dumplings simmer in the pot likker and steam until done.

I have concluded that cornmeal dumplings are unique to eastern North Carolina. Prove me wrong, if you will, because I've told you I'm no scholar. I have found a few people outside of the region who know what a cornmeal dumpling is. One is an older gentleman from Davidson County who is a vendor at the farmers' market in Winston-Salem.

"I know what you're talking about. My grandma made'm when the thrashers came. She would pat'm out and lay'm in the pot and when she took'm out and put'm on your plate, they had her fingerprints on top of'm." He smiled at the thought.

The fingerprints were the proof that he knew what he was talking about. Everyone who has eaten a cornmeal dumpling remembers, I hope with a smile like my friend, seeing the fingerprints of someone they loved impressed in the cornmeal.

"Where was your grandmother from?" I asked him. "Som'eres in eastern North Carolina, I believe," he replied.

Cornmeal dumplings were rarely served to company at our house, but they were a staple for us, and when my Aunt Stella was coming, she usually called ahead to make sure "Sister" had dumplings for her. I guess Mother figured, and rightly so, that dumplings were pretty common fare—an acquired taste—and hardly something anybody would write home about, except our Miss White, of course.

The one place where I've seen cornmeal dumplings in public, one might say, is at dinners on the grounds at Siloam Baptist Church in Bertie County. I called my cousin Joseph Leggett's widow, Mamie Clyde, who used to teach adult Sunday School every third Sunday at Siloam, and asked her about it.

Mamie Clyde said some folks at Siloam do still bring dumplings to church dinners, but mostly that's the old folks, and they are dying off fast. She named a couple of the Speller matriarchs from the area—distant cousins, I think. They pile up platters with fresh greens and arrange the dumplings around the side. Seems most young cooks just don't make them, and Mamie Clyde confessed that she never has especially liked them herself. She did say that

Cobb's Corner in the Williamston Holiday Inn—just across the Roanoke River from her place—serves cornmeal dumplings that locals think rate.

You have to cook something in the pot to make dumplings and not many people do slow cooking anymore, especially fresh greens, cabbage, or collards. I cook dumplings with string beans, butter beans, and field peas, too. The field peas turn the dumplings a sort of sick green color, but cooked in the pea likker, they absorb a lot of flavor and taste mighty good. I throw in a piece of country ham and some new potatoes, and I have a meal. Add fresh okra to give body and flavor to the pot likker, and you have the best country cooking imaginable. If you are worried about presentation, using yellow cornmeal will brighten up a platter.

My sister-in-law, Nancy Porter Leggett, in Greenville, makes delicious dumplings, and my Aunt Stella did before she died. But I don't know anybody else who does now besides my Bertie County cousins. My good friend Ron Grooms wasn't raised on them, but he took to them right off and can smell my dumplings cooking a mile away. He can eat a passel, too. You come to see me, and I'll fix you some.

Thank you for the "A" in American Lit, Miss White, and may you rest in peace. I know St. Peter was expecting you, knew your first name, traded you "birth teeth" for those ill-fitting, store-bought ones, and ushered you right to the kitchen table. For sure, they serve cornmeal dumplings up there, else, between you and me, what is Heaven for?

Cornbread in Buttermilk

Michael McFee

Smiling, he would slowly pour
the sour pale-yellow liquid
into our tallest glass

then pinch golden chunks
of the still-oven-warm wedges
into it until brimming,

stirring that thick tart soup
with an iced-tea spoon
he'd use to sip and nibble

down to the crumbly dregs
as if he were a boy again,
licking his chalky lips—

how could dad stomach it?
His emptied coated glass
gagged me when I sniffed.

Salt

Michael McFee

It was the taste their country tongues craved,
my parents and their parents and ancient kin:
not sour, not bitter, not funky umami,
not (like us, their spoiled television kids) sweet

but salt, pepper's twin, sugar's quiet cousin
seeping from fatback into simmered green beans
or pinched into steaming dishes by the cook
or flurried hungrily from our grainy shakers.

They'd even salt fruit, fat knife-sliced wedges
of an apple or (better) a juicy watermelon
on the picnic table, that seedy red meat sweaty
with melting crystals: summer in the mouth.

I'd pick up stray grains with a licked fingertip:
Who is the Morton Salt girl? Does she own a mine?
My mother just laughed and shook her head.
Our blood must have been briny as the Dead Sea.

There are five basic tastes in the human palate;
that salty umbrella girl never really existed—
now I know. Now I watch my sodium intake
as the doctors instruct. But how I crave it.

One day, like my parents and all their parents,
I'll become the salt of the earth, pale seasoning
waking the hidden flavor of the family plot
until I too lose my savor, forgotten underfoot.

Pork Skins

Michael McFee

Before we get down to the bacon,
the chops, the tenderest of loins,
long before slow conversions
to sausage or barbecue or country ham,

there's this pesky question of skin
to be gotten past somehow,
a greasy rind that must be dealt with:
and since our hungry ancestors

ate all of the pig but its squeal and tail,
somebody somewhere sometime
took sharp knife to scraped hide
and cut it into bite-sized rectangles

he cooked down then popped up,
curling salty parchments
he chewed and dryly swallowed,
pronouncing them (choking a bit) good:

and so they were, and so they still are,
these little fried clouds
filling my mouth with the crunchiest
hint of pig, a noisy meringue

that needs no sweet pie for flavor,
its shining airy cells dusting
my chest and fingers with pale gold,
the apotheosis of the epidermis.

Rinds

Fred Thompson

Growing up in Greensboro, North Carolina, I was one of the few kids on my block who actually knew about pork rinds, or pork skins, as more citified folks called them. Since I ate them with regularity, I was also an oddity until I could get these crackly, faintly greasy, wonderful treats in my buddies' mouths. Both my parents were raised on farms in eastern North Carolina, and pork rinds were the tortilla chips of their youth. Plus, my dad worked for Frito-Lay, so we had a steady supply of the company's Baken-ets Fried Pork Skins. Most Saturday nights, as my dad stoked up the grill to charcoal some steaks, he'd open a bag to accompany his Jack Daniel's. Not to leave us behind, Dad would fix limeades for my sister and me, and the sweet-tartness tasted great with the skins. But these were nothing like the pork rinds that we nibbled on at my grandmother's house.

To really appreciate pork rinds, and have them in their absolute glory, you really need to go to a hog killing. This ritual has been performed for centuries in rural America, and even though today most hogs are taken to a slaughter-house, a hog killing is much like an Amish barn-raising. It is about neighbors helping neighbors and having a good time in the process, a community event. While my dad left the farm when he returned from World War II, he had two brothers that continued the family traditions. Dad's heart was never too far from his roots, and our family visited often, especially during hog killing.

With the first cold snap of the year that is predicted to last several days, hogs become bacon, hams, pork chops, and such. The parts of the beast that were perishable, or that didn't yield great results in the smokehouse, were eaten by the folks gathered over a couple of days. This is when I first noticed the importance of the rind. The women did all the things that the men couldn't stomach, and all of the cooking. In no time after the noble critter met his end, a black washpot of hot lard was bubbling with the hog's skin inside, held down in the grease with boat oars. Fresh out of the fryer, and coated with a little salt, they found their way to the menfolk, who would crack open some moonshine from my uncle's still and celebrate the victory of man over beast.

As the processing went into the second day, pork rinds became the snack that all of us longed for. That second go-round with rinds was always paired with some homemade wine. Scuppernong, muscadine, peach, and strawberry wines were the most common. They cut through the lard and salt, and just as fruit makes a good glaze for a pork roast, the sweet wines enhanced the pork rinds' flavor.

Pork rinds are chic nowadays. The first President Bush took them to the White House. And the low-carb craze made them the snack of choice. The store-bought variety are good, but nothing compares to the real, unadulterated rinds you find in Ziploc bags on the counter of a Southern barbecue joint, which were probably smoked before they were fried. Many an old rural meat market or gas station will have rinds, a big bag for two dollars. You might have to ask for them, but check out the Hispanic markets and Cuban enclaves.

For me, a cool evening on the porch, a bottle of a California big-fruit Zinfandel, and these sheets of crackling pig magic may be the best way to escape back to when "urban" wasn't a word.

In food writing there is an established genre of articles with titles like "My Mama's _____ " or "Cooking _____ with Mamaw." The individual pieces are heartfelt; they can move the reader almost to tears when they're well written— and often when they're not. But reading a dozen of them more or less back to back produces a very different effect. After a while it takes a very unusual food or a very unusual mother to hold the reader's attention.

Late-Night Chitlins with Momma

Audrey Petty

Ours came frozen solid in a red plastic bucket. Butchered and packaged by Armour. Ten pounds in all. Cleaned, they'd reduce to much less, not even filling my mother's cast-iron pot.

We usually shared them in the wintertime, Momma and I. Negotiations regarding their appearance began weeks in advance, around the dinner table. My mother would tell my father she was considering fixing chitlins for the holidays. My father would groan, twist his mouth, and protest in vain.

"Why you got to be cooking them?"

My two sisters backed him up with exaggerated whimpers, calls for gas masks, threats to run away from home.

"I'll cook them next Saturday," Momma would say, suddenly matter-of-fact. Daddy would plan that next Saturday accordingly: out of the house for hours, in protest, then coming back with the Sunday papers, opening the living room windows wide before heading upstairs to read and watch football in his La-Z-Boy, behind a closed door.

My mother turned to me, smiling and winking. "You'll help me eat them, won't you?"

I nodded in time to my sisters' gagging noises. I stuck my tongue out at anyone who cared.

I was actually a pleaser, plagued by the classic middle-child complex. With the exception of fierce bickering and the occasional smack-down match with my sisters, dissent tended to make me nervous. Maybe my love of chitlins all began with me feeling sorry for my mother. In terms of labor and attention, cooking proper chitlins is as involved as cooking paella or fufu or risotto Milanese. Cleaning them took hours. Hours. So I'd keep Momma company while she rinsed the tangles of pig intestines in the basement sink. And I'd sit with her in the kitchen once they'd simmered down to something that needed watching. By that time, the house was filled with their sharp scent. "Potatoes will absorb the odor," Momma would insist during the negotiation phase. Everyone knew that *absorb* was too optimistic a word. The smell was pervasive—vinegary and slightly farmy. When one of my sisters would storm in, holding her nose, proclaiming her disgust, I'd puff out my bony chest and call her stupid.

I'd stay up late with Momma, and we'd eat the chitlins off of small saucers as a bedtime snack. For all their potent smell, their flavor was calm and subtle. They had a distinct taste; they didn't remind me of anything. Their texture was pleasing, tender but not soft. My mother's were never greasy, though I marveled at how the leftovers emerged from the fridge, congealed in a murky gelatin. Momma would warm up a few in a frying pan, and we'd douse them with hot sauce and put some cornbread on the side. They never failed to build a craving after the first bite. Precious, strange and furtive food, I longed for them even as I consumed them.

I am a first-generation Northerner. My mother was reared in a middle-class family in El Dorado, a boomtown in southern Arkansas; my father, in a coal-mining camp in Alabama. The two met and fell in love in the late '50s, while students at Talladega (a historically black college in Alabama), married, and then moved to Chicago. My sisters and I came of age in Hyde Park, at the time one of the city's few intentionally racially integrated neighborhoods. My dearest friend was Jewish (and white). We shared Sassoon jeans, watermelon Now and Laters, Judy Blume books, a mania for Shawn Cassidy, and plenty of secrets. My mother grew to love Karyn, but in the first days of our acquaintance, her anxieties about our closeness showed itself. She had lots of questions about how I was treated by the Levins. Were they kind? Had they made me eat the matzo ball soup? Did Karyn have other black friends? What about her parents? Gradually it emerged: she was trying to prepare me for the prospect of rejection, once recalling to me how little white girls in El Dorado customarily grew out of their friendships with little black girls. At the time, my only response was confused irritation. Karyn was my best friend.

As my sisters and I reached adolescence, my parents became more visibly concerned about our assimilated ways. While the Jackson 5's *ABC* had been our very first album and we still crowded around the television on Saturday afternoons to watch *Soul Train*, we also knew the entire content of "Bohemian Rhapsody." I even played air guitar. None of us showed much interest in attending a Talladega or a Howard or a Spelman. And, at seventeen, I fell for a boy with blond hair and blue eyes. He also fell for me. On more than one occasion, my sisters and I were summoned to a dialogue that began with my father's question: "Do you all know that you're black?" As adults, my sisters and I laugh about it now. My parents do too. But their uneasiness was real and deadly serious, and I'd sensed it for years. Maybe I ate chitlins to please Momma and Daddy.

My grandfathers died before I was born; my grandmothers, when I was quite young. I have missed their embraces, their indulgence, and seeing my face in theirs. I have especially missed their stories. The down-South tales my parents passed on to me and my sisters were rather limited. We'd hear about my uncle Booker T. setting the mean goat after my father or how my mother's nickname came to stick. We learned that my father, his siblings, and his cousins worked the family farm in Columbus, Mississippi, and how the sections of the farm had names. The Five Acre. The Melon Patch. The Prayer Cut. We learned that my mother's father was a high school principal and an avid fisherman, and that my mother's mother taught piano and Latin. My parents gave us their South as best they could: in their politesse and their hymns and verses. In their ways with words. They gave us only what they hoped would be nourishing: a sip of pot likker for our growing bodies and black-eyed peas for good luck at New Year's dinner.

I never saw anyone's chitlins but my family's when I was coming up. At least a few of my classmates must have eaten chitlins at home, but I, for one, never raised the subject. Chicago was a Great Migration city, where a wave of black folks had begun arriving in the early 1900s and had been redlined to black belts on the South and West Sides. That was my story and the story of so many of my childhood friends. We all had roots and people down South. And we ate like it, too. I remember red beans and rice at Kim Odoms's house, fried gizzards at LaTonya Mott's, and my junior-high business teacher eating take-out rib tips from Ribs n' Bibs during our fourth-period typing class. I remember hot sauce on everything. But chitlins were their own category of soul food. Chitlins were straight-up country. If you called someone country, you were calling that someone out. Country meant backwoods, backwards, barefoot, 'Bama-fied. K-U-N-T-R-E-E.

I once believed that my father didn't like chitlins because of how they smelled. That was his core complaint, but as I got older, I began to contemplate my father's childhood and I formulated a more complex theory. My father had eight brothers and sisters; his father was a miner and a preacher and his mother was a domestic worker (a fact I discovered only this year). I assumed that Daddy rejected chitlins as suffering food—a struggling people's inheritance. It wasn't until just this year that I finally learned the truth. "He had a bad plate of chitlins as a boy," my mother told me. "He never got over it."

When my mother cleaned our chitlins, she never failed to stress how important it was to clean them well. This meant washing them, one intestine at a time, with a mild salt water solution. "You don't just eat any old body's chitlins." I knew this rule by heart. I've eaten chitlins at the hands of my mother and my aunts Mary and Annie Bell (my father's sisters, who would occasionally make a pot when we'd all gather for Christmas). When a cafeteria called Soul by the Pound opened and quickly closed down on State Street, my mother was not at all surprised. "Black people don't live that way. Risk-taking for no reason at all. Flying from bungee cords or buying all-you-can-eat chitlins made by God knows who."

My mother has not cooked a pot of chitlins in fifteen years. Perhaps the ritual ended the year I lived in France and sorely missed Christmas with my family. My mother and I shared a good laugh when I told her about chitlins in France, how they called them andouillette de Lyon and topped them with dijon mustard. I smelled them before I saw them, in a Left Bank bistro. Et voilà!—there they were, on a nearby plate, wrapped tightly as sausage. I trusted the chef at Les Fontaines, but I couldn't imagine eating his chitlins. Not without my mother's company. And not without Louisiana-style hot sauce as generous seasoning.

As my mother has gotten used to the idea of me going public with our chitlin habit, she's reminded me that she cooked hers with onion and a green bell pepper or two, and she also splashed in cider vinegar to taste. I've learned how some people add white bread instead of potatoes for the odor. And I've shared Momma's excitement about the new technology in chitlin processing. "They really clean them now. More expensive, but you don't have to do all that work."

She doesn't have to ask me twice; we have a date for chitlins this December.

No Bones about It

Carol Penn-Romine

As a child I thought the real miracle of Jesus feeding the multitudes with five loaves and two fishes was that no one was reported to have choked on a fish bone. Given my abysmal track record of trying to eat fish, this was understandable.

Growing up in rural Tennessee, I always had the same experience: an adult would plop a hunk of fried crappie or trout onto my plate and say, "Watch out fer them bones, hon."

This admonition always accompanied fish, never pork chops or meatloaf. I heard more than enough horror stories of people swallowing the tiny, pinlike bones and getting them stuck in their throats. It didn't help that my older brother terrified me with tales of folks who had sprouted leaks like a lawn sprinkler. Summertime family gatherings filled me with boundless anxiety, for I grew up in a clean-your-plate-there-are-starving-children-in-Asia household in which dodging food was not an option.

"Y'all come on over for supper," Aunt Maisie's summons would arrive over the party line. "Uncle Beevo's caught a mess of catfish and we can't possibly eat 'em all." (Even as a small child, I realized there was something suspect about being obliged to eat a mess of something so it wouldn't go bad.) We'd arrive and find Uncle Beevo out back with a catfish suspended from a pine tree, a nail driven through its lower lip, peeling off its skin like you'd remove a tube sock.

"This is gonna make some mighty fine eatin'!" he'd proclaim as the slimy skin would reluctantly let go of the fish with a fwpp!, fly over his shoulder, and affix itself to the pickup truck. I'd fill up on hush puppies and brown-'n'-serve rolls and hold out for the peach cobbler.

And so my bias against fish followed me into adulthood and finally into culinary school, where I was forced to face my fear. While other students turned pale over the sweetbreads and raw oysters demanded by classical French training, I found myself growing weak at the prospect of handling whole, fresh fish, complete with every bone God had given them. But then came the moment that forever liberated me from my dread of coughing up a fish bone like a cat working on a hairball. I learned to fillet fish, the single most valuable skill I picked up in culinary school.

I would drive out to the massive Asian food market in Los Angeles's San Gabriel Valley and buy several whole fish at a time, trying to explain to the Fellow with No English behind the seafood counter through pantomime that I wanted him to leave the fish intact, not an easy message to convey through hand gestures alone. He would stand there blinking at me in front of a bank of aquariums filled with all manner of wriggling dinner possibilities, then finally shrug and wrap up my selections in newspapers that only he could read. I'd carry my purchases home and fillet, fillet, fillet, then line up the delicate portions of raw, boneless fish in neat rows across the cutting board and admire them like a kid arranging his collection of Matchbox cars. My fear was vanquished, and in its place blossomed a glowing admiration for what the French call "fruits of the sea."

In fact, I've now come to regard all types of fish as a single species, a remarkable creature that swims the waters of this planet, in every ocean, lake, and stream. It is an amazing and clever animal that sometimes tastes like halibut and at other times like sole or salmon. This creature is versatile, always in season, and plentiful throughout the world, with little risk of ever becoming overfished and endangered. It comes in all sizes and, most delightfully, it has no bones. This superb species of animal even has a crisp little French name. Fillet!

After all these years, I still don't understand why fish was routinely hacked into serving-size lengths, with everyone left to run the fishbone gauntlet. Why didn't Uncle Beevo simply fillet them? That way none of us—himself included—would have faced the prospect of an emergency-room visit after someone had tried to remove a bone from someone else's throat with tweezers and gotten them stuck down there too. Alas, all those who collectively made up Uncle Beevo are long gone, so there's no one left to ask.

I love returning home to our family farm in Tennessee, far from the frenzy of Los Angeles. My favorite meals still center around salt-cured smoked ham, pork barbecue, and, of course, the humble catfish. Mercifully, in the intervening years since I moved away, some compassionate missionaries have visited and taught folks there how to fillet. Forget the loaves and fishes—now, *that's* a miracle.

The Way of All Flesh

Hal Crowther

It was a lesson in humility, finally, a lesson in the way our highest and (so-called) lowest impulses are quartered so close together that you can't embrace the one without waking up the other.

A poet drove me to it. Duke's Jim Applewhite, intending no harm, read his poem "How to Fix a Pig" for an audience of writers and creative writing students at Virginia Commonwealth University in Richmond:

> When that vinegar and wood ashes
> smoke starts rising,
> And blowing in a blue wind over fields,
> It seems like even the broom straw
> Would get hungry.

Several hundred were charmed by the poem; one was undone. One had been carrying—burning in his pocket like a forbidden woman's phone number—a flyer for the World Invitational Rib Championship at the Virginia State Fairgrounds. It might have remained there until, like so many meaningful scraps of paper, its hour of possibility was past. But Applewhite's eloquence started a salivary chain reaction on a level far deeper than will or reason, in the region "under sleep," in Eliot's words, "where all the waters meet."

Without ever making a conscious decision to attend the World Invitational, I found myself at the fairground gates at 11:30 Saturday morning, the second car in line. The gates opened at noon.

I can't say what I expected. What I found, in a cloud of hickory smoke and airborne cholesterol no poet could properly honor, was like nothing so much as a red-light district in some foreign port where sailors come on shore leave.

If you know New Orleans's Bourbon Street or Baltimore's Strip you have a sense of it. There's no point in feigning innocence or indifference here. No one comes to window-shop in the Rib District. They know you when you come.

"Hey, step over here. This is the place, Mac."

"Just take a look, that's all."

"Free samples. One taste, sir!"

Beckoning from the shadows, framed by the flames of the cookfires, the rib runners are like pimps or Bourbon Street shills, like St. Anthony's demons. The Prince of Darkness is Cleveland's Lemeaud "Hot Sauce" Williams, a handsome black man wearing skintight black pants like a wet suit, wheedling seductively from a thick cloud of hickory smoke.

"It's hot, hot, hot," cackles Hot Sauce. "You like it hot, don't you, Jack? Hey, you in hog heaven now. High on the hog. Come get it while it's HOT."

Under Hot Sauce's awning, under Hot Sauce's beaming, crooning, proprietary scrutiny, I made short work of a half rack of baby back ribs smothered in a sweet, electric-red sauce with a deep jalapeño burn that operates on a five-second delay. Across the table, another big white man, with a big gold chain, was on his second rack.

"These are good, but try the Iowa tent," he offered, mopping hot sauce from his mustache. "Their mustard sauce is . . . unique."

Like lonely men in a brothel, passing in the hall, we exchange guilty glances and helpful tips but never look each other in the eye. Gluttons and lechers share the furtive camaraderie of the damned.

The glutton has one advantage, though: he can sample almost every attraction on the street. The Rib District's twenty alchemists, at their fires ringed around a sandy no-man's land of woodpiles and electric cables, were transmuting mere meat into a rainbow of delicacies I'd never dreamed of, in every color at the warm end of the spectrum, from near mahogany through burgundy to gold and hot pink. Smoked and soaked and purified by fire, the ribs become something almost mythic, more than flesh. "Meta-meat," a friend suggested. If Hot Sauce Williams was my Rubicon, the Australians were my Ides of March.

"Over here, myte—you. Free tyste. Don't pass this by."

The Aussie's greasy napkin cradled something that once was meat. It was beef, I think, no rib attached. He said it had been marinated, smoked, and cooked slowly for two days. The first bite awakened impulses from the collective unconscious, racial memories from bloodstained ancestors crouched by their cookfire a million years ago, while giant hyenas fought in the darkness for the castoff bones.

I'm a man of some willpower who rises at 6:30 to run three miles, who once lost ninety pounds, who lets years elapse between one piece of cheesecake and the next. I've been training to become a vegetarian, gradually and successfully eliminating red meat from my diet. My relapse in the Rib District naturally brought me shame. My body felt mutinous, my pulse sluggish, as if fat cells that recently belonged to hogs were building roadblocks and damming streams in my arteries. I looked at the demon rib chefs themselves, at 300-pound Billy Bones from Red Keg, Michigan, and 350-pound Ray Green, the swollen football lineman whose Sweet Meat Cooking Team from Euless, Texas, won the 1989 grand prize for Best Ribs in the World. The life of the flesh takes its toll.

But there's a wisdom beyond shame in the Rib District. A man must come to face his limitations. In spite of my hypochondria, in spite of my belief that animals have rights, I'll never talk that vegetarian rot again. It's like boasting that you're a good husband who would never cheat on his wife; as long as you know there's one woman who could always trip you up, you're nothing but a hypocrite blowing smoke.

Besides uniting the most vermilion of rednecks and the most soulful of soul brothers in a rare common passion, the invitational serves as a great leveler of all our pretensions. There's a sensitive side of me that objects to rib-eaters cheering for Robinson's Racing Pigs while the contestants' luckless littermates are reduced to charred bones a few feet away; it objects to Little Piggy puppet shows for kids with sauce and hot fat still staining their T-shirts. The World Invitational is spectacularly low-rent, a visual dialectic on the difference between "tastes good" and good taste, between tasty and tasteful.

But when did I start assuming that high-rent was where I belonged? In shame in the Rib District, I sensed that I was spending too much time with people who talk about houses and careers. And though I honestly enjoy them both, maybe too many evenings eating poached scallops and drinking Vouvray. You can't live on scallops and Vouvray any more than you can live on Mozart—the well-nourished spirit cries out for Mose Allison and B. B. King.

Worst of all, I had fallen into one of the self-worshiping heresies of the Reagan generation. I wasn't caught by the acquisitiveness, the hunger for wealth and possessions. What I'd absorbed was the accompanying myth that rich people don't ever have to die and give it all up. There's a connection between greed and fanatical good health, between earning more dollars you won't need and more days on earth you won't enjoy.

In the Rib District, a different voice whispers that you need meat; it whispers that you are meat. It whispers that the Lord wouldn't have made the meat so sweet and the swine so fine if he hadn't wanted us to enjoy them. Is that voice the Lord, the devil, or Hot Sauce Williams? Do I care? Ask me if I'd trade six months of my life for what I received at the World Invitational. If they were healthy, full-speed months in my fifties, maybe not. If they were medicated, couch-potato, TV-lounge months in my eighties, I'd turn them over in a heartbeat. If a long life is so great, why are more old people killing themselves than ever before? (A 25 percent national increase between 1981 and 1986.)

At this existential moment the Jukebox Naturals, the quintessential redneck band this event demanded, wailed their opening anthem across the fairgrounds:

It's later than you think, Son
Better have some fun
Time marches on
Soon you be dead and gone.

I took it seriously, as an omen. I'll go on running at 6:30 and avoiding butter. I'll never be as wide as Billy Bones or the Sweet Meat man mountain from Euless, Texas. But excommunicated by the vegans and shunned by the fastidious, I may grow bigger. Lord willing, I'll never again be a sanctimonious cholesterol cop, shaming others for their greasy diets. Moderation in all things, my late, meat-loving arteriosclerotic father counseled. Even moderation should be practiced in moderation. Show me the great poetry that celebrates the mortification of the flesh.

By the Silvery Shine of the Moon

Jim Myers

My first dance under the fiery light of moonshine was almost twenty years ago, near the Tennessee-Virginia border.

A friend who grew up in that pointed corner of the state dropped me off at a place where he swore they made the best moonshine he had ever tried. It was about a hundred yards off the narrow highway, down a gravel road. As he pulled away, peeling off to go get some gas, I stood there looking at a low trailer that hadn't been moved in likely forty years. Mists crawled down the holler, and I felt like I was participating in some strange rite of passage.

After a knock on the door, and no answer, I started to turn and go back to the main road to wait for my buddy. Then I heard a terse "Eyeah" from inside the trailer. I opened the door and found the vestiges of an old bar. Behind it stood a large man taken straight from Moonshine Central Casting. Mesh trucker hat. Dirty T-shirt. Overalls wrapped around a giant belly that sorely tested the tensile strength of the straps. I started to stammer and his giant paw reached behind the bar and pulled out a small fruit jar half-filled with diamond bright liquid.

It all felt so dangerously exciting, like a teenage boy buying his first box of condoms, and all I really just wanted to do was score some 'shine and get the hell out of there. That's when I nervously started to fumble with a wad of crumpled bills. And the man says, "Well, aren't you going to try it?"

"Oh yeah," I say, and suddenly I'm embarrassed at my nervousness, and now I'm sweating in the cool, dank air of that trailer. I slowly remove the lid and the smell braces my nostrils. Memories of rubbing alcohol and gauze swabs come to mind. It's an unpleasant, burning smell. I take a sip and it stings my lips. Then it feels like it's punching a hole in the back of my throat. It's terrible, and now all of a sudden I feel like I've been poisoned, and Oh!-

My!-God! what have I done, and I'm going to die right here in this trailer and how could I have been so stupid.

And all the while he's watching me. He's studying my reaction, which I clearly can't hide because the edges of tears are forming in my eyes. "Burns, don't it," he deadpans.

And I'm thinking, you're damned right it burns, and who on God's green earth drinks this stuff, or worse yet, who pays for it? That's what I'm thinking. But all I can do is just nod, and cough out a "Yeah, it burns."

There's an awkward pause and he pulls out another fruit jar, a full one, and puts it in front of me. With the slightest hint of a grin he says, "Now try mine."

Moonshine is indeed alive, fairly well, and more than present in this modern world. Not only is this mule not dead, but this mule still delivers a mighty kick.

Coupled with my earlier experience and motivated by Joe Dabney's work, I developed quite a thirst for homemade spirits. The more I learned, the more fascinated I became with the drink, and with the people behind the jars. And I tried to understand the reasons why, in this day of readily available liquor, moonshine still persists.

Central to the question is the tenet that people like to drink. And then, of course, there are people who like to cook, who will gladly cook the mash that will later soothe our savage thirsts. There's complexity and nuance when it comes to moonshine, and like other parts of our culture, it's not static. It evolves. Still, moonshine persists with a tenacity that defies all the cultural markers that tell us otherwise.

Where is it?

■ You find it today in tack rooms in barns, hidden under saddle blankets, waiting to take the chill off a long night with a sick horse.

■ You find it in trailer parks set among the kudzu, cheaper than bonded whiskey and closer than the closest wet county.

■ You find it in the glistening half-a-million-dollar tour buses of country music stars with pressed jeans and outlaw images.

■ You come upon moonshine in the homes of antique dealers who like to entertain their starched-collar friends and Yankee visitors with a dangerous taste of the past.

■ You find it in the dorm rooms of University of Tennessee

students who venture out to Cocke County for menu staples like "love juice" and marinated cherries.

- And—though the carefully controlled, billion-dollar image of NASCAR would like you think otherwise—moonshine persists at infield parties as the blessed communion wine that once fueled the dirt-track racers in the days of thunder.

Moonshine isn't dead, but it does seem to be killing off some of the old moonshiners. One old maker outside Senatobia, Mississippi, died in the summer heat of 2005. Another, near McMinnville, Tennessee, was recently taken, along with his recipe, by a heart attack.

Then, on a trip to L.A. (Lower Alabama), I arrived to the bad news that one of the most respected and prolific makers had suffered a massive stroke, two days before I was going to meet him. I think he knew it was coming, too, because his son had said the week before, "Daddy's ready to talk, and he ain't never talked to no one, including me." When I arrived, I got the bad news. The son realized I had traveled all that way for nothing, and, putting his hand on my shoulder, said to me, "Daddy cain't talk no more, he's mostly just propped up in bed drooling out the corner of his mouth." I tell the son how sorry I am, and after a short pause he says, "Well, you can come by and look at him if you want to," as if I'm some moonshine-watcher from National Geographic who wants to see the maker in his natural habitat.

But trips like that are never a loss. You ask around and you end up talking to other folks. That's how you learn about Slatts Blackwell, who back in the 1950s ran a tugboat up and down the Alabama River, picking up 'shine at night and carrying it as far away as New Orleans. You hear about how old Slatts had his boat rigged with explosives, and sure enough, when those federal boys tried to board him, he lit the fuse and swam to shore. The agents were quick enough to figure out what was happening, and luckily got off before that boat went up, and then went down.

You hear about a horse trainer near Grove Hill, Alabama, who just a few years ago ran a still underneath a trap door in the floor of a grain shack next to his hog pen. The underground room connected to a small passage that took you out through a hole on the edge of a hollow, allowing a quick escape when you heard the sound of boots shuffling above you.

You learn that Monroeville, the town that gave us Truman Capote and Harper Lee, is still no stranger to moonshine. They call it shinny, and during the humid doldrums, they make shinny-shakes with ice cream.

You talk to the sheriff up in Clay County, Tennessee, and he tells you about a man called "the Worm," who ran some fishing lodges up above Dale Hollow Lake. Lots of folks knew the Worm kept moonshine up there and that, if you knew who to ask, there might be some Mexican marijuana, too. But two men thought they just might break in and help themselves to some of the Worm's collection. Those boys liked it so much, they went back that same night for some more, and that's when the Worm answered with his shotgun. When deputies arrived they found two scared men, bleeding from birdshot, and silly drunk on 'shine. (That episode earned the Worm the ATF trifecta: multiple charges on alcohol, pot, and firearms.)

But it just about takes reports of gunfire to invoke the full weight of the federal agency that was established to control and tax illicit whiskey. Today they use the enforcement term of alcohol "diversion," meaning that the steady flow of liquor and money can't be diverted away from the government hands that demand their piece of the action.

Of course, there are those moonshiners looking to do nothing more than turn a buck. Let's not fool ourselves. There's still some bad stuff out there that will make your gums bleed and leave you hopping like a jake-legged dancer. Many of those makers who care more for profit than taste have turned their entrepreneurial drive to the modern scourge of methamphetamine. There's nothing warm and nostalgic about that, and it's taking a real human toll, seen especially at places like Vanderbilt Hospital's burn ward, where helicopters air-lift postexplosion victims, sometimes for their second and third visits. For the small-time makers, though, the U.S. attorney for middle Tennessee has only prosecuted one moonshiner in the past six years, and that was only because they found him in flagrante while investigating his cash crop of cannabis.

And just maybe, there's a softening of sorts. A few years ago, just south of Nashville in tony Williamson County, where land grabs and Starbucks have sent the price per acre soaring, a grand jury failed to return an indictment against Clifton "Greasy" Ladd. The sixty-three-year-old said he was sorry, cooperated fully, and claimed he made the moonshine (and grew the three marijuana plants) to give away to friends. You can't indict a man for being neighborly, now, can you?

Even President Bush found it in his heart to pardon Tennessean Kenneth Copley for some still-fired indiscretions forty years ago.

No, moonshine's not likely going anywhere anytime soon. As long as people like to drink it remains a fascination that lingers. Not only is it a palpable link to the past, it's a taste of independence, of defiance, and of man's god-given right to make liquor if he wants.

Moonshine's not dead. In 1994 a working still was found in metropolitan Nashville, just off busy Murphy Road. And about fifty miles west of the city, at a minimum-security correctional facility, investigators remain stymied about whether it was the guards or the inmates who were running a still found in an underground room covered with gravel and overgrown with weeds.

Yes, moonshine remains. And if you remain unconvinced, you need to meet Ralph Garner, a.k.a. Robin of Sherwood. Caught more than a dozen times over the past fifty years, he says, "When I'm not in the pen, I'll be making whiskey." Today, if he happens to be making it, he works with his nephew Potsie along the bluffs that mark the rise of the Cumberland Plateau in an area that is indeed called Sherwood Forest. Even the state ABC agent who's run Ralph behind bars can't help but speak of him with fondness. Field Supervisor Don Earle keeps one of Garner's seized stills on display. But that doesn't stop Robin Hood either, fired by a pride in making whiskey and the burn of mountain recalcitrance. "I can build a still cheaper than I could pay all that bond," says Garner. Unrepentant, he adds, "I'll be making whiskey till I die. They know that. Don knows that."

Moonshine is alive, and I think it's still well. Observers like Matt Rowley, who wrote a how-to tome, believe we may be entering an era where home distilling grows from an underground hobby to a legal right, with boutique concoctions made from recipes that honor quality. But there remain important stories to capture, people to meet who are aging links to our past, links that, when broken, will leave a terrible void.

That's why I was so excited to meet a seventy-eight-year-old gentleman named Zebbie in Moore County, Tennessee. By his own word he's not making moonshine or whoring anymore, not since he found "the light of the Lord Jesus Christ." But he'll talk, and his stories run seamlessly, with equal conviction, from preaching the gospel to tales of making love fourteen times in one day. I met him at his house, in a back corner of a hollow about fifty yards from the tree line that rises into the hills. I was greeted first by his menagerie of short-legged hounds, a funny-looking hybrid cross of beagles and red bones.

He's a handsome man, with gray hair slicked back and a pencil-thin mustache, waxed and curled. He grabbed my hand with his thick, bent fingers and led me inside. On a dresser by the door, shotgun and rifle shells were lined up neatly on a white towel. In between plaintive songs played on his old flat-top, he told his stories. Even though he's out of the business, he referred more than once to other operations, of stills "running right now," and that kind of revelation excited me.

He invited me to come back to see him for his birthday. I'll bring the moonshine so he can shake it and swirl it and tell me how the drop of the bead, a bead "as blue as indigo," shows the proof. I'll listen to him tell how they used to put the 'shine in a large pot and stir it up with a peach tree switch, cutting the high-proof hooch with branch water, stopping and checking it along the way until at last they got it down to the proof where they wanted, and put it in bottles and jugs to sell. That's what we'll talk about. Until then, I'll savor the taste of our last conversation.

"Well I oughta know a lot about it. I was raised on it. I followed my dad to the still right over across this mountain when I was about four, five years old. Him and my brother-in-law made whiskey in that one hole over thar for thirteen years, and never moved that still."

Downhome Places

Is There a Difference between Southern and Soul?

Shaun Chavis

Drive into Chapel Hill, North Carolina, on a typical March weekend, and you will see Franklin Street humming with students and alumni, many wearing Carolina sky blue. Spot a few people on street corners holding signs that read, "I need tickets," and you'll know the madness is only hours away from its peak. This is where Michael Jordan played basketball for Dean Smith, it's where legendary battles are fought on the hardwood every spring, and it's where pride bursts like the wide-open flowers of the dogwood trees.

The Tobacco Road rivalry is just one battle with Southern roots. You certainly don't have to drive far from Chapel Hill to walk across battlefields of the Civil War. And there is yet another ongoing fight with roots in the American South, one without territory or uniforms. It is a battle for identity and acknowledgment, both things any proud person would fight for. In October 2004 it erupted in Oxford, Mississippi, on the campus of Ole Miss, where writers, chefs, restaurateurs, historians, and other members of the Southern Foodways Alliance gathered to talk about race, food, and the South. Passions rose as people argued about Southern food and soul food, debating which cuisine came from where, who taught whom how to cook, and whether there ought to be just one name for both.

You might look at this scene and wonder why it exists. You'd rather go get some deviled eggs or fried chicken, and Southern or soul, as long as it tastes good and the sweet tea keeps comin' (or maybe you'd prefer Tennessee whiskey), who cares? Certainly there are better things to debate, and even so, you're not going to get into them now, not with that Jack Daniel's in your hand.

Dr. Jessica Harris is a member of the Southern Foodways Alliance, an author, and a culinary historian. She's got an explanation worth thinking about. "Your food is your heritage. We're passionate about it because in some cases we didn't get it when we were growing up. Certainly for African Americans, it is one of the few things we can claim, and need to claim, and we are discussing it. I think the passion comes from that. And certainly there is a subcutaneous discussion: somewhere in that room, someone's granddad owned someone else's granddad. All the more so, we grew it, cooked it, served it, cleaned up the waste it caused, and didn't always get to eat it. That's a big problem."

The notion of getting rid of either name, Southern or soul, is enough to offend, because you're not just talking about renaming food. "It's an emotional, valid, African American identity. It's an emotional trigger," said Nathalie Dupree, SFA member and cookbook author. "I think the emotionalism is that white people, too, think this is their food."

In Chapel Hill, one street over from Franklin, on Rosemary, is a restaurant Michael Jordan himself enjoyed, a place where food writer Craig Claiborne found a suitable plate of chitlins. It looks like a one-story house with a wrap-around porch filled with chairs and tables. A sign out front, shaped like a kettle, reads "Mama Dip's Traditional Country Cooking." On a typical weekend, you may circle a few times looking for a parking space, and then wait forty-five minutes for a table. Yet the lobby still fills with people of all ages and races, some wearing their Sunday best, some wearing Carolina colors, all dressed with devotion. A board lists the day's specials: fresh flounder, fresh oysters, collards, corn pudding, pineapple coconut cake, rum raisin bread pudding, and blueberry cobbler. At the bottom, in sky blue letters: "Go Heels!" A gray-haired white gentleman calls out, "There she is. Dip, come on out heah!" Out of the kitchen comes a black woman in her mid-seventies, six feet and one inch tall, wearing a brown and black dotted short-sleeve blouse. This is Mildred Council, also known as Mama Dip.

No one's ever uncomfortable at Dip's, because comfort is what you get on your plate: fried green tomatoes, served piping hot as any fried food should be, with the taste of the sun's warmth in them. The mac and cheese is so creamy, you want a spoon to gather all the sauce. A light sweetness kisses the yams. The biscuits are small by America's commercial super-sized standards, but what's size got to do with goodness? They are two inches across, if that, and just as high as they are wide, ideal carriers for butter or the savory juices on your plate. Peach cobbler in March is just as delicious as in August, because Council buys locally grown peaches and freezes them for meals like this. The cobbler's so good, you don't want to eat anything else for the rest of the day so you can savor its lingering flavors.

You'll find some of the same ingredients used at Magnolia Grill, a restaurant that's about a twenty-minute drive away in Durham. The simple green building gives little hint of what Ben and Karen Barker have built inside. Here, the couple interprets Southern food with the elegance and creative mix appropriate for fine dining, and they have done it to national acclaim. Just as you might feel warmly welcomed at Mama Dip's, you're no less cared for at Magnolia Grill. Paintings on the walls spill their colors into the room; warm lighting and thoughtfully placed tables create a space just as right for treating your mother on her birthday as it is for charming a lover. The Barkers give passionate attention to the food as well: Ben knows exactly what's on your plate before the waiter carries it to your table. "I hope to retire before I can't see all the food go away from me," he says.

Magnolia Grill's menu changes with the seasons. They cure pork themselves, and preserve locally grown produce for use in off-season months. At any time, you may find greens, ham hocks, grits, pork chops, or sweet potatoes mingling with other, more exotic flavors: twice-baked grits soufflé with wild and exotic mushroom ragout, aged sherry-mushroom emulsion and shaved confit foie gras, for example, or curried sweet potato bisque with shrimp, toasted coconut, and sultana chutney. For dessert, the Southern combination of peanut butter and bananas may be served in the form of a phyllo napoleon, with a milk chocolate sauce. Magnolia Grill is a place where, the Barkers are very aware, visiting Yankees may taste traditional Southern ingredients for the first time. "I guarantee you we're the only white-tablecloth restaurant in the Triangle that serves creasy greens," said Ben.

This corner of North Carolina is as much Ben Barker's home as it is Council's. Barker grew up a few hours' drive away. "My grandparents and my aunt and uncle ran a tobacco farm, and had sharecropped it with neighbors I grew up with who were black. . . . I was mostly taken care of, when I would stay with them, by Louise, who was the black lady that minded me like a ma. But I never really thought that there was any difference in the food that we ate, that she fixed or that my aunt fixed or that my grandmother fixed. Their style of cooking was the same, the ingredients that they chose to use were the same."

Move the foie gras aside, and you'll see Magnolia Grill and Mama Dip's share some roots. Both Ben Barker and Council draw on common history and flavors to create their cuisines. Barker's food is Southern, and some call Council's food soul. She, however, doesn't, not even in her cookbook, *Mama Dip's Kitchen*. "When the cookbook came out, I called the food country cooking, and then when people started coming in, especially if they were black, they would call it soul food, and I was telling them that my cooking is country cooking because I didn't hear about soul food until in the '60s, during the demonstrations. Blacks came to be more visible on television and out in the world. That's when they started calling it soul food. But our food, the food I cook is just country, because I cook fresh food, fresh vegetables."

You'd be right to think there's not much culinary difference between Southern food and soul food. Pick up a copy of Nathalie Dupree's *New Southern Cooking*, and you'll find recipes for black-eyed peas with duck giblets, old-style greens and pot likker, fried green tomatoes, and peach cobbler. Thumb through *Sylvia's Soul Food* by Harlem restaurateur Sylvia Woods, and there are recipes for black-eyed peas and rice, collard greens with cornmeal dumplings, fried green tomatoes, and peach cobbler. Or consider the works of Edna Lewis, the Virginia-reared granddaughter of slaves who treated New York to her culinary talent first in the 1940s at Cafe Nicholson. Her published recipes include black-eyed peas in tomato and onion sauce, greens, fried tomatoes, and peach cobbler. (Lewis, by the way, didn't use the term *soul food* in her books.)

People started using the term *soul food* in the '60s, when black Americans were redefining themselves. Men were "soul brothers," women were "soul sisters," and they grooved to "soul music." New Jersey poet and civil rights activist Amiri Baraka is likely the first person to put the words "soul food" into print. In 1962, he wrote an essay addressing another writer's criticism that the problem with "Negroes" in America was that they had no language of their own and no characteristic cuisine—both elements of cultural identity. "This to me is the deepest stroke, the unkindest cut, of oppression," Baraka wrote, and he pointed out items brought to America from Africa, such as watermelon. He listed the foods on the black American table: sweet potato pies, greens, hoppin' John, hush puppies, and fish sandwiches, all "soul food." Baraka didn't define a cuisine as much as he exposed an element of black American identity, an identity much needed as an anchor during a time when blacks fought through a social storm to gain civil rights.

Just as people used the term *soul* to define themselves and create a community of acceptance and belonging, today groups of people who call themselves "neo-Confederates" are rallying around their own definition of "Southern": a culture they see as primarily "Anglo-Celtic." Their adopted language is the king's English, and their slogan is "heritage, not hate"—a message many don't buy. "It's by its nature hateful because it's exclusive," said John T. Edge, director of the Southern Foodways Alliance. "They use the term *Southern culture* and mean white Southern culture. Southern culture is a multiracial culture. When you talk about the South, you are, whether you know it or not, talking about white folks and black folks, Native Americans, and many other ethnicities. I think a term like *Southern food* embraces it all."

Harris, author of *The Welcome Table: African American Heritage Cooking*, is not sure she likes the term *soul food*. "Most African Americans in my experience did not say, 'I'm going to get some soul food' until the '60s," she said. "Bottom line, it was dinner. All cultures have food for the soul, and this is just the food for the soul for African Americans." To Harris, the term *Southern* can also fit. "All soul food is Southern, but not all Southern is soul food, in the sense that most African American food, in the narrow sense, has its genesis in the South. . . . There are dishes in the Southern culinary lexicon that are not soul food at all—country captain, for example."

It isn't as if the declaration of a cuisine called "soul food" in the '60s took its dishes off anyone else's table, nor has it kicked anyone out of the kitchen. Fighting over which food is mine and not yours isn't the point of the effort to link food and heritage—doing so, to many, is futile. Council, for example, sees her cuisine as American (though you could also call it Southern, soul, or country). "I don't like just to say it's just for blacks, that it represents blacks," Council said. "It's everybody's food. I wouldn't want to say that they took it away from us, like they took a lot of things, but they want to use it, use it."

"The better point made is that there is a debt of acknowledgment that white Southerners owe to black Southerners," said Edge. "It is a debt of acknowledgment that has not been erased. That's a different matter than saying, 'this food is black folks' food' or 'this food is white folks' food.'"

Ben Barker knows his taste for creasy greens came from his black neighbor Louise, and it's that memory, that flavor, he consciously tries to preserve. "I think it's important to try and keep doing that kind of cooking. Now, because I'm a white guy cooking it, does that mean it's not soul food? Maybe. But Louise used to cook that for me, because she'd gather the greens up on the way over to my aunt's house and she'd fix up creasy greens for lunch. I don't ever remember my aunt cooking creasy greens."

Barker's experience is one example of why it is so difficult to distinguish two separate cuisines. The food, and the people, are commingled. "There is so much integration of foods and attitudes in the South, which perhaps people from the North don't really realize," said Dupree. "In the South, for all of its flaws and difficulties, within the food there has been an enormous cross-over, not just from African Americans working in white homes, but it's from intermarriage, it's from people having farms next to each other. Everything here has been intertwined, which is what has made this a distinct culture."

Economy is also a common element in the foods of the South: what people ate depended more upon resources than ethnicity. "When I talk to some people, they think somebody called it soul food because we like food with the bones in it," Council said. "We like fish with the bones, we like our pieces of meat with the bones, we like the pig tails, we like the neck bones. What happened is that it was affordable. We're always getting the big packet of pork chops because it's cheaper. It's got more bones in it and it comes from the economy part of the roast, you understand. . . . It was about economy, you know, what we could afford. It wasn't about [race], because white people bought those big things too, and they ate them."

Barker agreed, again drawing on his family experience. "I think what most distinguishes [them] in general from an intellectual perspective is the choice of protein that you might use because of the cost of it. But because both families were farm families, the proteins that we ate were yard chickens and hog products that they raised themselves."

"The core is, these are the foods of poverty," said Edge. "Granted, African Americans have suffered more at the hands of poverty than perhaps many whites. There's a heck of a lot of poor white folks out there that are gnawing on pork chop bones and eating the hell out of chitlins, too."

Culinary historians have traced specific elements in Southern cuisine to their African roots. Okra, watermelon, peanuts, pumpkin, and black-eyed peas, for example, came to the United States from Africa. Techniques such as deep frying, seasoning food with small pieces of smoked meats, and making fritters all have some element of Africa in them.

Dig a little deeper, and you'll discover that peanuts were indigenous to South America and introduced to Africa by Portuguese explorers. The slave trade brought peanuts to North America. The use of nuts and seeds as a thickening agent is also an idea from Africa, but the Arabs have used ground almonds to thicken sauces since the thirteenth century and perhaps earlier. Is it possible the Arabs passed that practice on to others as they traveled through north Africa? Some scholars believe black-eyed peas may have come to Africa from Asia. And while we get the word *yam* from Africa, the actual vegetable never made the Atlantic crossing. The American sweet potato became the yam's substitute.

Truth be told, throughout history, someone's always taken ideas from someone else's kitchen. We still do it.

"You see this over and over again," Dupree said. "You go to an Afghani restaurant and you love the food. And then you get a recipe of something you liked, but you may not have all the ingredients, so you substitute. So then, whose recipe is it? Is it Afghani? Is it yours? The English have always cooked with small pieces of meat and greens. Turnips and rutabagas proliferate there. How do you put your finger on this? So then, you have to ask yourself, why do you want to put your finger on this? The answer is because African Americans have been robbed."

This is why a battle exists. "There are no people who have been less embraced, with the possible exception of Indians, than African Americans," said

Jessica Harris. "American food is changing like the country is changing. There are all sorts of things that are becoming American—pizza is American, sushi is becoming virtually American, mojitos. I think the slowness with which the food of African Americans has been accepted speaks to the slowness with which the people are being accepted. Go to a Barnes and Noble and look at the cookbooks—shelves and shelves of Chinese cookbooks, Cuban cookbooks, just about everything outnumbers African American cookbooks."

Chef Barker also senses a lag in racial reconciliation. "I feel like we've come a long way, and not nearly the way we should have come by now," he said. "It seems like to me there was such tremendous progress in the '60s, and then people became apathetic about what it takes to make us a whole country."

The very language used to describe Southern and soul food is a hurdle on the path to harmony, simply because of the politics behind the words. The term *soul food* gives African American heritage an acknowledgment it hasn't fully received, yet signals white Americans are excluded. *Southern* is used by some to encompass a multiethnic culture, and by others as a racist code word. "The South has a uniquely troubled history," said Edge. "Even those of us who don't spend a lot of time pondering that, it's kind of subcutaneous. It's still a part of our experience. I think we realize—some of us reluctantly so—how our food is weighted with this legacy."

If food is a point of contention, it can also be an agent of unity. The many culinary professionals who attend the Southern Foodways Alliance's symposia know this firsthand: they take raw ingredients, apply culinary skill, serve, and watch food build relationships and create lifelong memories. It's as awesome as any force of nature. Many in this crowd believe racial reconciliation will happen around the table, and, in fact, they left Ole Miss last October with a charge to start dialogues around tables in their own communities. "I think it will happen through food, intermarriage—let's face it, it is happening," said Dupree. "Society is becoming accepting of things that my generation couldn't, things that are very natural and normal. I think food is just one aspect of it. If you can come to my house and enjoy the food and be comfortable, then I think that we have a better chance of having a good conversation."

"I think the simple act of breaking bread together, of that kind of communion in not necessarily the religious sense but in the humanistic sense—I think that offers opportunities for all," said Edge. "The most intimate act we engage in every single day is eating, and it fosters bonds and breaks down some of those chasms."

"I can feel it," Council agrees. "Since the five years I've been out there, just the five years since I've put the cookbook out, this is what I feel all over the country." She likely knows this from daily experience. Mama Dip walks

through the dining room of her restaurant, going from table to table, often sitting down right next to her customers. "How y'all doin' over here?"
she says. The noise is thick: there is clinking of dishes and silverware from
the kitchen and a moderate roar of conversation. Now and then you hear
Council's laughter above it all. Sometimes she laughs so hard, she takes her
glasses off and wipes a tear from her eye. Council has long belonged to this
community. In the '40s and '50s, she cooked on campus and for local families.
Since she opened her restaurant in 1976, every North Carolina governor and
UNC–Chapel Hill chancellor has dined at her tables. It has taken her decades
to battle her way from being a domestic worker hidden behind kitchen doors
to being a businesswoman whose contributions are honored and sought after.
Even after this long time, she may have to confront stereotypes each time a
stranger to Mama Dip's comes in to eat. "I have a lot of white customers and
I have black customers," Council said. "I didn't want them to come here, 'let's
go get some soul food at Mama Dip's.' I want to be an American woman. You
understand? That's what I want to be."

This is an edited and shortened transcript of an address—a talk, really—given at the Southern Foodways Alliance symposium "Southern Food in Black and White" in 2004. It has been left informal, as it was delivered.

Movement Food

Bernard Lafayette

I want first of all to say, "Good afternoon," so you can tell I'm from the South. We always greet each other—"good morning," "good afternoon," you know.

When they invited me to come and speak to this conference, I said, "*Race* and *food*?" I could not imagine what y'all were doing. They said, "Well, you know, one unique thing about you is that you've been in jail twenty-seven times, so you could tell us about food in jail." So I guess I can make a unique contribution, after all.

When I was in the fourth grade I went up north with my parents. They all migrated from Tampa, Florida, to Philadelphia right after the war. I went to an integrated school. I remember one time this white boy hauled off and socked this black boy and I said, "Good Lord." Then another white guy stepped up and hit the white guy. And then a black one stepped up and hit the white guy for hitting the white guy. I was traumatized. The whole world went topsy-turvy.

Well, long story short, I got involved in the gangs and stuff like that and a couple of fellows I was with got shot and killed, so they sent me back south. They said, "Well, you have to stay with your grandmother and she's going to take care of you," but she was bedridden. So they said, "This is a good reason you should go, because you're going to take care of her," and so I became a nurse at the age of twelve, and it was really quite an experience because she taught me how to cook from the bedside. I also grew the food, because we had a victory garden from World War II. So instead of grandmother taking care of me I took care of grandmother, and she taught me how to take care of her. That's what happened. She had a big ol' two-story house with wrap-around outside porches and all that—that's what I grew up in and went back to.

I'm a good cook. I don't have any recipes. I just know how much to put in there—that kind of thing. I can cook possum. We call it "dressing" possum—you dress him up. A lot of folks don't know what they're eating and it's all right until it's over.

I can make biscuits, too. My grandma used to call them cat-heads and that made it difficult for me to eat, but they tasted so good I forgot about it. I can give you the recipe for biscuits, and also pie crusts, and hoe cake is what we used to do. And by the way, I cooked on a woodstove. I had to cut the wood and make sure I stoked the thing and all that—I had to do the whole thing.

Collard greens, cornbread, and cornbread cush—y'all know about cornbread cush, don't you? You know how you make your cornbread for dinner? Well, sometimes you don't eat all of it because you always make enough in case somebody comes around later on—you know, you feed everybody. That's what we do in the South. We always have extra. Cush is a breakfast dish. What you do is take the cold cornbread and crumble it up and just make mush out of it—put some more water in it and bring it back to the dough stage. And you get a great big ol' black skillet and pour some lard or bacon grease in there. We saved bacon grease; that's the best thing to cook it in. We always kept a coffee can full of bacon grease. You cut up some onions in that cornbread mush and then put it right in the pan and stir it up. Put some black pepper and salt in there. That's cornbread cush—leftovers.

We didn't throw away anything. We even took the leftovers of the hog and made soap. You ever heard of lye soap? Yeah, we cooked soap. Y'all talk about cooking: we had a pot outside in the backyard and we put in all kinds of leftover hog meat. You understand what I'm talking about?

Y'all probably never had any good ol' hog snoots, have you? And chicken feet and rice, y'all had that? What about fish head and rice? Now y'all from New Orleans, I know y'all got to had some fish-head rice. Y'all jiving—you know, that's all right, but I know. Another thing you should know is, I know black folk. And one time in Louisiana you had about two thousand black folks who went in one year across the color line and became white. They moved north. I see a couple of them in here now. But I ain't going to say nothing. Hey, your secret is good with me. No, if you're making it all right, that's cool.

We had a situation when we were demonstrating in Nashville. It moved fast in Nashville. We got the lunch counters desegregated in three months and then we went on to the restaurants. Then we had thirteen nights of demonstrations and desegregated all the movie theaters downtown. We were hot. We were hot. So when the Freedom Riders got in trouble down in Alabama and they blew up the bus down in Anniston and set it afire and tried to smoke the people out . . . They tried to cook the people. Did you know they put the bus on fire and then held the door so the people would get roasted? Those folks were serious down in Alabama. Yeah. So they said, "Well, let's have a cooling-off period"—Attorney General Robert Kennedy and the head of CORE, James

Foreman, and all of them—"because people are going to get killed." Those of us from Nashville said, "Things have been cold too long; if they're hot then let's go." So we rode on through the smoke into Mississippi.

Now I'm going to talk about some food in jail, but you know what happened with the Freedom Riders? I mean, some of y'all are old enough to remember, but for the young people I have to share this with you: they would not allow white people to sit in the back of the bus. I know it sounds strange, but it was a law.

Now just because a person was white—I mean, it wasn't their fault; I mean, why treat them that way? That was not right. Those little white kids sometimes used to try to run to the back of the bus and the parents would snatch them—"Come on, sit back up here." They said, "What? We want . . ." "No; you sit up here." I remember when I was growing up they had that situation. And guess what: all the black folks used to be able to see all the white folks because they were all sitting in front. Did y'all know that? We used to watch them. We used to hit each other—"Look at that!"

And you know what? Now, some of y'all from the North—those from the South don't know about this—but they got automobiles now where you can press a button and it heats up your seat. Did you know that? Yeah, it's new. They just came out with it. But you see what you ain't understanding is that we had hot seats all the time. That back seat—that's where the motor was. Why do you think black folks tripped over each other running to the back? It was nice and warm and toasty. Sure, you know that long seat back there? That was our couch. It was reserved for black only. When we had to ride from one place to another, we had a couch. We used to stretch out and take a nap back there.

In the Movement you had to know where you were going first—your destination. Decide on that, and then decide what you're going to do while you're on your way, so you have to act your way into thinking rather than thinking your way into acting. Sometimes you do that when you cook. The Freedom Rides started out in Washington the first week of May of 1961. The destination was New Orleans. We never made it to New Orleans, but that's why I got on the Ride in the first place. I was trying to get to New Orleans.

I remember my first entrance into Mississippi. As we crossed the state line, I shall never forget, the first sign I saw was a huge billboard that said, "Welcome to Mississippi, the Magnolia State," and a beautiful white magnolia blossom. "Welcome." And the next sign I saw said, "Prepare to Meet Thy God." But I came on down, you know, because you only got one life to live and the greatest fear is to die over some foolishness. Martin Luther King said that unless you found something in life so dear and precious and valuable that you were willing to die for it you had yet to live. Martin Luther King had a method about this thing—an incredible philosophy about how you defeat your opponents and people who would be your enemies by making them your friends. The goal was to win people over, so we experimented with that, and what happened was we got into the city jail in Jackson, Mississippi. I'll never forget.

Now the food was good. I don't care what nobody say, the food was good. We enjoyed it. They had some good ol' Southern cooking—hot biscuits. We kept asking for biscuits, and they gave us extra biscuits. One fellow made a chess set out of them. Yeah, what he did was wet the biscuits and remold them. Then you know the blank page in front of the Gideon Bible? He took that out and made a chessboard out of it. He still has that chess set.

We were actually in four jails in Mississippi. First the city jail, and then the county jail, and we ended up in Raymond, Mississippi, in a penal farm. There was a girl on that Freedom Ride, and they slapped her because she wouldn't say "yes, sir" or "no, sir." She was a little thing, about ninety-eight pounds. They slapped that girl—boy, we got so mad. We said, "Everybody is going to get whipped because we're not going to say 'yes, sir' and 'no, sir.'" Only two of us didn't get whipped. One was Leroy Wright, who was very aggressive—a big, tall guy. The only reason they let him go on the Freedom Ride was because I went with him—I trained policemen and all that kind of stuff. He got in there and acted up and scared the folks so bad they put him back in the cell. I was supposed to be his mentor; so how was I going to go in there and not get beaten? I came up with a very ingenious plan, and I will share this with you. They brought me in, set me in front of the desk; the warden was on the other side, and behind us they had about five Mississippi deputy sheriffs with blackjacks. They asked you a question, and if you didn't say "yes, sir" or "no, sir," they started beating your head. Blood was all over the floor when I got there, so you know—it was serious. So they asked me, "Are you from Nashville?" and I said, "I am from Nashville." They said, "Have you ever been in the army or military?" I said, "I've never been in the army or military." Every question they asked me I just repeated without saying "yes, sir" or "no, sir." They got thoroughly confused, so they said, "Get your black so-and-so out of here, you smartass"—you know, N-word type thing. So I said, "Well I'm sorry; I apologize." They ran me back to my cell, and when my friends saw I didn't get beaten, they said, "Well, what did you do? You must have said 'yes, sir' or 'no, sir.'" I said, "No, I didn't, either." I told them what I'd said, and they said, "Why didn't you tell us that?"

Then we moved from there on over to Parchman [penitentiary]. By the time we got to Parchman, we were gourmets. Yeah. We had fresh food. I knew the biscuits were made with buttermilk. Buttermilk biscuits, and we had grits, hot grits in the morning. They had built a brand-new maximum-security unit at Parchman and that's where they housed all of us. We were the first ones that ever used that facility. It was great. We were first class, you know. All the utensils were brand new—the coffee pot and everything else—everything. So we tried to show our appreciation, you know, by eating up all the food.

Now, if you're not getting along with those people who are in charge of you, you don't know what you are eating. I'm not talking about the cooks—the cooks were black—but I'm talking about those folks who brought it to you. What happened between the kitchen and the cell? So you got to be mindful of how you relate to people. So guess what we did? We made friends with the folk who brought us the food. We sang and we made up songs about the people themselves and all these jailers and the sheriff, the deputy sheriffs. Oh no, we didn't go around there acting all this black power and all that—no, not when you're in jail and you've got to get some food. That's the wrong time. There's a time and place for everything, you know—yes, sir. So we told them how nice they were. We called them "professor" because we were students. We honored them, and they gave us all the food we wanted.

Now some people don't believe this, but they brought us ice cream at night. You know, ice cream used to come in those little pints? Yeah. The jailer in Jackson would send a trusty out to get some ice cream. We were his friends, so he'd bring ice cream for us. What the trusty would do is take the ice cream and put it in a mop bucket with the wheels on it and then throw the mop on top and then roll it past all the other cells until he got down to us, flip the mop off, and then we'd reach in and get the ice cream. And we'd use the little cardboard top as a spoon. We had ice cream every night. Mississippi jail—you got to know how to work it.

But the real deal was this: he had a daughter who was in the eleventh grade, and he wanted to get his daughter in college. He had not had the benefit of going to college, and as a father he didn't know what to do. We were college students, so we would tell him how to apply and how to get the money and how to send off and get all that kind of stuff for these colleges. So it was a trade-off—he gave what he could give; he gave us ice cream. And I can tell you now that when we got ready to leave the jail he looked like he was losing his best friends. In fact, I remember the very words; he said, "Y'all come back to see me, hear?" And our response was the Southern one—"uh-hm; uh-hm, yeah, hmm."

There's another thing about food that I want to share and that is the hunger strike. In Mississippi they took Dion Diamond and put him in solitary confinement because he was very—you might say *aggressive*. He believed in nonviolence, but you know some people's mouths might be very annoying. We said, "Go get him [out]," and they wouldn't, so we went on a hunger strike—refused to eat. About the fifth day, Jim Bevel said, "I'm going to eat in the morning." Oh, people got upset with him because he was going to break the hunger strike, but he just ignored them. I always knew that this was a man of principle. He was very determined—very strong.

I'll tell you the kind of person he is before I finish that story. He grew up in Itta Bena, Mississippi. (We used to call it "itty-bitty.") He was one of seventeen children and his father became ill, and he was on his bed expecting to die. He sent for all the children. And Bevel wouldn't go. That was one of the times I really got angry with him. I mean, his father trying to die and, no, he's not going to go see him. I mean that's low-down. I said, "This is really just inconsiderate and disrespectful." You know what happened? Yep, about a month later the old man came down to see Bevel. Bevel said, "If I had gone up there with the rest of the children he would have just smiled and died."

So this is the guy who broke the hunger strike and what we discovered was this: there was a student in jail who had an ulcer and didn't want to let people know about his health problem. So he was suffering more than anybody else. And Bevel was strong enough to take the criticism and the ridicule for breaking the hunger strike so that somebody else could eat.

The only other experience I want to share with you about food in jail was at Parchman when they ran out of coffee. They got white potatoes and put them in the oven and parched them to the point they got brown, dark brown. And then they soaked them in a great big old vat of hot water until the water turned brown, dark brown. And that's what we drank for coffee. Put some sugar in there and some milk, how do you know? And, by the way, when we were in the county jail, they taught us how to make beer out of potatoes—white potatoes, uh-hm. You ferment white potatoes and you make beer, just the way the Pilgrims made liquor out of corn.

Now I'm going to give you a confession, okay? We had Freedom Houses where the civil rights workers would stay, but I never stayed at the Freedom Houses because the girls in the Movement couldn't cook. (Make sure the car is waiting out there when I get ready to leave.) But they were too busy—I mean, I understand. A lot of them weren't into that kind of thing, cooking stuff. They were just like the fellows and getting in jail and Freedom Rides. . . . I always found me a nice, quiet older family, you know, like Miss Logan in Jackson, Mississippi, and in Selma, Alabama, I stayed with Miss Robinson. These people practically adopted me, so I had a kitchen where I could cook. I'd be the houseboy and clean up and rake the yard and everything. So I had a nice quiet place to go home every night. In the Freedom House they used to stay up all night making noise, and you know I was a little Baptist preacher—eighteen-, nineteen-year-old preacher—so you know I couldn't be caught up in stuff like that.

You know what happened one time? We were in the midst of the Selma march and we got a phone call that there were some Southern white church people who were going to come and march in Selma. They didn't want any local people to join them—this was their own thing. They had a prayer meeting and they came and marched by themselves in support of the Movement. It was the strangest thing. They were still segregated, but they were for the right to vote.

But y'all should also know this. When the bus was burned in Anniston, Alabama, and someone was trying to hold the door to keep the people from getting off the buses, a white girl ran out because the bus was right in front of her house, and she got water for all the people who were choking—a little white girl. And there were whites who ran up and forced the other people to move out the way. She brought water to them and someone ran her entire family out of town. I wish I could find that family—I'm still looking for them. There were a lot of ministers who stood up, church people, right there in Montgomery, Alabama, and every place you can think of.

Some white people came down, like Mrs. [Violet] Liuzzo, who was from Detroit and went down to Selma and was killed. I knew this woman, okay?—a nice, lovely Italian housewife who was concerned about the right to vote. She left her home to come down there and all she was doing was driving folks back and forth. Anytime you needed a ride she was a ride; she was synonymous with ride. They killed her right there on the highway, shot and killed her. In fact, more white people died in the Selma Movement than black folks. They came from all over. They said if you're going to shoot people for the right to vote, we believe in democracy, so we are coming down to support that. See, that's why I can't get hung up on no white folk. The largest single group that we had on the Freedom Ride who was in jail in Jackson, Mississippi, was Jewish young women from Chicago. That's right.

An interesting little incident happened one time in Selma (this is appropriate for the topic race and food): one of the white ladies who had been marching was staying at the home of a black family, and the black lady got the spirit. It jumped on her and she told the white lady, "Take my baby; I'm going to get in this march." She had been supporting the white lady who was marching every day, and preparing food and everything. The white lady said, "Okay; it's your turn. You go ahead and march. I'll take care of the baby." She had this little black baby in her arms and then she panicked. She said, "Wait a minute; when do I feed it? What do babies eat?" They eat food, you know—whatever you can get. Black babies don't eat anything any different from white babies. But sometimes we forget that we have more in common than our differences.

Ricky Parker

David Leite

Ricky Parker leans his elbow on a shovel that's almost as tall as his lanky six-foot frame and wipes his brow with the sleeve of his shirt. He rests, but for only a moment, and scans the group of waiting customers lining the chain-link fence. His body, which appears cobbled together with limbs that telescope at the joints like a carpenter's ruler, is restless. Although he has just spent the past twenty minutes feeding hickory coals to several outdoor barbecue pits the size of a minivan, he barely misses a beat of narration. For Parker is always narrating—to onlookers, to his two sons, to friends who help out during busy times. To anyone, that is, who'll listen.

"Now, see, the important thing to remember," he says, nudging his chin toward the corrugated-metal-covered pit, "is don't disturb the ash that's already burned down, otherwise it swirls up and ruins the hogs." To demonstrate, he takes a shovelful of coals from the wood-kindling shed behind him and in one deft movement arcs them across the pit without causing so much as a cloud of cinders. A satisfied grin crosses his face, and he punctuates the lesson with his trademark phrase, "And *that*, my friends, is how it's done."

Parker, owner and pit master of Scott's Bar-B-Que in Lexington, Tennessee, just 110 miles east of Memphis, has been gaining attention and followers ever since John T. Edge, Southern food writer and director of the Southern Food-ways Alliance, pointed students, journalists, and food intelligentsia to Parker's pits several years ago. The reason? "Ricky Parker is a living, breathing Jack Daniel's–and–Mountain Dew–drinking barbecue dinosaur," says Edge. "He's the last, best hope for the survival of whole-hog barbecue in Tennessee."

According to Edge, whole-hog barbecue, which is also found in discrete parts of eastern North Carolina, owes its existence to the areas' extreme rural-ity and cheap, easy access to wood. "There have been fewer outside influences, fewer intrusions of change in Ricky's neck of the woods," he says, "which is why this form of barbecue still exists there."

This culinary microclimate is the locale featured in *Whole Hog*, a documentary film by Joe York that investigates Tennessee's whole-hog barbecue community. "Draw a line from Jackson to Lexington to Henderson," says York, "and it forms a triangle. That's ground zero for whole-hog barbecue." But even though this triangle cuts a sizeable 250-square-mile swath through the center of the state, according to York the technique is now so rare many people in Memphis and in nearby Nashville have no idea it's still being practiced. Pit masters, he says, switched to shoulders and ribs because of ease. "Cooking a whole hog using nothing but hickory coal doesn't exist anymore because there aren't people like Ricky who are stubborn and dedicated enough to make it happen."

Although Parker isn't from a barbecue family, he's nonetheless the scion of barbecue royalty Early Scott, who began cooking whole hogs in 1960. "At the age of sixteen, me and my dad got into it," Parker says in the film, "and I hit him with a baseball bat cuz he was whupping up on my momma. I went to school one morning, and when I come back, he had all my clothes sitting up on the front porch. So I called Mr. and Mrs. Scott, and I've been with them ever since." Parker took over the business in 1989 and operates it exactly as Scott did: the sauce recipe—an unusual combination of vinegar, cayenne pepper, black pepper, sugar, lemon juice, and salt—and barbecuing techniques have remained the same. And he continues to fire only whole hogs because, as he puts it, "If anybody walks in that door, they can have shoulder, ham, catfish [tenderloin], middling. They can have it fat, they can have it dry, they can have it juicy. Hell, if I served just shoulder, I'd be run out of business like all them others. People 'round here want what they want."

To meet this demand, Parker has to work nearly round-the-clock because most of the 180- to 220-pound dressed hogs are cooked from twenty to twenty-seven hours, depending on size as well as outside temperature and humidity. The hogs are rotated through three pits—fired at approximately 195 degrees, 165 degrees, and 135 degrees, respectively—until they're pulled up to the front counter, where employees serve Parker's fiercely loyal customer base.

"He's like a barbecue-cooking shark," says York. "He never sleeps, he never rests. He's always working." The job, though, takes a toll, and neglect is the price. Parker is often heard repeating, and usually in front of his wife, Tina, that he's more married to his work than he is to her or his three kids. In fact, his first wife divorced him because of his fanatical attention to his hogs. "Ricky can't stand disappointing people," says Lynn Pollock, a friend of Parker's who often lends a hand. "I remember one time we was fresh out of barbecue, and a customer came in. Well, Ricky just went in back and came out with the order he set aside for his family."

It's easy to look at Parker though the gauzy lens of nostalgia, at a way of life that's being replaced by hulking electric smokers, stainless-steel pits, and TV-celebrity rubs and sauces. But Parker possesses what few other local pit masters have and what will ensure his survival: an unerring instinct for marketing. For example, during the days prior to Fourth of July weekend 2004, a rumor circulated that Scott's was being ranked as one of the top three barbecue places in the nation. In no time the local media were alerted, and boxes of free T-shirts emblazoned with the honor materialized to be handed out to customers. The excitement built to such a fever pitch that on the holiday a line began forming more than an hour and a half before opening, and Parker sold a record forty-two hogs. That number was outstripped this past Fourth, says Pollock, when he sold sixty hogs, thanks to an additional pit that allows for more pigs to cook at once.

Emboldened, Parker agreed to be a featured presenter at the sixth annual Worlds of Flavor International Conference and Festival, held at the Culinary Institute of America in Napa. It was the first time Parker was out of his element, and the first time he was unsure of himself. "See, I'm sheltered here," he says of his rural location. "So I'm comfortable, and I can make other people comfortable. But in Napa me and my family walk into this thing that looked like a castle, and there was all these chefs from different countries. I turned to Tina and said, 'Hell, no, Momma, I can't do this.' I spun right around and walked out to have me a cigar and gather my thoughts." Whether it was advance word of Whole Hog, which premiered at the festival, or a case of his reputation preceding him, when Parker returned he was met with a surprising reaction. "Everybody turned around and started clapping," he adds. "They recognized me, and I don't know how." From then on, he says, he felt at home.

He disarmed the food cognoscenti in Napa with his barbecue demonstration, and it wasn't long before they sought him out again, this time for the 2006 Big Apple Barbecue Block Party, held in and around Madison Square Park in New York City. Now Parker was ready. When Blue Smoke's executive chef and partner Kenny Callaghan asked if he was up for the event, which was expected to attract more than 100,000 people, Parker said yes and gave a list of demands. "You just get me the wood, the hogs, and room to build my pit," he told Callaghan, "then stand back and watch me do it." Union Square Hospitality Group, the organizer of the event, was sure the city would consider an open pit filled with slowly cooking hogs a health hazard. (Unfortunately, the 13th police precinct agreed.)

Parker is equally adept at charming crowds back home, which, according to York, has won over the hardest-bitten skeptic. "Some people who eat Ricky's barbecue for the first time are put off because it's not what they expect," he says, referring to Parker's cayenne-packed vinegar-based sauce, which is nothing like the dry rubs of Memphis or the sweet molasses-and-tomato-based sauces of other parts of the country. "But they're drawn to his energy and the atmosphere he brings to the pit. He's out in front and is a complete live wire. You become passionate because he's passionate. In the end, his presence elevates the food to another level," he adds.

A clutch of new customers gathers along the chain-link fence as Pollock and Parker abut a large metal grid to the tailgate of a pickup. With one elegant movement, they haul a hog onto the grid, cut side up, and balance it on the edge of the pit. Parker waves a Black & Decker jigsaw at the crowd and without any warning to look away begins cutting off the bottom six inches of the hog's legs. Every so often the saw locks, bucking against bone and tendon. "Catch," he says, tossing each leg to his son Zach, as if they were rolls of paper towels.

Parker reaches for a short knife. "The trick here is not to go too deep," he says for the benefit of all, as he slits the hog down its spine to help it lie flatter, "otherwise the fat and juices leak out, and that don't make good barbecue." He then flips the grid up and over the side of the pit, and the carcass lands squarely gutted side down. Applause erupts from the onlookers. He smiles and nods, taking it all in.

"And *that*, my friends, is how it's done."

Home away from Home Cookin'

Deb Barshafsky

I refused to believe that cooking a mess of greens was any more challenging than navigating the parking lot of the produce stand at Kissingbower and Milledgeville roads. White-knuckled, I piloted my trusty Explorer across the furrowed field of red Georgia clay, coming to rest in a watering hole that could conceivably have concealed an adult hippopotamus. I descended from the safety of my four-by-four and stepped gingerly around the perimeter of the slowly evaporating puddle, watching in case a lone crocodile had commandeered the last wet spot within miles. But I was threatened only by the jagged edges of a few Michelob Light bottle caps and a Nestle's Crunch wrapper, skittering away in the wind.

Here, betwixt two tattered and sun-bleached flags touting BOILED PEANUTS and FRESH VEGETABLES, I found greens. Dozens of rubber-banded bunches of vibrant green greens. Chameleon green greens. Antifreeze green greens. And mess is right, I thought, staring at rows and rows of these sand- and grit-covered cruciferous vegetables. "These here are collards," explained one of two purple-knit-capped custodians of this shabby but popular little market. Collards are one of the oldest members of the cabbage family to be cultivated (he didn't tell me that).

After a little prodding, knit cap #1 attempted to walk me through cooking my first mess of greens ("you cut 'em 'bout right here"), but we were interrupted by a gleaming black Town Car, circa 1982, splashing up to the stand. The tinted window descended, revealing an elderly gentleman on the prowl for turnip greens. "In a few weeks," said my cooking instructor, and the Town Car headed south—a blur of bright hubs and red pinstripes.

What's the difference between a turnip green, a mustard green, and a collard green, I inquired, sticking close to the onion, a vegetable of a much more familiar variety. "Turnips got a root," he said. "And they got bite." He asked me what kind of meat I intended to use for flavoring. When he suggested a hog jowl, I realized I was in over my head. So I tossed a few sweet potatoes in a bag and headed to Calvin's. Because as contradictory as it may sound—when you want real downhome cooking, it's infinitely easier to eat out than to cook in.

HOT FOODS BY CALVIN

Calvin Green is the crown prince of Augusta's downhome cooking scene. His unassuming little Broad Street restaurant, Hot Foods by Calvin, was anointed by readers of Augusta magazine as the city's best spot for home-cooked victuals. The hardest-working overnight success in the Central Savannah River Area, Mr. Green should have been born Mr. Greens, for the man can flat cook some collards.

The youngest of six, Calvin (like Cher and Madonna and Emeril, he's achieved first-name recognition status) learned to cook at the ten elbows of his siblings. "You think I can cook?" he laughs. (Hot Foods by Calvin's Brothers and Sisters? Hmmm.) Calvin honed his culinary skills in the kitchens of Casi's, Calvert's, and the Augusta Country Club. But it wasn't until he stepped out of the shadow of Augusta's "fine dining" establishments and set up shop in the heart of Harrisburg that we, the hungry masses, began to fully appreciate his talents.

From 8 a.m. to 11 p.m., only nine hours short of 24–7 ("people gotta eat seven days a week"), Calvin dishes out fried chicken and candied yams and his heralded greens (eighteen vegetables in all) to folks from the neighborhood and folks who make the pilgrimage from contiguous counties to relish his, well, his hot food.

"I think you can divide this kind of cooking into three groups," Calvin said. "Downhome cooking, soul food, and just general Southern cuisine. You know what I'm saying?" (Calvin likes to say that—"you know what I'm saying?") Soul food, in his estimation, comes from "the soul of an animal." Knuckle of pig, chitlins, and the like. The closest he comes is oxtails. And you'll find nothing from the soul of a pig at Calvin's. The bacon on his $4.50 Everyday Breakfast Special comes from the soul of a gobbler.

Southern cuisine is sort of a nebulous umbrella category that he attributes, with a wave of his hand, to places like Piccadilly and the S&S and Harvest something-or-other. I didn't really follow this part of his explanation. I got the sense he was rolling quickly through these first categories to get to what he really wanted to talk about—cooking, downhome style.

"There's just something about that soft cooked taste," he said. "The corn-bread dressing, the collards, the yams, the squash, the okra." Most restaurants make their money off their meat, but Calvin lovingly tends to his sides. "That's what differentiates home cooking in my mind." No canned yams at Calvin's. "I'm not with that," he said.

CAFE 209

Don't be fooled by the name, a rather uninspired homage to this newcom-er's street address. There's nothing pretentious about Glen and Cassandra Brinson's eight-table eatery on Tenth Street. I think they should have simply called it Cassandra's, but then, I wasn't invited to the nomenclature plan-ning session.

When I arrived for lunch on Friday, eight of the nine tables were taken. Under a handwritten sign boasting "Augusta's best home cooking," a couple in business attire finished their flounder. I slipped in next to a woman in scrubs who polished off her apple crisp and bid the rest of us farewell. Two tables over, a gentleman in full-out Super Fly mode (complete with burgundy shoes) worked over a plate of barbecued chicken. This, I soon realized, is the kind of establishment that causes well-dressed and seemingly well-bred women to pick their teeth in public (table to the immediate left of Super Fly).

Glen, a mountain of a man whose huge hands dwarfed my fried fish and shrimp special (not an easy feat), knew why the seemingly incongruous no-tion of restaurant-prepared "home-cooked" foods attracts customers. "It [downhome food] makes 'em think about how their grandmamas cooked back in the days." That, and the fact that no one really wants to devote the time it takes to create the perfect glazed pork chop (come on Thursday) or a superior sweet potato soufflé (see you on Tuesday).

Cassandra, on the other hand, likes to think that Cafe 209 is filling a void in downtown's dining scene—that is, a dearth of establishments serving fresh vegetables. She told the story of one of her regulars, a lawyer, who told her colleagues "if you want to be strong and stand up here all day in court, you need to eat your veggies." So now they all eat at Cassandra's . . . uh, at Cafe 209.

Andy Williams ("just like the singer") recently discovered 209. He assured me that Wednesday, when baby back ribs play a starring role on the menu, is the must-visit day. I asked him how many times he's been to 209 and he laughed. "Well, I just started coming and I haven't stopped yet." He assured me that he doesn't come every day. "I've got to get to the House of Prayer, too."

The midday sun blazed through the purple, red, yellow, and turquoise stained-glass panes that form the windows at Madison's, a cafeteria-style restaurant located in the United House of Prayer for All People. The lightness, the brightness, the downright cleanliness of this place was astounding. Generally preferring a somewhat grimy atmosphere for my downhome fare, I nonetheless returned for the consistently good food. And I've yet to make good on my promise that I will one day be adventuresome enough to sample the neckbones.

The United House of Prayer was founded in the early 1920s by Bishop C. M. "Sweet Daddy" Grace. I'm not sure if this day kitchen was part of Sweet Daddy's master plan, but under his portrait and images of Jesus and the current bishop, S. C. Madison, the UHOP's faithful flock slowly moved through the line, devoutly requesting a dish of banana pudding or a slice of strawberry cake, a fried chicken quarter or some pig knuckles, maybe some greens and black-eyed peas.

On my most recent visit, another patron called after me as I readied to leave. "Coming back tomorrow?" Tomorrow? "It's Friday," he explained, as if my companion and I were challenged by the Gregorian calendar. We bit. "What's Friday?" "Fish," he said. "Come back tomorrow. Won't get in but come on back." (Really, this guy must be a plant.) His companion, pausing over a plate of liver and onions, clarified. "Well, you can get in, but the line is really long." "Long?" exclaimed diner #1. "It's out the door. Like a Beatles concert." On our way through the parking lot, next to the house built for Bishop Madison's visits to the church, we passed the fish man, rolling in cases of brim and whiting, seemingly oblivious to the weekly hysteria begotten by his delivery.

TASTEBUDS BY DENISE

My whirlwind journey through Augusta's hot spots for home cooking took me full circle, back to Kissingbower and Milledgeville roads, to Tastebuds by Denise—building C of a cluster of structures located across the street from Mann Methodist Church. I found the owner, Denise Moore, frying up four hand-formed burgers the size of Rhode Island. A diminutive woman, she could barely see over the colorful panel that separates the cooking area from the dining area. She must have borrowed someone else's hands to form these monstrous patties of ground beef.

Denise (let's just do the first-name thing with everybody in this piece) assured me that "you don't get taste like this from a can." This equals delectable, divine, delovely. Denise's menu warns you that some of her food has been known to cause people to "slap their own mommas." Denise does what the rest of us can't seem to find the time to do. She strolls up the street and buys collards from the fellows at the corner market. Although, lately, she's been frequenting a new place on Morgan Road where she gets more greens for her green. She buys those sandy, gritty greens and she washes them and trims them and folds them and chops them and seasons them ("with smoked turkey to keep them healthy") and boils them and serves them with a smile to those of us who are too lazy or too unskilled in the kitchen or simply too overwhelmed by daily living to find the time to cook our food at home. And that's just fine with Denise, who learned her way around a kitchen by her mother's side while her bedridden grandmother hollered instructions from the next room. If Denise didn't get it right, Grandmama made her do it again. And it all paid off. As she told me—"I'm good at it." You know what she's saying?

The Cypress Grill

T. Edward Nickens

The road to the Cypress Grill, in the two-stoplight town of Jamesville, North Carolina, scurries down a sandy slope shaded by tall oaks and poplars, their branches draped with Spanish moss. You'll know quickly if you've gone too far. The asphalt dead-ends at a boat ramp, which leads to the coffee-with-cream-colored Roanoke River. Here the river flows swiftly through one of the South's largest intact bottomland forests, its banks a greening veil of cypress and tupelo gum trees.

At the intersection of the road and the river is a little shack of a place built of weathered board-and-batten cypress siding, with a tin roof and hinged shutters propped open to reveal a black placard with orange lettering: "YES WE'RE OPEN." Seeing the sign, I breathe a sigh of relief. I'm not too late.

Whether I'm fishing for shad, paddling a back swamp, or bird-nerding the Roanoke's lowlands during the spring warbler migrations, I make a stop at the Cypress Grill every chance I get. For almost sixty-five years now the ramshackle diner has opened its doors for a few short months, January through April, to dish up an ephemeral pleasure: river herring, netted on their spawning runs from the open Atlantic. Historically, untold legions of the fish surged up the Roanoke, Chowan, Tar-Pamlico, and other eastern North Carolina rivers each spring, supporting a seasonal fishery that shipped salt-cured herring across the South and Northeast by the millions of pounds. Locals, too, flocked to the riverbanks to nail together makeshift "cook-up shacks" where the fish were fried over an open fire or a propane burner from an old tobacco-curing barn.

The foot-long river herring were an integral part of daily life. Farmers even used herring parts as fertilizer. ("When you plant yo' corn, put a herrin' to de hill / If dat don't do it, de good Lawd will," ran one line in the old fisherman's chantey.) By 1880 the Roanoke region's fishery landed tens of millions each spring, and not too many years ago you could take a washtub down to 'most any eastern North Carolina fish house and fill it with herring for a dollar.

No longer. Pollution, overfishing, and loss of spawning grounds—due to the construction of dams in the past half century—have reduced the numbers to all-time lows. These days, if you want an old-fashioned taste of herring, you head down the hill at Jamesville and hope your timing is right.

Like mine. "Oh yessir, we have herring today, sure do," Leslie Gardner tells me. He stands between shelves groaning with tea pitchers and homemade pies. The interior of the Cypress Grill is crowded, homey; the air is spiced with the scent of vinegar and fried fish. There are a half dozen booths painted stark white and eight tables with straight-back chairs. A hand-lettered poster hawks tickets for the Jamesville EMS and Rescue Raffle. Sunlight bores in through a few knotholes in the siding.

Leslie is lean and gray-haired, with salt-and-pepper eyebrows and faded jeans held up by a belt with a 1972 Eisenhower silver dollar buckle. He and his wife, Sally, have rented and run the Cypress Grill for twenty-seven years, bolting the doors each season in time to put in a new tobacco crop. (They decided to retire from tobacco farming a few years ago.) Originally constructed about 1936, the building burned down in 1946 and was soon rebuilt. It may just be the only seasonal herring shack left in this part of North Carolina.

When the Gardners first took over, herring were an easy score. Each morning at first light, the Gardner boys launched their skiffs on the river to net fish before they went to school. These days, Leslie loads up his pickup truck at fish houses on the nearby Chowan River and Albemarle Sound, making the run every single day the restaurant is open. "You know how it is," he tells me. "If I ever skipped a day, then I'd want to skip two, or three. I told myself way back that I wouldn't start that. There ain't no need to have old fish."

Especially when you need so many. On a typical day, up to five hundred herring will take a hot dip at the Cypress Grill, most under the watchful eye of a short and chipper lady named Julia Price. "Other than raisin' young-uns," she says at a near-holler over the boisterous sizzle of frying fish, "I've been right here, off and on, for more than twenty years." It takes a certain alchemy to turn an overgrown, bony sardine into a regional icon, and Julia is happy to play sorceress. First, she explains, notches are slashed into the fish, perpendicular to the backbone. The cuts let the hot oil bubble deep into the flesh, softening the herring's bones. Some folks request fish barely fried—this is called "sunny side up"—so that the skin can be scraped away to reveal the flesh beneath. But far more ask for their order "cremated," cooked so long that the fish turns a deep chestnut brown, and hardens up so you can eat one like a cob of corn, bones and all. "They want it burnt slap up to cracklins," Julia says, with a can-you-believe-it look on her face. "It don't matter to me, though. I don't eat the things anyway."

Just then, waitress Linda Perry sticks her head through the order window. She's laughing hard and holding an order ticket. "Fellow out here says he wants his herring 'a total loss,'" she says. "Wants 'em brickbat hard." Julia grins, and scoops three freshly fried fish back into the pans. "Brickbat hard, huh? Well, we'll see about that!"

To be sure, river herring are an acquired taste. And for many Cypress Grill regulars, it's a taste acquired during a time now past, and every bite of fish evokes an era when these silvery harbingers of spring were counted on to keep a belly full. This has always been a poor region. For the first half of the twentieth century, tenant farming and sharecropping made cash money hard to come by. As late as 1943, less than 35 percent of the region's farms had electricity, and without refrigeration fresh meat was only an occasional pleasure. It wasn't unusual for salt-cured herring to find its way to the plate three times a day. "Fish and collards," grimaces Sally. "That's what people lived on."

"Tiny" Harrison remembers. She's sitting in a window booth with two friends who drove her here from a nearby rest home. Born near Jamesville in 1909, she dresses in Sunday go-to-meeting clothes for her annual pilgrimage to the Cypress Grill. "We stored our fish out in the smokehouse, with tins of lard and sausages hanging off the rafters," she recalls. "To me, it's a real taste of home."

I take a seat across from Tiny, with a view of the river. My plate comes heaped with herring and tubular sacks of herring roe, rolled in cornmeal and fried. When I pick up knife and fork, Tiny gives me a quizzical look. "No, no," she reminds me, "with your fingers."

Of course. How silly of me. I pick up a fish, forked tail between thumb and forefinger. Sheathed in cornmeal, the herring is steaming hot, and I have to hold the first few bites between my teeth for a few seconds. No one ever mistook river herring for chicken. Fresh from the pan, each bite has a smoky punch, an unrepentant flavor of fish. I savor each mouthful. I may not know what it feels like to watch net corks bob and dance in the river current, or to fill a crock with fish and salt. But for the moment, I can taste the brine of the sea, the salt of toil, the urgency of rivers pregnant with spring rains in the satisfying crunch of a not-quite-cremated herring.

When Leslie stops by my table, I ask him about the most herring he's seen one customer eat. There's one lady, he says, that eats ten or twelve at a time—"and she's no big girl, either." For years Mort Hurst, a local county commissioner and noted big eater, asked Leslie if he might eat all he could for a fixed cost. "But he's the collard-eatin' king of the world," Leslie tells me. "Set a world record for eating Moon Pies. We won't let him do it. He'd just stick it to us."

People love their herring, I say, and Leslie just grins. "Sure do." Like this one fella, he recalls, who came in for supper just before he was scheduled for heart surgery. "He wanted a good fill of herrings before he went into the hospital," Leslie explains, "and it just so happened that we ran short. He made a horrible ruckus, hollering and yelling. I felt sorry for him, I did. He told me, 'Mister, if I wasn't in the condition I'm in, I would fight you.' I could see why he needed a heart operation."

Leslie fills my cup with iced tea, and when I ask him how things have changed over the past fifty years, he has to think for a moment. Instead of hog lard, the fish are fried in heart-healthier vegetable oil, he tells me. The previous proprietor poured a concrete floor over the old sawdust one, and Leslie himself installed an automatic fish scaler about twenty years ago. "But we've tried not to get real modern."

Before I head out the door, I amble over to a table where Sally introduces me to Mack and Donna Smith—"Some real herring eaters," she says. The Smiths are polishing off a half dozen fish, and pondering pie. For the past ten years they've made the forty-five-minute drive from their home to the Cypress Grill every Friday night the place is open. "Every Friday night," Mack says, proudly, holding a half-eaten herring with two hands. He's a trim fellow in a crisp shirt, and he can, in fact, recall the only two Fridays he and Donna missed their appointed hour. In March of 1994, Donna had neck surgery and couldn't make the trip. "But we didn't go without, we still ate herring," he says with a resolute nod. "It just so happened that the local fire department had a few."

As long as herring are still around, he tells me, "we'll eat our share," and in his voice I sense the fear of a fishless Friday. "Sometimes we almost get to the point where we want to come in the middle of the week, but we don't. Looking forward to it just makes these fish better."

That, I figure, and looking back.

Compare and Contrast

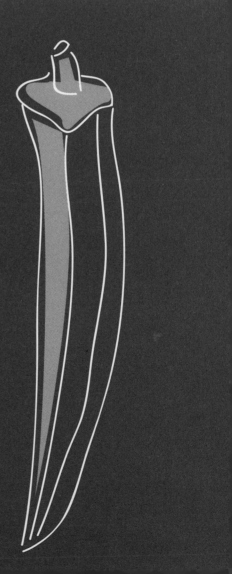

Roll Over, Escoffier

Jim Ferguson

Tell me what you eat, and I'll tell you what you are.
   Anthelme Brillat-Savarin, The Physiology of Taste *(1825)*

Not long ago I read that to judge from Southern cookbooks
published in recent times, one would assume beef Stroganoff was
a traditional dish. My heart sank. The dishes herein are a rebuttal
of that assumption and my affirmation of an active Southern
heritage. I want to know what season it is, what day it is, where I
live and how I got there; nature has a beautiful and perfect order
of which we are all only a small part, and never lords.
   Bill Neal, Bill Neal's Southern Cooking *(1985)*

I once had the good fortune to audit a course on the sociology of the South
at the University of North Carolina at Chapel Hill. Actually, it was a bit of an
intellectual breather from five-years' work on an increasingly ponderous tome
concerning Burgundian culinary traditions and tradents—the latter represented
by three megachefs in the region. The course turned out to be a sort of revelation—a serendipitous epiphany, really. I discovered that despite Yankee roots, I
am a Southerner—which got me to musing about similarities between the part
of the South I know and Burgundy. There are such obvious things as finding
our familiar red clay at the monastery of Pierre que Vire just south of Vézelay.
But there are fundamental social substrates as well. In this course, we heard of
the importance to the Southerner of sense of place (*terroir* in French), family
ties, and religion, all of which help define the Burgundian character. I could
hear Marc Meneau of L'Esperance say that the Nivernais, though politically a

subdivision of Burgundy, did not belong because the cuisine was different. The famed Troisgros kitchen has three generations of family working side by side. And were it not for the knowledge and diligent labor of Bernard of Clairvaux's Cistercian monks and nuns Pinot Noir and Chardonnay would not be as avidly consumed (and grown) in the South as they are today.

Something written by Bill Neal, a North Carolinian whose sophisticated literary and culinary endeavors brought national attention to Southern cuisine in the 1980s, seemed to speak to another bond: "But true Southerners hold historical and cultural bonds to heart, above geography; they remain Southern wherever they are—New York, Chicago, Paris, London—and their food is part of their cultural identity." The French "Tell me what you eat . . ." could as easily be our "Tell me what y'all eat . . ." Upon further reflection I realized that more than a simple love of things culinary was at work here—it is an appreciation of the same kinds of earthy, elemental foods that these two cultures share. Our love of the Burgundians' cuisine mirrored their response to what we brought—there was common cause at the kitchen table.

In the fall of 1994, we took North Carolina country ham, sausage, and barbecue along with grits and Virginia bacon on that trip to France. Ellie, my wife and collaborator on this project, took premeasured and sifted flour to bake biscuits. We were at Restaurant Greuze in Tournus—two Michelin stars for decades—home of Jean Ducloux, France's exalted champion of traditional cuisine. Ellie had twenty minutes in the convection oven to bake her biscuits in between gougères and brioche for the luncheon service. I was fixing bacon, sausage, country ham, and redeye gravy. We were cooking breakfast for twenty, including Jean Ducloux. When I asked for strong coffee to deglaze the country-ham pan, the assembled staff from executive chef on down was incredulous. Someone swore they heard Escoffier gasp or weep—they weren't sure which. Ducloux halved his first biscuit the wrong way, but he was in ecstasy as he devoured the next five. He also could not get enough redeye gravy.

Later, in Roanne, Ellie had taken a jar of her freshly made okra pickles (with Gary Murray's tiny okra from the Carrboro Farmers' Market) to Pierre Troisgros, one of France's longest-running Michelin three-star chefs. I explained that the recipe was similar to his mother's recipe for cornichons (the tiny French sour gherkins) that is to appear in the Burgundy book. Eyes twinkling, he unscrewed the Mason jar and liberated the topmost pickle. Five or six more quickly followed as this titan of French gastronomy smacked his lips with ill-concealed relish. Soon, Michel, his son and chef de cuisine, appeared in the office to discuss plans for the luncheon and dinner offerings that would greet the international parade of culinary pilgrims at this legendary shrine. Before he could utter a word, Pierre handed him the jar and said, "Taste these, they're incredible." Michel packed away five or six, and Pierre popped one or two more before replacing the lid. I offered a suggestion about refrigerating the remainder. It was unnecessary—the jar was empty the next day.

On the same visit, Pierre was besieged in the kitchen by twelve Japanese men who were trying to sell him cheese. Talk about carrying coals to Newcastle! I was on the line, sautéing country ham and preparing redeye gravy during the dinner service—again for the staff. When the ham was cut into bits and served, Pierre discreetly left the cheese on the table, put pieces of ham on slices of baguette, dotted them with redeye gravy, and instructed the Japanese to taste them. He then finished five of them himself—allowing as how they were delicious and that it never would have occurred to him to deglaze a pan with coffee.

In May of 1996, the sous chef at Restaurant Greuze came up to me and said, "Do you remember that sauce you taught us to make? We make it every day now for the staff lunch." Could it be that these Carolina crackers taught them something about "what they are"?

Imagine that. Forget, Hell!

Wie Geht's, Y'all?
German Influences in Southern Cooking

Fred R. Reenstjerna

While a great deal has been said about Celtic and English influences in Southern culture, less attention has been paid to other significant European influences. Most especially, German culinary traditions were established in several key regions of the South by the mid-1700s, and these traditions continue to this day.

German settlement in the eighteenth-century South was the result of English colonial policy in the Carolinas and Virginia. South Carolina planters lived in fear of Native American and slave uprisings, and they wanted colonies of white militiamen available on their borders. They devised a Township Plan, recruiting colonists from German Europe to settle in an arc ranging from along the Savannah River over through Columbia and down to Orangeburg, South Carolina.

Most of the townships failed, in part because they were put down in swampy landscapes bearing little resemblance to the homelands of German settlers. One settlement that did take hold, however, was Saxe Gotha Township. The region between the Broad and Saluda rivers is known as the Dutch Fork even today, reflecting its German origins. Comprising modern Lexington County and Saluda County (and the land now under Lake Murray), this settlement took root as a center of evangelical Lutherans—and their food.

Take, for example, chicken and dumplings. This mainstay of mountain culture, which is actually served throughout the non-German South, is a stew of chicken and vegetables covered with pieces of a thick flour dough that is cooked by the steam of the boiling broth. In the Saxe Gotha region, by contrast, "dumplings" are flour noodles about two inches square. The region has become so homogenized since 1970 that food stores no longer carry dumplings in that size, but they did in my youth. I know this because my mother, once assigned to bring the dumplings to a family dinner and too busy to make a batch by hand, bought a package of prepared dumplings and sprinkled some flour over them to make them look homemade. Nobody knew the difference. Today, however, the only "extra-wide" noodles in food stores are barely an inch across.

This kind of "dumplings" is only one German culinary tradition. Liver pudding, quite a distinct food from pork sausage, is another characteristic of Saxe Gotha. Its distinctly South Carolinian feature is that it combines rice with ground pork organ meats, mixed with red pepper and other seasonings, all stuffed into casing. Commercial liver pudding in food stores is pretty bland, but "real" pudding is available at Caughman's meat plant outlet ("The Meat'n Place") and Four Oaks Farm. These places are within a mile of each other in Lexington County and are operated by old Saxe Gotha families (the Caughmans and the Mathiases).

But the most distinctive German food to come out of Saxe Gotha is liver nips. Clearly of central-European heritage, liver nips are still cooked in central South Carolina. Basically, "nips" are a paste of ground beef liver, stew beef, eggs, and flour, spooned into boiling beef broth. Cutting into the paste with a spoon was referred to as "nipping" some of it off—hence liver nips. They are also called liver dumplings nowadays—an interesting reminder of the Southern-style chicken and dumplings discussed above. As the nips cook, some of the material falls off into the beef broth, producing a kind of thick sauce (or a really lumpy gravy, if you're disrespectful).

Two critical elements in liver nips are the seasonings and the amount of flour. Nips are heavy on thyme and other herbs; cooking nips fill the kitchen with a heady, herbal, almost sausagelike aroma. The amount of flour is critical in final consistency, and recipes vary from family to family. Some people prefer a "tight" nip, made with lots of flour, while others prefer a looser nip. The finest nips ever, at least according to our family tradition, were made by Mrs. Clara Harmon. Regrettably, her grandson does not like liver nips, so that branch of the nip evolutionary tree has come to a dead end.

Liver nips are properly served with "mix bread," so named because the dough is mixed rather than kneaded. The central element of mix bread is cooked grits, mixed with flour and yeast and left to rise twice before baking. These ingredients yield a product with a tough crust and a spongy interior—ideal for sopping up the broth associated with liver nips.

Few commercial establishments serve chicken and German-style dumplings, and fewer still offer liver nips, but one place still serves both. Shealy's Restaurant in Leesville, South Carolina, maintains the traditional cuisine of old Saxe Gotha Parish in an all-you-can-eat, family-style buffet. The Shealy family began catering the Gilbert Peach Festival over thirty years ago, long before the suburbanization of Lexington County, and they have continued serving authentic food at their restaurant.

Recent (1997) menu modernization at Shealy's has included the addition of barbecued ribs to traditional (pulled-pork) barbecue, but the buffet still includes chicken and dumplings on occasion. Thursdays are liver-nip days, and you can tell from the turnout that not all Lexingtonians have moved to the area in the past twenty years (even though it may seem that way during rush hour on Highway 378). The wide expanse of family-style tables allows people to move among the seats, making the obligatory greetings to individuals in their ken (which usually means about 75 percent of the diners at any given moment).

Because Germans have been in the South for over 250 years, they have blended more completely into Southern culture than, say, Germans in Pittsburgh or Detroit. Nonetheless, their unique culinary contributions to the diversity of Southern cooking remain distinctive, to be recognized and enjoyed.

Living North/Eating South

Jessica B. Harris

Cultural geographers have carefully drawn maps detailing the iced-tea line and delineating the boundaries between the white and yellow cornmeal zones. I grew up in a Southern culture that has eluded the balkanizing of these cartographers. You see, I'm a New Yorker who grew up eating Southern. The descendant of the enslaved and free Africans who made their way north in the Great Migration, I grew up in a Southern culture that was preserved in amber and that was and still remains a vibrantly alive region of the African American culinary world. Generations of families long separated from the South still raise their children in ways that continue the culinary traditions and still allow them to head south to sop biscuits and gravy, suck chewy bits of fat from a pig's foot spattered with hot sauce, and yes'm and no'm with the best of 'em.

Grandma Harris was an old-line Southern matriarch. It didn't matter that she lived on the third floor of the South Jamaica projects in New York: her world was deeply rooted in the traditions of her South. She grew peanuts, okra, black-eyed peas, and collards in her garden allotment out back, would brook no contradiction about manners, and made sure that all of her grandchildren knew how to cook. In her home New Year's was celebrated with a mix of collard, mustard, and turnip greens that she'd cooked to accompany the hoppin' John and chitlins that were obligatory. Daily meals were simpler, hog maws stewed down with white potatoes or vegetables cooked down and made into a meal with the addition of a piece of "streak-a-lean-streak-a-fat." Breakfasts, if you were lucky, included her world-class beaten biscuits, which she would whack away at while "Pressing on the Upward Way" and wading in the "Deep River." They were split in two and dipped in a pool of Alaga syrup into which bits of butter had been cut. Other times, when she was busy, a piece of the previous night's cornbread was fried up in some bacon fat out of the coffee can that had pride of place at the back of the stove. Crisp edges and crumbly bread made the perfect accompaniment to thick pieces of hand-cut slab bacon and grits.

Grandma Jones came from a different South. Descendant of free people of color of Virginia, she prepared glaze-glistening hams and great roasts and served them with her own put-up condiments like pickled Seckel pears and watermelon rind pickles. Parker House rolls showed up on her table more than cornbread, but there was always a crystal pitcher filled with minted iced tea or some other cool drink. She had a Southern sweet tooth and made her own peanut brittle and fudge and great quantities of coconut-frosted yellow cakes. It was another world, but it was still the South.

My New Jersey–born mother, who grew up in a parsonage, came from a world of church suppers and roast chicken Sunday dinners, but she accommodated herself to my father's tastes as well. On top of this she was a trained dietitian, so dinners at our house could be anything from pigs' feet served with a hot German potato salad seasoned with celery and bacon, to fried butterfish or porgies served crisp out of the skillet accompanied by a salad and the two or three vegetables that were obligatory on every plate, to roast beef with Yorkshire pudding! My father knew he'd only get hog maws once a month or so, but that was enough; he contented himself with smothered pork chops and stewed collard greens and slow-cooked string beans seasoned with ham hocks. Chitlins were rare, but less so when we moved and a second stove was put in the basement to keep the smell down. Breakfast was his meal and my mother would bake a batch of biscuits with a large hand-formed hoecake for him every Sunday morning.

I savored it all and sucked it all up and so it isn't surprising that when I finally settled on a neighborhood, it was one filled with traditional African American families. There are a multiplicity of greens as well as raw peanuts at my Korean market, and an array of pork products at my butcher. Every morning, as I go to work, I pass a parked truck festooned with the sausages, hams, greens, and yams that an entrepreneur brings up from the South and sells to a neighborhood where many still long for the foods from what will always be sweet home. I watch gleefully as sweet potatoes (that he persists in calling yams) and greens turn to watermelon, then to fresh raw peanuts and black-eyed peas in the shell, and back again.

I have long contended that one's history turns up on the plate. If so, my passport may be stamped Yankee, but there's no denying that my stomach and culinary soul and those of many others like me are pure Dixie. We may be in the North, but we eat South. We not only eat it, but we grow it; when we can't, we demand it in our butcher shops, greengrocers, and supermarkets.

Why Jews Don't Get Quail

Marcie Cohen Ferris

I am a Southerner, born and raised in a small cotton-growing town in north-east Arkansas, where eating pork barbecue is evidence of one's regional up-bringing and loyalty. Being Southern but also Jewish complicated this act of solidarity a bit for my family, but not enough to keep any of us out of the Dixie Pig, a barbecue institution in my hometown. Barbecue, at least the kind they serve in northeastern Arkansas (chopped meat with a spicy vinegar-based sauce), is delicious. As a Jewish eater, looking beyond its un-kosher status for a moment, pork barbecue makes sense to me. (May I not be hit by lightning.) Occasions for eating barbecue are usually joyful, good people are present, portions are plentiful, the side dishes are tasty, and con-versation is animated.

But wild quail—this is a foreign world for Jews. This is not to say that Jews do not eat quail. Many Jews in the South enjoy quail in their local upscale bistros or downhome "meat and three" cafés. Jewish farmers who live in the Mississippi Delta hunt and eat dove, another small game bird. But for the rest of us Jewish Southerners, quail eating, not to mention quail culture, is a foreign experience. Perhaps this has to do with Jewish law, which does not condone hunting purely for pleasure. After Biblical times Jews considered hunting cruel and therefore "un-Jewish." Moreover, meat that is not slaughtered ritually by a *schochet*, a Jewish butcher, is considered unclean or *treyfa*. For most Jews hunting, and eating wild game—even farming, for that matter—are difficult to associate with one of their own. But I recently crossed over into this world when my husband, Bill, and I visited a quail-hunting plantation owned by one of his boarding-school friends in Thomasville, Georgia.

I had reservations about taking this trip when Bill first described it to me and quail entered the conversation. "There will be quail hunts and a big quail dinner." I knew I was in trouble. Jews don't get quail. Why all that effort for such a tiny bird? How do you eat them? Where's the meat? Are you supposed to eat several or daintily consume one and feign fullness? Can you pick it up with your fingers? What do you do with all those tiny bones, the unsightly pile of carnage left exposed on your dinner plate? I knew I'd be hungry, and what if they served quail for every meal? I know it's one of those Southern dishes that is interchangeable between breakfast, lunch, and dinner. Who knows? It could be twenty-four-hour quail—quail all the time.

I reluctantly agreed to join Bill. I packed snacks.

I am not wholly unfamiliar with quail. My mother-in-law, Shelby Ferris, always serves quail at least once during our annual visits to the Mississippi farm where Bill grew up. She prepares them beautifully, lightly dusting each with flour, seasoning them, and frying them in a cast-iron frying pan until they are golden brown. The quail is served with buttered grits, hot biscuits, and Shelby's wild plum jelly.

My first encounter with quail at these family occasions was a turning point. I had never eaten quail. When someone is eating lobster or crawfish for the first time, people offer directions to the uninitiated, but how could you not know how to eat quail? You're a Southerner. I watched as everyone enjoyed their quail. I went back for seconds on grits. My epiphany unfolded: "I am Jewish. I have married a Gentile who eats quail. God help me. I'm a foreigner. Who are these people at the dinner table?"

Breakfast ended and so did my epiphany. We decided to ride horses. Oh, no. It was back. "How do you get on a horse? What if I look stupid? How come Jews don't ride horses? Who are these people?"

In Thomasville, Georgia, I was in for the quail-eating, quail-hunting, quail-fest of my life. It was a quail-a-rama. As soon as we arrived at the plantation, we were taken to join the other guests, who were eating lunch lakeside. It was a picnic—but what a picnic. There were white tablecloths and finger bowls. Ellery, our host, greeted us warmly. "Have some fried alligator nuggets."

Jews don't get fried alligator nuggets either.

Alongside the platter of alligator was another platter of fried chicken, a fresh green salad, black-eyed peas, cheese grits, and biscuits. There was fruit compote and home-baked sugar cookies for dessert. I ate everything, including the alligator nuggets, which were delicious. I figured it was a culinary warm-up act for the quail that were to come.

After lunch, we joined one of the quail-hunting expeditions. There was a mule-drawn wagon, a wagon driver, one huntsman who directed the hunt, eight English pointers to find the quail, two Springer Spaniels to retrieve the dead quail, two guest hunters, and Bill and me, interested onlookers. We spent the rest of the afternoon in the piney woods, following the pointers as they encountered coveys of quail. We returned home at sunset. The beautiful Spanish-revival home was built in 1905 and is filled with period antiques and rugs. A center atrium is a tropical paradise of banana trees, sweet olive, and camellia bushes. The dead quail from the afternoon's hunting were left on a table in the entryway, where the cooks gathered them to clean and prepare for dinner the next day. I was struck by the incongruity of the dead birds on a table in such a beautiful space. But it wasn't strange to anyone else. The entire plantation exists for this experience, and the dead quail symbolized a successful afternoon.

The quail disappeared by the time we had dressed for dinner. An old plantation bell that hangs in the center of the atrium ceiling rang three times to announce cocktails. The hunting party had cleaned up remarkably well—men in ties and jackets, women in dinner-party attire. It wasn't hard to imagine Bill's boarding-school friends as they looked at age sixteen—clean-cut young men, anxious to succeed, fearful that they would not keep up with their companions. But they did make it, and that night they joined together around a table to become friends again after so many years apart.

The bell rang again and we took our places at the family dining table, where birds and hunt scenes appeared on the china and in beautiful quail-shaped salt and pepper shakers. There was rare roast leg of lamb, rice, and carrot parcels tied with green onion ribbons. Dessert was a dramatically presented prune soufflé, a traditional recipe in the Sedgwick family. Everyone cheered as the puffy dessert made its grand entrance. I could see the family gathered around the same table in the 1930s cheering the same way as the soufflé was served. The combined influence of home economists, domestic science, and the Depression had produced such desserts, symbolizing health and frugality, saved from utter drabness by enormous quantities of whipped egg whites and sugar.

I asked if I could see the kitchen after dinner. I entered a bright blue service pantry filled with sets of china, glassware, and serving dishes, and then walked into the working kitchen with its large industrial-style stove standing next to the old cook stove purchased soon after the house was built. A message board on the wall reminded, "night crew and day crew, check birds on table in atrium." Beyond this room was the children's dining room, an informal space, where children were free to eat outside the formality of the main dining room. The head cook's desk here was covered with stain-spattered community cookbooks, complicated grids that list the weekly menus, and a frequently referenced binder filled with family recipes. If a home has pockets of memory, this was one of them. The voices, cooking smells, gossip, and harried instructions that had filled this room for over a hundred years permeated the cabinets and well-worn work surfaces.

Our last day at the plantation was marked by more memorable meals. At breakfast, a fantastical arrangement of chicken and eggs was the centerpiece. Hard-boiled eggs sat amidst a delicate arrangement of straw, and placed nearby were two china baby chicks. There was a large platter of scrambled eggs, served with sausage and bacon, grits, and hot muffins. At lunch, another soufflé—this one cheese—was served with warm stewed tomatoes and a green salad. The apple crumble was just right, so perfect in its mixture of crunchy topping and melt-in-your-mouth filling that I asked for the recipe. In the evening we dined on quail wrapped in bacon and cooked on a special grill just outside the kitchen. I carefully observed my dinner companion's quail-eating form. I did my best, including a quick swish in the finger bowl. The last soufflé appeared—this one chocolate, what Ellery describes as "chocolate soup," also an old family favorite. Once again we cheered, this time for the soufflé, for the extra whipped cream, and above all for these days when time slowed down, old friends gathered, dogs were loyal, and all seemed right with the world.

Southern by the Grits of God

Timothy C. Davis

Picture me: I'm sitting in the parking lot of a rundown convenience store—a "Stop 'n' Stab," as a friend of mine calls such establishments—eating a shrink-wrapped pimento cheese sandwich and quaffing a twenty-ounce Coke. Not haute cuisine, to be sure. Not-so-haute cuisine, more like it.

As I sat there and chewed the sandwich—made of that processed pimento cheese spread author Reynolds Price claims tastes like bug spray—my repast came back to haunt me. Not that the sandwich was so bad, mind you. What bothered me is why I ordered the sandwich in the first place. There were plenty of ham-on-ryes, "Italian" subs, and other hermetically sealed goodies to choose from. Yet I bought a pimento cheese sandwich, so bland in its entire packaging, taste, and preparation that I cannot think of a single adjective—the food writer and the pornographer's favorite part of speech—to describe it. It simply existed, a Sartre of sandwiches.

I bought it, I decided, out of guilt.

Telling someone you're from the South instantly used to cause people to view you with red(neck)-tinted glasses. Now, it's a foot in the door, a book deal, a record contract, a cooking show.

As far as I can tell, this languid love affair is a matter of "authenticity," a tenuous concept people will usually eagerly gobble up no matter how hackneyed the premise or the packaging. As marketing slogans go, it's one of the best.

Of course, the American South has always been portrayed as a fertile delta when it comes to matters of artistic authenticity—it's why there are "Southern Lit" sections in bookstores across the country (usually right beside another rather segregated section, that of African American literature) and graduate degrees in Southern studies at major universities.

Yes, we're painted with a pretty broad brush. Thing is, like Tom Sawyer, we've learned how to turn chore into "cha-ching!" Like Tom, we've managed to turn whitewashing a fence into whitewashing our friends.

What we discovered is this: we can fleece these Yanks! Pop a paint pen in that old gas station attendant's hands. Folk art! You grew up in a trailer? Write a memoir! You make a pretty decent pork shoulder, and people call you Mama? Open a café! (Just make sure the facade is appropriately "weathered" and you offer sweet tea. Always sweet tea.)

Food, by God, is the last frontier. Just the other day I heard Emeril Lagasse inform his Pavlovian audience that he just loooved him some pimento cheese—oh yeah, babe!—and that the concoction was in fact so good that he could, and I quote, "eat it on a tire." (Whether he would eat it shrink-wrapped from a convenience store cooler is another question entirely.)

An admission: I love pimento cheese. I love it on brown bread, I love it on Ritz crackers as a midnight snack. I love grits, too, whether with eggs and sausage or topped with shrimp in true Lowcountry style. I like livermush (fried only), Red Velvet Cakes, and Cheerwine, and Sun Drop, and Dixie beer. And, God knows, I love me some barbecue.

It's just that, sometimes, you gain a reputation and you can't shake it. This is never good, even when the reputation is a positive one. You can't be truly yourself once you gain a reputation, because at that point you've already begun to serve what we here in the Bible Belt call the "two masters": you and the idea of you.

Steve Almond, in his great sweets-heavy book *Candyfreak*, says this: "I do know an unfortunate number of Southerners as a result of attending a university in North Carolina, and virtually all of them, when I mentioned candy bars, assumed that the Goo Goo Cluster would be at the top of my list. It was not. Part of the reason for this is that candy bars are not often grist for literary culture and thus have been spared the relentless invocation of other such Southernisms as kudzu, moonshine, Co-Cola, and Shiloh."

Someone buy that man a Moon Pie.

I can't complain, really. I get calls when there's a Southern Story to be penned, and I usually don't turn these opportunities down. However, my prose is often switched midway through the editorial process to a "first person" narrative—authenticity!—and I do sometimes notice a few more "ain'ts" and "shoots" and "doggones" on proof sheets than I originally remembered writing. I don't usually fight it, preferring to let the publication get the story they want, provided I'm not turned into some sort of quasi–Bo Duke savant who just happens to be able to type purty when I'm not mouth-breathing.

However, like the many painters and artists and writers down here, I am a battler. The battlefield? Restaurants and art galleries and blues halls, bookstores, universities, and record stores. We don't win too many fights around here, as a little conflict about 150 years back will attest. We're good at turning the tables, however. Would you like sweet tea with that?

Ziti vs. Kentucky

Cindy Lamb

Trying to make that meal-planning choice between the varieties of pastas can be challenging. I was lost in the semolina swirl of linguine, bowtie, angel hair, and mostacholi when I sensed the gentleman next to me was frustrated, grunting, sighing—not enjoying his search. Paul Newman's wise face looked upon the situation from his place among the sauces. It should've been a hint.

"What'cha looking for?" I asked. I'd noticed the thirtysomething guy earlier in the produce section. He seemed odd in his dark-tanned skin, sunglasses wrapped around his head despite the adequate yet annoying fluorescent lighting.

"Ziti!" he said, pushing the "T" out in a puff of disgusted breath.

He stared back at me through his shades, looking like a fly. I had a knee-jerk reaction that surprised me by forming the words in my brain, "He's not from around here, is he?"

After ogling the shelves around the penne, cappellini, and macaroni, I furrowed my brow to appear concerned but willing to talk noodle shop. "I've not seen ziti being offered on many local shelves this past year," I said. I continued by suggesting he substitute one of the aforementioned pastas for his casserole. He glanced at his list and acquiesced, tossing the bag of small shells in his cart. "That's what happens when you don't live in places like New York and Chicago!"

In this moment of good neighborly spirit mixed with venomous Louisville cockiness, I said quietly, "*What* happens?"

As if I'd pulled a rope from his mouth, the words came out in one long complaint. "You just can't *get* the same stuff, the same *quality* stuff when you want it. There's just no *choice* here, you never have *anything*."

Silence. Save for the computerized boops of the U-Chek lane, only tension punctuated the moment.

I pushed my horns back down beneath my scalp, expressing myself with the simple arrangement of consonants, "Hmmm." Rolling my cart away from the heat, I felt my own surge of piss and vinegar rising. Not a good combination to think of in a grocery store, mind you, but I couldn't help thinking about the plight of all the good folks from international port cities who find themselves, for one reason or the other, stranded in Louisville, Kentucky—Ziti-Challenged Capital of the Earth. I sensed the dig at all of us, that we were responsible for his failed recipe because we were—what, hicks?

I wheeled my basket past the bakery and held back from punching a bag of pecans. "Maybe he just needs to go *back* to Chicago!" Huff. Puff. "I hope he wants some good *bourbon* back there!" A savvy mother guided her children around me as I passed the Little Debbie end cap in a blur.

Maybe it was the breeze from my own velocity through the store—hell, I'd made it from desserts to the dairy case in record time, practically carving my own personal Mason-Dixon line along the way. Then, my cultural karma raised its colorful head.

When I returned to my home state of Kentucky from over a decade in Los Angeles, to live in rural Russell County, I could barely shop at the local Kroger without rolling my eyes and whining. "What? No *cilantro*?" I actually had to spell it and do a little botany workshop right in the express lane, explaining the friendly cousin of parsley to several frightened checkers and a beleaguered produce manager.

I would continue for several months to impress people with the great uneaten: quiche, quesadillas, red wine, balsamic vinegar, basmati rice . . . ANY rice . . . herbal tea, iceberg-free salad. I felt like the Michael Moore of high-quality, healthy foods in a part of the country raised on lard, grease, white sugar, whole milk, and cigarettes. I was practically a California citizen, after all, and I had to help these people out. I had a lot in common with that Chicagoan at one time.

Maybe this particular week I was a little sensitive about the displaced thousands in the wake of the hurricane—how they might be looking for a bottle of water while this man's ziti could only be found in a gourmet market in town. Maybe I should've continued the conversation to find out how I might direct him to a more rewarding retail experience here in flyover country. Maybe I should've asked him why he was visiting or living in Louisville. What did he really enjoy about it? Maybe next time.

Manners are one of our natural exports here in the South. I'll mind them.

Oddly enough, I cooled in the oily mirage of the asphalt parking lot. I thought of home, two hours and almost a half century south of Louisville. The lard, grease, and sugar made my grandmother's and mother's cooking some of the best in the land. Biscuits, green beans with ham hocks, iron skillet corn pone, chicken fried steak, sorghum molasses and butter, sticky white made-from-scratch birthday cakes. Sure, it took a few years off your life, but the time around the supper table was worth it. And all the ingredients were available at Houchens, roadside markets and flatbed trucks, Piggly Wiggly, or a neighbor's garden.

God bless the man who ticked me off at the grocery in my rear view mirror. I do want to speak with him again. If it was you, I apologize for leaving in a curt manner. And, if I find you, I'll accept *your* apology for dissin' my city.

We have everything we need, just not everything *you want*.

Dennis Water Cress

Christopher Lang

Before it was ever known as "Rocket City," Huntsville, Alabama, could claim the unusual distinction of being the "Watercress Capital of the World." Long considered a traditional Southern treat, this tasty leaf grows naturally in swampy lowlands and was once a significant cash crop in Alabama's Madison County. At one point, over 2 million bunches of watercress were shipped annually from the Huntsville Depot to every state east of the Rockies. This enigmatic crop built a family business that would last a century.

In 1874, Frank Dennis was a young entrepreneur who sold watercress to hotels around his home in West Long Branch, New Jersey. Dennis grew the watercress on his own land, but because the plant was considered a delicacy and a health food (it was thought to stave off scurvy), demand became so great that he soon decided to expand the operation. He continued expanding for almost three decades, buying up farms in Pennsylvania, Maryland, Virginia, and West Virginia. But harsh winters and short growing seasons eventually forced Dennis to seek more temperate climes, and his eye was drawn to north Alabama.

The growing season lasted from December until May, and limestone springs made the Huntsville area ideal for growing watercress, especially since as many as five crops could be harvested in that time. In 1908, Dennis bought a series of ponds and dammed lakes in north Alabama stretching from Moore's Mill to Meridianville, with the largest and most developed ponds scattered around Jeff, Alabama. For the next half century, those ponds would make Huntsville synonymous with the Dennis Water Cress Company.

Before modern machinery the process of cultivating watercress was strenuous work. Ponds had to be built using plow horses to form earthen dams, which regulated the flow and height of the natural spring water. Once the dams were built, field workers would bring in wagonloads of watercress and scatter them over the shallow ponds to take root. Within a week, the plants would start to grow, and the pond level would be raised to a half foot. In four to six weeks, the area became a massive green carpet ready to be gathered.

At harvest time, cutters wore hip boots and worked in tandem across the ponds. With sharp knives and twine, they collected the leaves in bunches and delivered them to the packing house to be washed and cooled. Because the watercress had to be shipped while it was still fresh, the packinghouse was located near the Huntsville Depot on Monroe Street. There the watercress was packed with ice in barrels that were then covered with burlap for express shipment across the country by railroad.

Although the Dennis Water Cress Company maintained its headquarters in Martinsburg, West Virginia, Huntsville became the main office during the winter. When the Dennis family came down, they would stay at the Russell Erskine Hotel in downtown Huntsville, just a few blocks from the packing-house and the Huntsville Depot.

In 1922, Frank Dennis died and his son Charles Edward Dennis (known simply as C.E.) took over the burgeoning family business. The younger Dennis, who possessed a keen interest in farming, turned out to be an indefatigable promoter of the company. Besides packing and shipping improvements, he developed new methods of soil conservation, insect and weed control, and water purity. He also introduced several marketing innovations. Under his leadership, the company honed its brand image, producing matchbooks, playing cards, wildlife calendars, and recipe books all emblazoned with the Dennis logo. C.E.'s enthusiasm for the business soon earned him the nickname "the Watercress King." A remark he once made in jest reveals his almost missionary zeal: "When I get Dick Tracy or Superman to eat watercress like Popeye eats spinach, then I'll be a contented man."

From its inception, the Dennis Water Cress Company aimed to supply the most prestigious eating establishments across the country. Although the company sold wholesale to merchants, hotels, restaurants, steamships, and railway companies, it also supplied famous restaurants and chefs. Antoine's and Brennan's in New Orleans both used Dennis-brand watercress. So did the Waldorf-Astoria in New York, the Drake hotel and the Palmer House in Chicago, and even the White House in Washington, D.C. But perhaps the greatest breakthrough the company achieved in expanding its business was placing watercress on the Defense Department Procurement List, which provided guidelines for standard items to be stocked in commissaries. Supermarket grocery chains were quick to follow such suggestions. As the popularity of Dennis Water Cress expanded, Huntsville became known as the source of the best watercress available anywhere.

In contrast to the first forty years, the 1960s were a sluggish decade for the company. Before his death in 1951, C.E. incorporated the Dennis Water Cress Company and persuaded his daughter and two sons to take over after he died. By that time, however, the run was almost over. As the novelty diminished and watercress became more widely available, demand for Dennis-brand watercress gradually declined. Ineffective chemical fertilizers and increasingly cold winters also hurt production. In 1965, many of the watercress ponds were infested with leaf spot fungus, and after a bitter lawsuit Railway Express, once the key to quick distribution around the country, discontinued shipping the plant. These factors and more led to the demise of the Dennis Water Cress Company.

On July 10, 1969, the *Huntsville Times* lamented the end of an era as the last box of Dennis watercress left on an airplane bound for New Orleans. The company was moving to south Florida to take advantage of a milder climate and better trucking and road transportation. Most of the ponds in Madison County would be sold, except for a few in New Market, where the springs generated 20 million gallons of water per day at an ideal temperature of sixty-eight degrees Fahrenheit.

Surveying the abandoned packinghouse on Monroe Street, which would soon be demolished to make way for a new road, the *Times* reporter remarked, "So Huntsville moves forward with budding industrial plants in all directions as a once-proud plant on Monroe Street sits and waits to be destroyed in the face of progress. The equipment is for sale. One cold room is shut down, and the other houses enough watercress for about four bridge parties."

In 1973, nearly a century after Frank Dennis began selling watercress from his home in West Long Branch, New Jersey, a rival company bought out the Dennis Water Cress Company. B&W Quality Growers took over the watercress market. Still the largest growers of watercress today, B&W Quality Growers operates in six states from Pennsylvania to Florida—including a few ponds in New Market, Alabama.

Frank Stitt

Pat Conroy

There are austere rules in the writing of novels that vex the young writer every
bit as much as the rules of finesse and discipline and cuisine vex a headstrong
apprentice. Young masochists are drawn toward melodrama and coincidence;
thus young writers and young cooks have much in common. As do older
writers and master chefs.

I speak now of coincidence and the detached collisions of fate. In the early
'80s, I spent an extraordinary week in New York City, where I attended plays
and thrilled to an opera with my agent, Julian Bach, having dinner at the Four
Seasons afterward. Like a birdwatcher, I keep a list of great restaurants that I
would like to eat my way through during my passage on this earth. I crossed
off Lutèce and La Côte Basque on this journey, during which I presented the
full outline of *The Prince of Tides* to my lovely editor, Nan Talese. But Julian
Bach and Nan Talese were not coincidences, rather part of the natural architecture of my life.

On the Delta flight back home to Atlanta, fate cleared its throat as I heard
a handsome young man in the aisle seat across from me whistling softly. I am
not the kind of man who starts up conversations with strangers on airplanes
and who then pulls out pictures of his children to show to any passenger
within earshot. When I travel, I prize my anonymity and solitude and have no
desire to be seated next to a compulsive chatterbox. The whistling from the
right drew my attention, but it was the stack of cookbooks that riveted me.
In a neatly stacked pile, the young man was looking up recipes from the very
best cookbooks published in that year. These were on the cutting edge and
the outer rim—it was long before the dawning of the era of the celebrity chefs
and the Food Network, but that revolution was in the air. Already, extra-virgin
olive oil had started to appear in Southern supermarkets, bringing sex, at last,

to Southern kitchens. Arugula, watercress, and daikon radishes were making shy appearances in produce departments in my part of the world, and Paul Prudhomme had already made his mark in New Orleans, initiating the era when you could not meet a red fish that someone had not blackened. In my hometown of Atlanta, the glittering era of Pano & Paul's had begun, Buckhead began to strut with restaurants bucking for four stars, and I heard a Frenchman say you could get a better Russian meal at Nicolai's Roof's downtown location than you could in Moscow. Cuisine was breaking out all over the South, as luxuriant and uncontrollable as kudzu. The man across the aisle from me was about to change the history of his home state of Alabama forever.

"Sir," I said, watching him scribble in his notebook, "those cookbooks you're reading, they're wonderful."

"I think I just spent the best week of my life working in the kitchens of these four chefs," he said. "It's amazing what you can learn in just a week. My name is Frank Stitt, sir."

"Mine is Pat Conroy," I said. "Are you a chef?"

"Yes, I am, though I've never run my own place," Frank said. "I'm about to open a restaurant."

"Can I ask where?"

"Birmingham, Alabama," he said.

"It's a wasteland for good food," I said. "I was there a month ago."

"It won't be a wasteland anymore," Frank replied with a confidence that both surprised and delighted me.

"If you're any good at all," I remember saying, "you're going to be a very rich man."

Frank appraised me with care and then said, "I'm good. I'm very good."

He said it with a measure of conviction and authority that carried much weight with me. Frank declared it like a man with keenly earned self-knowledge, an awesome respect for the art of cooking, and a firm knowledge of the great gift he was about to bestow on his home state. He spoke with enthusiasm about the chefs who trained him in France, and he was already comfortable speaking in the vocabulary and techniques of Escoffier, Joel Robuchon, and Alain Ducasse. I could not mention a restaurant that he did not have knowledge of. His long apprenticeship was now over and Frank Stitt was coming home to deliver the goods to Alabama.

Highlands Bar & Grill changed the way the people of Alabama thought about food. It was a revolution in the center of a neighborhood that was going slightly to seed but was about to start its renaissance. The quality of its restaurants is an important gauge for a city to measure its call to greatness. Frank Stitt put Birmingham on the culinary map the day he opened his restaurant. Later I heard from a white-shoe lawyer in one of those Atlanta law firms with enough WASP names to start a hive that the Highlands was better than any restaurant in Atlanta. That's long before the kinks were worked out and long before Frank hit his amazing stride. I made it to the restaurant in the first six months of its existence and discovered that Frank Stitt was a far, far better chef than anyone who had ever crossed the Chattahoochee River from Georgia or entered the Birmingham city limits under the cover of darkness after a lost weekend in New Orleans.

Here is what you get in a Frank Stitt meal and what you get with every recipe in his magnificent cookbook, *Frank Stitt's Southern Table*: the full measure and passion of a man on fire with devotion to his chosen work. He gives you all the artistry at his command every time you sit down for a meal, and he does not tolerate lapses in the kitchen or produce that is not the freshest available. I have eaten at Highlands Bar & Grill over twenty times and have never eaten a single meal that was not superb—the restaurant remains the best reason to move to Birmingham that I can think of. I would call Frank Stitt the best chef in America, but that would cause undue jealousy in the ranks of other chefs whose powers of cruelty are exceeded only by genocidal despots and serial killers with bad tattoos. So let me simply state that I think that Frank Stitt is *one* of the best chefs in America, and America is starting to come around to my position.

I have watched with interest the growing reputation of Frank and his restaurant on the national scene. Whenever I go to Birmingham, I return to Highlands or its sister restaurant, Bottega, where I look forward to the changes and improvements in the menu. Frank works miracles with pork, as I discovered when I ordered a tenderloin with a bourbon and molasses glaze that I thought was the best thing I ever put in my mouth. But I had said the same thing about the soft-shell crab with brown butter and bacon vinaigrette and, on the same night, the basmati rice salad with chilled crabmeat, crescents of avocado, roasted peppers, and slivers of olives and mushrooms folded into a lemon mayonnaise that was both delicate and fragrant. I could write poems about the seared duck breast and his Louisiana rabbit simmered in red wine. Even the lowly Southern dish of grits Frank uses as a palette that he fills with slices of country ham and tosses with wild mushrooms, with a dusting of Parmesan cheese, grated fine.

At Highlands Bar & Grill, there is a sensibility at work in the smallest of details. When Frank offered me a watermelon margarita, I could think of no more nauseating a combination of tastes than a sweet fruit and tequila. Naturally, I was wrong and watermelon has seemed a noble fruit, as kingly as pineapple, since that encounter. Frank's bar makes a better gin martini than New York's Plaza Hotel, and his Chilton County Bellini is far superior to the one served at Harry's Bar in Venice, where it was invented. You can enjoy those drinks at the best raw oyster bar outside New Orleans, where the Apalachicola oysters have been harvested from the Gulf of Mexico on the day you consume them. They are cold and salty and Gulf-born. Just when you think that an oyster on the half shell is the most perfect food on earth, Frank will present you with baked oysters with watercress and a bread crumb crust, or his oyster pan roast with crawfish and buttery croutons, or spicy baked oysters with caramelized onions, pan juices, and chiles.

But then there are the lamb shanks with favas and the cobia with beet relish and how can I leave out the Gulf trigger fish or the magic he works with South Carolina quail or his ravioli with sweet potatoes, mustard greens, and country ham? I cannot do justice to Frank if I fail to praise his foie gras with cornbread or his roast leg of lamb with spring vegetable ragout, or the wine list that grows and mellows and deepens in complexity with each passing year. I have even failed to mention the desserts, which are often the weak spot of restaurants with the raw ambition displayed by Highlands Bar & Grill. But Frank's desserts are the stuff of both dreams and paradise, and I have heard men say aloud in front of their wives that they would marry the pastry chef as they scooped up clouds of the cinnamon crème anglaise or moaned over the crème brûlée. The waiters are classy and well trained. Frank's beautiful wife, Pardis, runs the front with elegance and panache. His chef de cuisine is masterful and the cooks know what they are doing. The knife work is deft and Zenlike, and every night the men and women of Frank Stitt's Highlands Bar & Grill know that they are in the process of making both history and art.

The food world is coming around to my opinion formed so many years ago. Recently I was in another airplane to Atlanta when I read that *Gourmet* magazine had named Highlands Bar & Grill the fifth-best restaurant in the nation. In the same year, Frank won a James Beard award for being the best chef of the Southeast. The inimitable R. W. "Johnny" Apple of the *New York Times* made one of his baptismal visits to the restaurant and left shouting kudos and benedictions like all the rest of us.

Over a year ago, my wife and I joined Frank and Pardis for a spectacular meal at Alain Ducasse's restaurant in New York. It was a meal for the ages, and a great joy to watch Frank smell each dish as it arrived steaming from the kitchen, his eyes lighting up with lapidary pleasure as each dish arrived on our table. The restaurant is as formal and plush and forbidding as Highlands Bar & Grill is welcoming and all-inclusive. The meal was Proustian and fabulous and indescribable, as all the great meals are.

When Sandra and I said farewell to Frank and Pardis Stitt that night and walked toward our hotel with all the clamor and splendor and mystery of the great city swarming about us, we both agreed that Alain Ducasse is a splendid chef, but we also both agreed that he is no Frank Stitt.

Benediction

The Reverend Will D. Campbell

What took you so long?

Forty-eight years ago tomorrow my family and I "crossed the bridge," according to Bill Emerson, who was then covering the South for *Newsweek*. The Mississippi state troopers took us to the Tennessee state line and threw us across, and the Tennessee state troopers were there batting us back over.

That didn't really happen.

It is a great honor. It has been my life to receive a number of so-called honors but until and unless one is honored by his own people he or she is not honored at all. I've never forgotten that you were my people, and I have never been so honored before, and I thank you. And I ain't going to cry—yet.

But all that introduction was made up. I was really born in New York City, in the SoHo district. It's true: my mother was a dancer for the Rockettes—she danced at the Radio City Music Hall—and my father was in the Secret Service guarding Mr. Garfield. And one day there was a terrible accident, you know, and Mr. Garfield didn't make it, so then we moved to Mississippi and started picking cotton down in Amite County. And if you believe that I have some beautiful oceanfront property up in the Smoky Mountains that I could interest you in.

A man who left his mark on this university [Governor Ross Barnett] used to say, "I love Mississippi," and he and I didn't agree on very many things, but we did agree on that. And I never lost that passion for this place. Lots of things have changed since we left here forty-eight years ago; lots of things have not changed. We are talking this weekend about food, and still talking about race. I don't know where and when that will end—not in my lifetime.

Did you ever beg? I have a friend who sees his vocation as policing the parking lot of the big cathedral where his wife is on the vestry, and he puts on his work clothes, fishing clothes, whatever, and picks up the trash in the parking lot. This cathedral is right on the edge of the city, where people stand with signs, "Will Work for Food," and most of them are telling the truth; they will, because they're hungry. On one occasion my friend stopped to pick up a little brownie, and a real street person came out of an alley and yelled out at him, "Hey, man, don't eat that!" And he handed him a paper bag and inside was a fast-food hamburger and a small Coca-Cola, which probably represented his entire day's work. Begging is hard work. You ought to try it sometime. I did. I didn't like it.

But what a sermon. "Hey, man, don't eat that!" Not a sermon, a sacrament. Take this bread: I'm offering it to you—for you. While the others were in church (did I say church?—well, who's to say?)—while the others were inside the building and my friend was picking up their trash, one who equated himself with this fellow gave his day's earnings. "Hey, man, don't eat that!" Here, this sacrament. It's for you.

How much time do I have here? What the hell, I'm the chaplain—I can go as long as I want to. And then we'll take up a collection. I'm the boss.

I was about eight years old, down in Amite County. It's not notorious for great wealth. It was not then; it is not now. It was the middle of the Depression and we were small cotton farmers. And I remember after these seventy-two years watching a little classmate at recess time. None of us had any money, but this chap's grandmother had some kind of widow's pension or something, and she would give my friend nickels and dimes and he would buy little "knick-knacks," we called them. And on this occasion he had a loaf of bread. I had never tasted loaf bread—sliced bread. We ate biscuits and cornbread made from our own corn, our neighbor's mill. And this boy came out with sort of a half loaf and it was just a thing of beauty. Not like these big old loaves you buy today where it takes two people to take them to the car, just a little half loaf. And Curly was at the top of the steps and I was at the bottom, and he was eating this bread one slice at a time, and I watched him. And I thought, my God, that must be tasty. That must be good eating. And I figured out a way to maybe get a bit of that for myself. When he got almost to the bottom I said, "Could I have the heel?"—the butt piece, you know. I thought he would be full by then and be glad to share a little bit—make him feel good, too. But instead he turned and said, "No, that's my favorite piece." And I hated him. As I made my way back to the classroom I fantasized about him choking to death, on that last slice of bread that he wouldn't share with me. And I saw him on the ground writhing and turning blue and choking and then—dead.

Now if the picture is not coming across, I will explain. We as a nation hold the full big loaf. And the small-people countries of the world—poor countries in a world where 300,000 children are soldiers, usually with handguns because they're too little to carry the big guns that we manufacture and are willing to share with them to kill one another and others; where other children, mainly little girls, get not one hour of education, not a minute for reading and writing and arithmetic, to say nothing of laughter and paper dolls and Ring-around-the-Rosie—we hold the big loaf and we go to the little countries and we spray their plants and kill them and call it controlling our drug problem, when all we're doing really is holding on to the big loaf and starving a lot of people. You want to talk about food? Let's talk about food.

We've got the loaf, and one thing I have learned as some kind of bootleg preacher (and I guess this act today is about as authentic as I've ever been—I may not be so timid to be introduced as Reverend Campbell anymore)—the one thing I have learned about Mr. Jesus in all these years since I was first ordained to this office when I was sixteen years old in the East Fork Baptist Church by my daddy, my grand-daddy, and uncle, and a country-preacher is that the One I vowed then to try to serve, there was one group of people he detested, he didn't like: religious people. Just read the Bible; it's there. You know, when we're told so-and-so is a good man, he reads the Bible every day, I say, well, when in the hell is he going to get to the Beatitudes?

Jesus didn't like religious people. And we talk about those dirty old Sadducees and Pharisees—those weren't the bad people. Those were the *good* people. Those were the religious people. Those were the righteous people.

Well we could go on, but we're talking about food and race—still talking about race, that nonexistent sociological thing that we have called race. And it's risky to talk [when you have] the same incurable skin disease I have and many of you have. It's risky to talk across racial lines because so often it sounds as if we are patronizing. I love the film *Driving Miss Daisy*, but in reality, if you look at it, the message, the deep-seated message, is, oh, they—they love us. No matter what we do to them they love us. They come and lick our hands, you know, and we pat them on the head. That's a lie. "They"—whoever—don't always love us, any more than I loved little Curly who held the whole loaf and wouldn't give me one slice. We hold the whole loaf, and we deprive, and we don't know.

I didn't say how many people will starve today while we're here, because we don't know. We know the number is large. I'm talking about dying from the lack of food or water, or a simple vaccine. With a fraction of what we're spending in this—call it a war . . . I don't know what it is. I spent three years in the Second World War. I know something about war. I know something about dying children. I saw a little boy brought in 3 o'clock one morning when I worked in the operating room. The sergeant in charge came and woke me up and said the colonel was doing an operation, and it was my turn to scrub up and help with this operation. I got there and got scrubbed up with my gloves and was getting the instruments and handing them to this crusty old Southern colonel—I'll never forget him: hard, tough, and saintly. He said, "What happened to this kid?" I said, well, he was a houseboy for a planter and he dropped an ashtray and his master kicked him and ruptured his spleen and he's going to die. And the old colonel just said, "Hmm—seems a high price to pay for a god-damn ashtray."

We have the big loaf.

The little vignette with which I'll close is not to say how they love us no matter what we do to them, but visualize, if you can, a handsome ebony-skinned woman with gray peppercorn hair standing in a graveyard somewhere in Mississippi, or it could be anywhere in this nation, with the rain mixing with her tears as it drops on her once lovely breasts, now wilting and sagging with age. And this is her soliloquy as she stands back behind the crowd:

> I wonder if she knows now, knows I didn't just cook for her. Oh, I did cook for her, all right, but that ain't the most I done for her. I really did love her. I helped her raise all her kids, bathed them, combed their little cotton heads, washed their clothes, ironed them, got them ready for school, and I helped every one of them girls get married, fixed their ruffles, curled their hair, and it was me that told them what to do and what not to do on their wedding night and they never forgot it. Not a one of them ever forgot it. One of them moved off to California and the other one to Louisville or one of the big places up north. The other one is just over in the next county, but it didn't matter where they was, whether they were near or far, they always come to see me when they come home—most of the time before they got to her house.
>
> I really did love her. But she almost took that away from me one time—almost took it away. Every time I'd do something that rubbed her the wrong way she'd rail out at me like some old witch setting in. If my husband had knowed she talked like that, Lordy God, he'd have burned her house down and never let me go back. I always just kept it to myself.
>
> But I almost lost it one day. I made the coffee and taken it to her bed like I always did. And she come dragging in the kitchen in her gown after 9 o'clock, way past time for me to be gone, yelling for her breakfast. I put it down in front of her and when I did she took the fried egg in her hand and throwed it at me hard as she could and said the egg was cold. That egg wasn't cold, because I had just taken it off before she come in. It missed me, but it landed on the stove burner I left on in case she wanted something else. And

it commenced to sizzle, a little smoke, and there wasn't no way I could keep it from stinking up the whole house. She kept yelling at me, telling me to do something. There wasn't nothing I could do but stand there and wait till the burner cooled off, so I could take it off and clean it up. I never was no mind to talk back to her, no matter what she said, but something or other got into me that day—I reckon the old devil hisself. I took my apron off and hung it where I always did and told her I didn't know what to do. But if she did she could damn well do it herself. She followed me out the door just a-hollering, "You wait until I tell Calvin! He knows how to take care of impudent wenches!" Calvin was her youngest boy and he paid me. I went straight to his house and told him I wouldn't be back and told him I couldn't take it no more. He almost cried while he was counting out my pay. Little cotton-head Calvin always was a sweet white child, his little wife right there beside him. She told me they didn't blame me, that they didn't know how I put up with so much for so long.

The next morning I was right back. I was already tired 'cause I stayed awake all night talking to my Jesus. He told me he knowed she was mean, all right, knowed she said hurtful things to people that was just trying to help her, but he said she was old and couldn't look after herself and if I'd go on back he'd help me out the best he could. Then he said something I won't never forget. He said if you just love the folks that's easy to love that really wasn't no work at all. He said if you love one you have to love them all.

About the time the sun was coming up I seen him plain as day. My Jesus, he was sitting there on the side of my bed. He put his hand on my shoulder and he said, "Will"—he called my name; he said—"Will, there's one thing I learned two thousand years ago. Don't let mean white folks make trash out of you." Then he put his hand on my shoulder and patted me again and called my name, shrugged his big old pretty shoulders and gave me a big wink and I got up and I looked around and he was gone.

Now here I am standing in the rain back behind the crowd in this cold graveyard, bawling with the rest of them as they lay her down. All the while the preacher was talking I kept looking around for my Jesus to wink at me again. But he never did.

Contributors

Brett Anderson is a James Beard award winner. He is restaurant reviewer and features writer for the New Orleans *Times-Picayune*.

R. W. Apple Jr. was associate editor of the *New York Times* and author of *Apple's America: The Discriminating Traveler's Guide to Forty Great Cities in the United States and Canada*.

Jim Auchmutey is a reporter for the *Atlanta Journal-Constitution* and author of two books on Southern food.

Deb Barshafsky of Georgia is the food writer for *Augusta* magazine. She recently launched www.bitegeist.com, focusing on her culinary adventures and observations.

Shane K. Bernard serves as historian and curator to the McIlhenny Company, maker of Tabasco-brand products since 1868.

Rick Bragg's books include *All Over but the Shoutin'* and *Ava's Man*. In 1996, he won a Pulitzer Prize for feature writing.

Wendell Brock is theater critic for the *Atlanta Journal-Constitution*. "Deep Roots," republished herein, was featured on NBC's *Today Show* and on the radio show *The Splendid Table*.

Rick Brooks is the *Wall Street Journal's* deputy bureau chief in Atlanta. He moved to North Carolina when he was seven and has kept moving farther south ever since.

The Reverend Will D. Campbell, a native of Amite County, Mississippi, is a preacher, author, and activist. Among his books is *Brother to a Dragonfly*.

Shaun Chavis spends her time in newsrooms and kitchens. She studied gastronomy at Boston University and specializes in food journalism.

Pat Conroy, the author of seven books, won a James Beard award for food writing in 2002.

Hal Crowther, author of *Cathedrals of Kudzu* and *Gather at the River*, was 2006 finalist for the NBCC prize in criticism.

Timothy C. Davis's work has appeared in *Gastronomica*, *Saveur*, and the *Christian Science Monitor*. He lives in North Myrtle Beach, South Carolina.

Candice Dyer is a Georgia-based writer. Her work has appeared in *Atlanta* magazine, *Brightleaf*, and *Paste*, among other publications.

John T. Edge is a contributing editor for *Gourmet* magazine and director of the Southern Foodways Alliance at the University of Mississippi.

Lolis Eric Elie, a columnist for the New Orleans *Times-Picayune*, is the author of *Smokestack Lightning: Adventures in the Heart of Barbecue Country*.

Amy Evans is a photographer, painter, and cofounder of Pieceworks, an arts outreach organization for the Deep South. She is the oral historian for the Southern Foodways Alliance.

Beth Ann Fennelly is the author of three books, two poetry, one nonfiction. She is an associate professor of English at the University of Mississippi.

Jim Ferguson is a lecturer in the Department of History at the University of North Carolina–Chapel Hill. He has taught the honors seminar in food and culture since its inception in 1997.

Marcie Cohen Ferris is assistant professor in the curriculum in American Studies at the University of North Carolina–Chapel Hill and associate director of the Carolina Center for Jewish Studies.

William Ferris teaches history and folklore at the University of North Carolina–Chapel Hill and works with the Center for the Study of the American South.

Peggy Grodinsky is food editor at the *Houston Chronicle*.

Tom Hanchett is staff historian at the Levine Museum of the New South in Charlotte, North Carolina.

Jessica B. Harris is a food historian and cookbook author who lives in New York City and New Orleans. Among her books is *Beyond Gumbo: Creole Fusion Food from the Atlantic Rim*.

Jack Hitt is the author of *Off the Road* and is currently at work on a book for Crown entitled *The Pursuit of Happiness*.

Mary Hufford, a writer and community coordinator, teaches in the folklore program at the University of Pennsylvania. She is completing a book on deep community forestry in southern West Virginia.

Dan Huntley is a columnist with the *Charlotte Observer*. He is the coauthor of *Extreme Barbecue*.

Bernard Lafayette is an ordained minister who earned his Ed.D. from Harvard University. He was a cofounder of SNCC and a leader of the Nashville sit-ins.

Cindy Lamb is a Kentucky native whose bluegrass has been sown in Los Angeles and Seattle. She currently lives in Louisville, where she works as a writer and a doula.

Christopher Lang of the Washington, D.C., area is an independent researcher who serves on the Speakers Bureau for the Alabama Humanities Foundation and the SUPER Teach Institute.

Matt Lee and **Ted Lee** live in Charleston and New York and are the authors of *The Lee Brothers Southern Cookbook*.

Carroll Leggett, a public relations professional, is a columnist for *Metro Magazine* who often writes about eastern North Carolina culture and foodways.

David Leite is the publisher of the James Beard award–winning website leitesculinaria .com. He has written for many publications.

Edna Lewis was a noted Southern chef and writer. Her published works include *The Taste of Country Cooking*, *In Pursuit of Flavor*, and *The Gift of Southern Cooking*.

Michael McFee's most recent book, his thirteenth, a collection of one-line poems, is *The Smallest Talk*, published by Bull City Press.

Jerry Leath Mills is emeritus professor of English at the University of North Carolina–Chapel Hill. He is author of the essay "Equine Gothic: The Dead Mule as Generic Signifier in Southern Literature of the Twentieth Century."

Jim Myers is a food writer living in Nashville, where he covers restaurants, spirits and beer, and Southern food culture for *The Tennessean*.

T. Edward Nickens is a North Carolina–based journalist who writes frequently for magazines including *Smithsonian*, *Audubon*, *Field & Stream*, *Men's Journal*, and *National Wildlife*.

Molly O'Neill writes for the *New Yorker*. She was the longtime food columnist for the *New York Times Magazine*, and she is the author of the memoir *Mostly True*.

Frederick Douglass Opie is an associate professor of history and author of the forthcoming book *The Origins of Soul Food*.

Carol Penn-Romine is a food writer and culinary tour guide with her company, Hungry Passport Culinary Adventures.

Audrey Petty eats, writes, and teaches in Urbana, Illinois. Her work has most recently appeared in the *Massachusetts Review* and *Best Food Writing 2006*.

Julia Reed of New Orleans is author of *Queen of the Turtle Derby and Other Southern Phenomena* and she writes often about food.

Fred R. Reenstjerna was a native of South Carolina. He earned a degree in library science from the University of Maryland and made it his life's work to put people in touch with the information they needed.

Fred Sauceman of Johnson City, Tennessee, is the author of two recent books in the series *The Place Setting: Timeless Tastes of the Mountain South, from Bright Hope to Frog Level*.

Fred Thompson is a freelance food writer and columnist for the *News & Observer* in Raleigh, North Carolina. His newest book is *Barbecue Nation: 350 Hot-off-the-Grill Tried-and-True Recipes from America's Backyard*.

Mary Tutwiler writes about food, travel, language, culture, and, alas, hurricanes, for the *Independent Weekly* in Lafayette, Louisiana, and the New Orleans *Times-Picayune*.

Judy Walker, food editor at the *Times-Picayune* in New Orleans, has written five cookbooks.

Robb Walsh is restaurant critic for the *Houston Press*. Among his books is *The Texas Cowboy Cookbook: A History in Recipes and Photos*.

Simone Wilson, native of Germany, has lived in Memphis since 2001. She has written about food and food-related subjects for the *Memphis Flyer*.

Terri Pischoff Wuerthner is a tenth-generation Acadian whose work has appeared in *Bon Appétit*, *Gastronomica*, *Snail*, and the *Washington Post*.

Acknowledgments

First of all, thanks to the authors of these pieces for letting us use their works, and for writing them in the first place. Thanks also to those members of the Southern Foodways Alliance and other friends who helped us track down articles and essays to consider, especially John T. Edge, the SFA's director, whose personal clipping file has enough material for several volumes. Bless the libraries at Louisiana State University in Baton Rouge and the University of North Carolina at Chapel Hill, which we used extensively to track down fugitive pieces. And thanks to the Atticus Trust for underwriting, in part, this volume of *Cornbread Nation*.

Mary Beth Lasseter, associate director of the SFA, acquired permissions and contributors' biographies for us. That's a tedious and frustrating job, and we'd say it's a thankless one too, except that we're thanking her here, profoundly.

Finally, we're grateful to the University of Georgia Press, especially to the director, Nicole Mitchell, for her act of faith in undertaking this project; to our editor, Courtney Denney, who kept things running smoothly; and our copy editor, Liana Krissoff, who saved us from a number of inconsistencies and solecisms.

The following is a list of permissions to reprint the essays and art that appear in this book.

All photos courtesy of Amy Evans, operating under the auspices of the Southern Foodways Alliance.

"Spring," by Edna Lewis. Excerpted from *The Taste of Country Cooking* (Knopf, 1976). Reprinted by permission.

"Tabasco: Edmund McIlhenny and the Birth of a Louisiana Pepper Sauce," by Shane K. Bernard. Originally published in *Louisiana Cultural Vistas* (Fall 2005). Reprinted by permission of the author.

"Boudin and Beyond," by Mary Tutwiler. Originally published in the *Times-Picayune* (April 27, 2003). Reprinted by permission of the author.

"First You Make a Roux," by Terri Pischoff Wuerthner. Originally published in *Gastronomica*, vol. 6, no. 4: 64–68. © 2006 The Regents of the University of California. Used by permission. All rights reserved.

"A Lunchtime Institution Overstuffs Its Last Po' Boy," by R. W. Apple Jr. Originally published in the *New York Times* (April 27, 2005). © 2005 by the New York Times Company. Reprinted with permission.

"The Natural," by Brett Anderson. Originally published in the *Times-Picayune* (June 12, 2005). © 2006 by the Times-Picayune Publishing Company. All rights reserved. Used with permission of the *Times-Picayune*.

"This Isn't the Last Dance," by Rick Bragg. Originally published in the *Washington Post* (September 2, 2005). Reprinted by permission of the author.

"Letter from New Orleans," by Lolis Eric Elie. Originally published in *Gourmet* (February 2006). Reprinted by permission of the author.

"From the Crescent City to the Bayou City," by Peggy Grodinsky. Originally published in the *Houston Chronicle*, vol. 105, no. 76 (December 28, 2005). Reprinted by permission of the publisher.

"A Meal to Remember," by Judy Walker. Originally published in the *Times-Picayune* (August 24, 2006). Reprinted by permission of the author.

"Comforting Food: Recapturing Recipes Katrina Took Away," by Rick Brooks. Originally published in the *Wall Street Journal* (August 26, 2006). Reprinted by permission of the author.

"Willie Mae's Scotch House," by Jim Auchmutey. Originally published in the *Atlanta Journal-Constitution* (January 29, 2006). © 2006 by the *Atlanta Journal-Constitution*. Reprinted with permission from the *Atlanta Journal-Constitution*.

"Crab Man," by Robb Walsh. A version of this article appeared in the *Houston Press* (July 13, 2006). Reprinted by permission of the publisher.

"Lowcountry Lowdown," by Jack Hitt. Originally published in *Gourmet* (December 2005). Reprinted by permission of the author.

"Carolina Comfort, out of Africa," by Matt Lee and Ted Lee. Originally published in the *New York Times* (August 17, 2005). Reprinted by permission of the authors.

"Sugar: Savior or Satan?" by Molly O'Neill. Originally presented at the 2005 Southern Foodways Symposium at the University of Mississippi. Reprinted by permission of the author.

"Molasses-Colored Glasses," by Frederick Douglass Opie. Originally presented at the 2005 Southern Foodways Symposium at the University of Mississippi. Reprinted by permission of the author.

"The Genie in the Bottle of Red Food Coloring," by Beth Ann Fennelly. Originally published in *Great with Child: Letters to a Young Mother* (W. W. Norton, 2006). © 2006 by Beth Ann Fennelly. Used by permission of W. W. Norton & Company, Inc.

"Store Lunch," by Jerry Leath Mills. Originally published in *A Family Cookbook*, by Rachel Victoria Mills (1997), and later published in *Southern Cultures*, vol. 4 (Spring 1998). Reprinted by permission of the author.

"The South's Love Affair with Soft Drinks," by Tom Hanchett. Printed by permission of the author.

"The Moon Pie: A Southern Journey," by William Ferris. Presented at the 2005 Southern Foodways Symposium at the University of Mississippi. Printed by permission of the author.

"Mountain Dogs," by Fred Sauceman. Originally published in *Marquee Magazine* (May–June 2006). Reprinted by permission of the author.

"Scattered, Smothered, Covered, and Chunked: Fifty Years of the Waffle House," by Candice Dyer. Originally published in *Georgia Music Magazine*, no. 2 (Fall 2005). Reprinted by permission of the author.

"Let Us Now Praise Fabulous Cooks," by John T. Edge. Originally published in the *Oxford American*, no. 52 (Winter 2006). Reprinted by permission of the author.

"Molly Mooching on Bradley Mountain," by Mary Hufford. Originally published in *Gastronomica*, vol. 6, no. 2: 49–56. © 2006 by the Regents of the University of California. Used by permission. All rights reserved.

"Deep Roots," by Wendell Brock. Originally published in *Saveur* (August–September 2005). Reprinted by permission of the author.

"Tough Enough: The Muscadine Grape," by Simone Wilson. Originally published in the *Memphis Flyer*, no. 869 (October 21, 2005). Reprinted by permission of the author.

"Making a Mess of Poke," by Dan Huntley. Originally published in the *Charlotte Observer* (June 2, 2004). Reprinted by permission of the author.

"Green Party," by Julia Reed. Originally published in the *New York Times Magazine* (January 11, 2004). Reprinted by permission of the author.

"Something Special," by Carroll Leggett. Originally published in *Metro Magazine* (June 2002). Reprinted by permission of the author.

"Cornbread in Buttermilk," "Salt," and "Pork Skins," by Michael McFee. Printed by permission of the author.

"Rinds," by Fred Thompson. Originally published in *Wine & Spirits Wine Lover's Guide to Pork* (Fall 2005). Reprinted by permission of the author and *Wine & Spirits*.

"Late-Night Chitlins with Momma," by Audrey Petty. Originally published in *Saveur*, no. 89 (December 2005). Reprinted by permission of the author.

"No Bones about It," by Carol Penn-Romine. Printed by permission of the author.

"The Way of All Flesh," by Hal Crowther. Originally published in *Unarmed but Dangerous* (Longstreet Press, 1996). Reprinted by permission of the author.

"By the Silvery Shine of the Moon," by Jim Myers. Originally presented at the 2005 Southern Foodways Symposium at the University of Mississippi. Printed by permission of the author.

"Is There a Difference between Southern and Soul?" by Shaun Chavis. Originally published on www.eGullet.org (May 16, 2006). Reprinted by permission of the author.

"Movement Food," by Bernard Lafayette. Originally presented at the 2004 Southern Foodways Symposium at the University of Mississippi. Printed by permission of the author.

"Ricky Parker," by David Leite. Originally published in *Food Arts*, vol. 19, no. 5 (June 2006). Reprinted by permission of the author.

"Home away from Home Cookin'," by Deb Barshafsky. Originally published in *Augusta Magazine*, vol. 28, no. 2 (April–May 2001). Reprinted by permission of the author.

"The Cypress Grill," by T. Edward Nickens. Originally published in *Smithsonian* (December 2000). Reprinted by permission of the author.

"Roll Over, Escoffier," by Jim Ferguson. Originally published in *Southern Cultures*, vol. 3 (Spring 1997). Reprinted by permission of the author.

"Wie Geht's, Y'all? German Influences in Southern Cooking," by Fred R. Reenstjerna. Originally published in *Southern Cultures*, vol. 4 (Summer 1998). Reprinted by permission of the publisher.

"Living North/Eating South," by Jessica B. Harris. Printed by permission of the author.

"Why Jews Don't Get Quail," by Marcie Cohen Ferris. Printed by permission of the author.

"Southern by the Grits of God," by Timothy C. Davis. Originally published in *Creative Loafing* (July 13, 2005). Reprinted by permission of the author.

"Ziti vs. Kentucky," by Cindy Lamb. Printed by permission of the author.

"Dennis Water Cress," by Christopher Lang. Originally published in *Alabama Heritage*, no. 66 (Fall 2002). Reprinted with permission from the publisher and the author.

"Frank Stitt," by Pat Conroy. Originally published in *Frank Stitt's Southern Table Recipes* (Artisan Press, 2004). Reprinted by permission of the author.

"Benediction," by the Reverend Will D. Campbell. Originally presented at the 2004 Southern Foodways Symposium at the University of Mississippi. Printed by permission of the author.

Southern Foodways Alliance

The Southern Foodways Alliance (SFA), an institute of the Center for the Study of Southern Culture at the University of Mississippi, documents and celebrates the diverse food cultures of the American South. Along with sponsoring the Southern Foodways Symposium and Southern Foodways Field Trips, we document Southern foodways through oral histories, films, and archival research.

Established in 1977 at the University of Mississippi, the Center for the Study of Southern Culture has become a focal point for innovative education and research by promoting scholarship on every aspect of Southern culture. The center offers both B.A. and M.A. degrees in Southern studies and is well known for its public programs, including the annual Faulkner and Yoknapatawpha conference and the Conference for the Book.

The fifty founding members of the SFA are a diverse bunch: they are cookbook authors and anthropologists, culinary historians and home cooks, chefs, organic gardeners and barbecue pit masters, food journalists and inquisitive eaters, native-born Southerners and outlanders too. For more information, point your browser to www.southernfoodways.com or call 662-915-5993.

SFA FOUNDING MEMBERS

Ann Abadie, Oxford, Miss.
Kaye Adams, Birmingham, Ala.
Jim Auchmutey, Atlanta, Ga.
Marilou Awiakta, Memphis, Tenn.
Ben Barker, Durham, N.C.

Ella Brennan, New Orleans, La.
Ann Brewer, Covington, Ga.
Karen Cathey, Arlington, Va.
Leah Chase, New Orleans, La.
Al Clayton, Jasper, Ga.

Mary Ann Clayton, Jasper, Ga.

Shirley Corriher, Atlanta, Ga.

Norma Jean Darden, New York, N.Y.

Crescent Dragonwagon,
Eureka Springs, Ark.

Nathalie Dupree, Social Circle, Ga.

John T. Edge, Oxford, Miss.

John Egerton, Nashville, Tenn.

Lolis Eric Elie, New Orleans, La.

John Folse, Donaldsonville, La.

Terry Ford, Ripley, Tenn.

Psyche Williams Forson,
Beltsville, Md.

Damon Lee Fowler, Savannah, Ga.

Vertamae Grosvenor,
Washington, D.C.

Jessica B. Harris, Brooklyn, N.Y.

Cynthia Hizer, Covington, Ga.

Portia James, Washington, D.C.

Martha Johnston, Birmingham, Ala.

Sally Belk King, Richmond, Va.

Sarah Labensky, Columbus, Miss.

Edna Lewis, Atlanta, Ga.

Rudy Lombard, Chicago, Ill.

Ronni Lundy, Louisville, Ky.

Louis Osteen, Charleston, S.C.

Marlene Osteen, Charleston, S.C.

Timothy W. Patridge, Atlanta, Ga.

Paul Prudhomme,
New Orleans, La.

Joe Randall, Savannah, Ga.

Marie Rudisill, Hudson, Fla.

Dori Sanders, Clover, S.C.

Richard Schweid, Barcelona, Spain

Ned Shank, Eureka Springs, Ark.

Kathy Starr, Greenville, Miss.

Frank Stitt, Birmingham, Ala.

Pardis Stitt, Birmingham, Ala.

Marion Sullivan, Mt. Pleasant, S.C.

Van Sykes, Bessemer, Ala.

John Martin Taylor, Charleston, S.C.

Toni Tipton-Martin, Austin, Tex.

Jeanne Voltz, Pittsboro, N.C.

Charles Reagan Wilson,
Oxford, Miss.

ABOUT JOHN T. EDGE

John T. Edge (www.johntedge.com) is director of the Southern Foodways Alliance. He is the author or editor of seven books, including *The New Encyclopedia of Southern Culture: Foodways* and *A Gracious Plenty: Recipes and Recollections from the American South*. Edge contributes to a wide array of publications, including *Gourmet*, the *New York Times*, *Oxford American*, and the *Atlanta Journal-Constitution*.